Estate Planning
SMARTS

Praise for *Estate*

"A terrific guide for people who are just beginning to grapple with estate planning, as well as those who have (or think they have) their affairs in order."
— *The Wall Street Journal*

"This book is a great supplement to traditional law school casebooks. It helps students bridge the gap between abstract theory and practical application. My students also enjoy reading the celebrity case studies, illustrating situations that could come up with their future clients."
— **Mary F. Radford**
Professor, Georgia State University College of Law

"Simple – but not simplistic – this is a book you can feel comfortable giving as a business-generating, action-oriented gift."
— **Steve Leimberg**
President, Leimberg Information Services

"I will encourage my clients to read this book because an informed client makes better decisions."
— **Dennis I. Belcher**
Past President, The American College of Trust and Estate Counsel

Planning Smarts

"Deborah L. Jacobs is very smart, knowledgeable and careful, and writes beautifully."

> — **Natalie B. Choate**
> Estate planning lawyer and author

"Absolutely fantastic! An incredible resource for both financial advisers and their clients."

> — **Jeffrey H. Thomasson, CFP**
> CEO and Managing Director,
> Oxford Financial Group, Ltd.

"I was knocked out.... This is a book for you to own and read, and to give to clients as a basis for discussion of a wide range of planning issues."

> — *Nick Murray Interactive*

"This book is a treasure! Buy it and pass your own treasure on to the people and causes you love."

> — **Deborah J. Merritt, Professor**
> The Ohio State University Moritz College of Law

"This is a category killer: a book so good there's no need for anyone else to cover the same material."

> — **Kaye A. Thomas**
> Tax lawyer, author, founder of Fairmark.com

DEBORAH L. JACOBS

Estate Planning
SMARTS

A Practical, User-Friendly, Action-Oriented Guide

A Note to the Reader

This book is intended for educational purposes, to provide useful ideas in the area of estate planning. Every effort has been made to ensure that the information contained in the book is complete and accurate at the time of publication. However, neither the author nor the publisher is engaged in rendering professional advice or services to the individual reader. The book is sold with that understanding. Neither the author nor the publisher can be held responsible for any loss incurred as a result of tax, estate planning or investment decisions the reader makes. To prepare your estate plan, you should rely on a lawyer licensed to practice in your home state. This notice is also meant to comply with IRS Circular 230.

This book is available at special discounts when purchased in bulk for premiums and sales promotions, as well as for fund-raising or educational use. Special editions or book excerpts can be created by the author to specification. For details, visit *www.estateplanningsmarts.com* or contact deborah@estateplanningsmarts.com.

Fourth edition published April 2015 by DJWorking Unlimited Inc.
Third edition published October 2013 by DJWorking Unlimited Inc.
Second edition published April 2011 by DJWorking Unlimited Inc.
First edition published December 2009 by DJWorking Unlimited Inc.

Publisher's Cataloging-in-Publication
(Provided by Quality Books, Inc.)
Previously catalogued as follows:

    Jacobs, Deborah L., 1956-
        Estate planning smarts : a practical, user-friendly,
    action-oriented guide / by Deborah L. Jacobs.
        p. cm.
        Includes bibliographical references and index.

        1. Estate planning—United States—Popular works.
    2. Trusts and trustees—United States—Popular works.
    3. Tax planning—United States—Popular works.   I. Title.

    KF750.Z9J33 2009   346.7305'2
                                QBI09-200049
    LCCN 2015903834
    ISBN-10: 0983697027
    ISBN-13: 978-0-9836970-2-2

Edited by Joshua Mills
Copyedited by Deborah Markson-Katz
Designed by Laura Zavetz

To Ken and Jack

Acknowledgements

W riting a book is labor-intensive and sometimes lonely work – no less so, I discovered, with subsequent editions. I am deeply indebted to the many people who provided me with information, guidance and encouragement as this book went through four editions in six years, reflecting dramatic changes in the law during that time.

For help with the heavy lifting in the first edition, I am extremely grateful to Lawrence P. Katzenstein, Gideon Rothschild and Howard M. Zaritsky, estate planning lawyers who spent an enormous amount of time commenting on drafts of various chapters and the Glossary. Lloyd Leva Plaine, who died in 2010, left a deep imprint on Chapter 14 and on me personally.

Special thanks to these experts, who gave generously of their time and reviewed draft chapters of the first edition: Susan T. Bart, Lawrence Brody, Natalie B. Choate, Michael N. Delgass, Keith Bradoc Gallant, Wendy S. Goffe, Jonathan E. Gopman, Steven B. Gorin, David A. Handler, Richard Harris, Stephanie E. Heilborn, Bernard A. Krooks, Carlyn S. McCaffrey, Michael D. Mulligan, Barry C. Picker and Pam H. Schneider.

When updating material for subsequent editions, I went back to Wendy Goffe, Larry Katzenstein, Barry Picker, Gideon Rothschild and Howard Zaritsky, all of whom were generous with their time – again.

Other experts joined this illustrious group in the fourth edition: Thomas W. Abendroth, Gerry W. Beyer, James D. Lamm, Paul S. Lee and Robert E. McKenzie.

Every writer needs an editor. Four have profoundly influenced this book. Robert W. Casey, then an editor at Bloomberg, started me on the estate planning beat 17 years ago, answering my initial objections by challenging me to "learn something new." In the process, he taught me a great life lesson.

Janet Novack, the Personal Finance Editor of Forbes, was my sounding board and edited dozens of articles that I wrote during the year that the estate tax was in flux. In 2011, she hired me. Her astute questions, during the three years that we worked together at Forbes, helped refine my thinking about this area of the law and many other subjects.

To bring all four editions to life, I had the privilege of working with Josh Mills. A veteran editor, he has a rare knack for helping writers dream big and realize their potential.

Deborah Markson-Katz brought fresh eyes to the fourth edition and copyedited this book from cover to cover. Her tireless effort, attention to detail and good cheer in the face of a deadline are unparalleled.

Estate Planning Smarts looks unlike any other personal finance book, and I have Laura and Craig Zavetz to thank for that. Laura designed a book that graphically conveys a life well lived, even as the text deals with the subject of mortality.

Craig deftly implemented Laura's highly creative vision and also designed the book's Web site, www.estateplanningsmarts.com. He is the Web master who helps keep the book's site up to date.

In producing all four editions of this book, I relied on Wayne Kirn, an expert production manager. He's seen it all.

Jane Schuck of Brentmark Software and Nicole Maholtz of Pensworth have featured *Estate Planning Smarts* in their booth at professional conferences and energetically promoted it to the community of lawyers and financial advisers. As this book caught on, Nicole assumed the role of national sales director, handling bulk orders. When Jane was struck down by cancer in 2014, I lost a cherished colleague and a dear friend.

During the six years since the first edition of this book was published, I have taken great pleasure in hearing from readers and meeting them at speaking engagements. I appreciate their comments and suggestions – letting me know when I hit the mark and where I fell short. In life and in print, there's always room for improvement.

And where would I be without my husband, Ken Stern, who has always been my biggest booster? His marketing know-how gave me the confidence to undertake this project, and the stability that he brings to our home life has enabled me to take greater risks in my professional one. Our son, Jack, who grew from child to young adult since the first edition of this book, gives special significance to terms that are integral to the estate planner's lexicon: family, legacy and the next generation.

Table of Contents

Shape the Future With Your Estate Plan

L ast I heard, no one lives forever. Estate planning, which deals with providing for ourselves as we age and taking care of loved ones after we are gone, is a constant reminder of that fact. So it's easy to understand why many people think this is a morbid topic and put off doing anything about it. Nearly 2.6 million Americans die each year, and many haven't signed the basic documents needed to protect those they care most about.

I didn't use to think much about this, either. Longevity ran in my family; it seemed like hardly anyone ever died. When my grandmother tried to talk about her will, I would brush her aside with a dismissive "stick around." To me, people who took an interest in other people's wills were money grubbers. Those who wrote wills themselves were flirting with the grim reaper. In short, I found the whole subject extremely unpleasant.

Then, in the space of three months, I became a parent, I lost a parent, and I found myself in charge of a trust that my grandmother had set up for my aunt, which my father had overseen until his death. Soon after, I was asked to write about estate planning on a continuing basis for two magazines. Realizing how important these issues had suddenly become in my own life, I agreed.

Today, after being immersed in this field for 17 years, I see estate planning as a way to shape the future. It can minimize the hardships of your old age and distribute assets to family, friends and the charities you support. If you are married or in another committed relationship, estate planning is about leaving a financial cushion for your spouse or partner. It also includes providing funds for a child's or a grandchild's education. For parents of young children, estate planning is a way to make sure someone will care for them if you suddenly perish.

Essential Documents

Regardless of your personal balance sheet, a good estate plan should include the following key documents.

- **Will.** The cornerstone of many estate plans, it should transfer assets, appoint a guardian for minor children and name an executor or personal representative – the individual or institution that takes charge of your estate after you die and distributes property as you have specified.

- **Durable power of attorney.** Appoints a trusted family member, friend or adviser as an agent to act on your behalf in a variety of financial and legal matters.

- **Health care proxy.** Sometimes called a health care agent or health care power of attorney, authorizes someone to make medical decisions on your behalf.

- **HIPAA release.** Gives doctors and hospitals permission to share medical records with specific people in addition to a person's designated health care agent. The acronym refers to the Health Insurance Portability and Accountability Act, the federal law designed to protect medical privacy; it prohibits doctors and hospitals from sharing medical information without a patient's permission.

- **Living will.** Also called an advance directive, expresses preferences about certain aspects of end-of-life care. Often this is covered in a health care proxy instead of in a separate document.

In many estate plans, trusts play a role. Although they are commonly associated with saving taxes and financing lavish lifestyles, they serve many other purposes. Most notably, they can safeguard your assets and provide for your care if you can no longer handle your affairs. They are also used to hold money for minors, forestall spendthrift family members, protect assets from former spouses or creditors, or even make provisions to care for a pet that survives you.

How to Use This Book

I wrote this book to guide you through what can be a difficult and very emotional process. That's true whether you are tackling estate planning for the first time or revising your plan to reflect changes in the law, your finances or your personal life.

The best place to start is with this book's Table of Contents. It can help you identify the chapters that apply to you. Each chapter cross-references others but is designed to be freestanding. I suggest you read the relevant chapters in sequence, though not all in one sitting.

At the end of every chapter is an action-oriented To-Do list based on material covered in that chapter. These are suggestions for next steps.

What about do-it-yourself planning? It's a question readers increasingly ask. In theory, you can use books or software and Web sites that create documents for free or for a fraction of what lawyers charge.

On the one hand, doing something on the cheap is better than doing nothing. On the other, do-it-yourself planning can cause trouble, even if your situation seems simple. There are many oddball things a layman wouldn't think of that can go wrong, especially with a will. These mistakes can end up costing your heirs a lot more than you saved in legal fees.

Here's a much safer alternative: Use this book as background before you meet with a lawyer. Referring to the To-Do lists, gather all the necessary information and think about the choices you need to make. That will make you a better-informed client and will help cut down on the billable hours your matter consumes. (Some readers have also used this book in conjunction with do-it-yourself products.)

Estate Planning Smarts is not a substitute for legal advice, but it can be a continuing resource. When there are new developments between editions, I keep readers current by tweeting (@djworking) and posting material on the book's Web site, www.estateplanningsmarts.com. You can register at the site to receive e-mail notifications of updates as they become available. This is a subject that affects us all. Let's keep the conversation going.

Chapter 1

Nothing Lasts Forever

*Read this chapter even if you
are hearty and clearheaded.*

M edical advancements that enable us to live longer, fuller lives also increase the likelihood that more of us will suffer from a diminished mental state. Mike Wallace, CBS newsman, and Ben Bradlee, former executive editor of *The Washington Post*, both of whom lived to age 93, developed Alzheimer's. An estimated 10 million Americans have dementia or cognitive impairment, with 2 million new cases reported every year, according to research by David Laibson, a professor of economics at Harvard University. More than 40 percent over the age of 80 have dementia and almost 70 percent are cognitively impaired, researchers say.

In This Chapter...

- Who Will Make Health Care Decisions?
- Who Will Take Over Your Finances?
- Whom Can You Trust?
- How to Organize Financial Records
- How to Manage Digital Footprints
- What Are Your Final Wishes?

Once you become mentally incapacitated, meaning that you don't know what assets you have, what you want to do with them and who your family members are, it is generally legally too late to change your estate planning documents. Unless you have made binding arrangements, your family may need to ask a court to appoint a conservator (also called a guardian) to oversee your finances. This can be an expensive, embarrassing ordeal, with unpleasant, even acrimonious, exchanges. So it is much better to be realistic. You can preserve your independence for as long as possible and design systems that will take effect if necessary.

Who Will Make Health Care Decisions?

Someone needs to be able to make medical decisions when you no longer can. To appoint this person to act as your agent, you will need a health care proxy – known in some states as a health care power of attorney. Legally, the health care proxy also gives the agent access to your medical records. (Some states have surrogate decision-making laws that give specific family members the right to make certain medical decisions for others.)

In the same document, or a separate one called the living will, you can express your preferences about end-of-life care. Although it is difficult to address every contingency, living wills typically cover pain relief and whether you would want treatments such as surgery, a ventilator, a feeding tube or resuscitation that might prolong your life but without necessarily ensuring your return to a functional state. Up-to-date versions of these forms for each state can be downloaded for free from the Web site www.caringinfo.org. Sign four copies of both this document and your health care proxy. Keep one copy of each and give one of each to your health care agent, your primary physician and a trusted adviser.

Although this type of planning is commonly associated with older folks, in fact this is a document that everyone 18 or older should sign. Why? Because in most states parents don't have the authority to make health care decisions for their kids once they turn 18 – even if they are paying the tuition, still have those kids on their health insurance plans and claim them as dependents on their tax returns. That means if a young adult is in an accident and becomes disabled, even temporarily, a parent might need court approval to act on his or her behalf.

Words to the wise: Before you send children off to college or to a gap-year program, ask them to sign a health care proxy (and a durable power of attorney, discussed on page 4). Much as you may hope that you've prepared children to take care of themselves, you may still be their fallback for emergencies. So make sure you have the necessary authority to play that role.

Who Will Take Over Your Finances?

If you become incapacitated, someone needs to be able to take over your finances – paying bills, authorizing stock trades and everything else. Nor will you necessarily have time to plan after the onset of symptoms – for example, if you suffer a stroke or a disabling fall. So plan for the unexpected. There are two separate documents to consider: a durable power of attorney and a living trust (revocable trust).

Durable power of attorney. This document authorizes a trusted family member, friend or adviser to act as your agent in a variety of financial and legal matters. The power of attorney may be effective from the moment you sign it or may specify that it is activated by a specific event, such as when you become incapacitated. Many people mistrust these documents, which give unbridled power to your agent. Some people sign them to appease their lawyers but never give them to the person designated to handle their affairs. If you're nervous about giving the signed document to your designated agent, leave it with your lawyer with instructions on when to turn it over. In that case, remember to tell your agent whom to contact.

Either way, make sure you name a second person who can become the agent if, for any reason, the first person cannot do the job. Some lawyers use pre-printed forms for the power of attorney and will include it as part of the estate planning package at no additional cost. If not, you can find one online by searching "free [your state name] power of attorney form."

Many financial institutions require that you fill out a specific power of attorney form for that institution. So does the IRS – it's Form 2848. The Social Security Administration has its own procedure for appointing and supervising what's called a "representative payee" for handling a beneficiary's funds; it won't accept a power of attorney.

In each case do the necessary paperwork but also sign a power of attorney to cover your other assets. A broadly worded power of attorney could give your agent the authority to implement a variety of estate planning strategies discussed in subsequent chapters, such as: disclaiming (turning down) an inheritance, changing the ownership of a Section 529 plan, making gifts, adding assets to a trust, pre-paying charitable bequests and amending retirement plan beneficiary designation forms. Ideally it should also give your agent access to online accounts (more about that later in this chapter).

Living trust (revocable trust). Some people will want to use this special type of trust in conjunction with the durable power of attorney. You'll find a primer on trusts in Chapter 6. Basically, here's how this one works. You set up a trust, designed for your own benefit, with the idea that a person or financial institution that you designate (the trustee) will ultimately manage the funds and distribute the money for your care. Until then, you can be a co-trustee or the sole trustee.

The trust can describe in detail how the assets are managed, how principal and income are distributed and who receives the property when you die. (A common misconception is that revocable trusts avoid estate taxes, which is not true.) It can also spell out exactly how to identify incapacity and who should determine it.

> ## Did You Know?
>
> You can use technology to keep your health care proxy, living will and HIPAA release handy: Send yourself an e-mail with the documents attached and save it on your cellphone. In an emergency, you can forward that e-mail to hospital administrators.

When you are acting as trustee, it should include a procedure to bring in a successor trustee should you become incapacitated.

Depending on your circumstances, these trusts can be unfunded, partially funded or fully funded at the time they are set up. For example, you can keep some cash to manage yourself and transfer other assets into the trust. Or you can leave the trust unfunded until someone certifies that you have become incapacitated. At that point, the designated agent could fund the trust for you.

The elderly or other people who find financial matters overwhelming might prefer to put everything in the trust except for life insurance, retirement assets and a checking account that holds the grocery money. This bank account is needed, if for nothing else, to deposit Social Security payments, since they cannot be made payable to a trust.

It would be a mistake to rely exclusively on a revocable trust and not sign a power of attorney. For example, if you do not initially put all the assets in the trust, it is important that the agent with power of attorney be authorized to add assets to the trust at some later point. And while the trust works well for assets under its umbrella, it does not cover quasi-personal functions, like filing tax returns, applying for Social Security benefits, signing a nursing home contract and even picking up mail.

While everybody needs a power of attorney in case of incapacity, the same is not true of a living trust. During life, a living trust is most useful to people who have many different kinds of assets, since financial institutions tend to be more accepting of trustees than they are of agents coming to them holding durable powers of attorney. If your financial life is relatively simple – say you've consolidated your accounts – a power of attorney may be all you need. But before you decide, read the following chapter to understand the role a living trust plays after you pass away.

Whom Can You Trust?

Choosing the right person – or people – to help you put all these mechanisms into action can be tricky. The individual with your health care proxy should be the same one designated in your living will. For this difficult job, you'll want someone levelheaded, who communicates well with doctors and is prepared to put emotions aside and implement your wishes.

There's no need or particular advantage to having the same person in charge of financial matters, too. When choosing an agent under a power of attorney or the trustee for your living trust, look for someone who is honest, well organized, good with paperwork and vigilant about meeting deadlines. A person's own financial acumen is less important than knowing how to hire experts when his or her own knowledge falls short.

Most people think first of naming a family member, especially a spouse or child. But that approach backfired for Brooke Astor, the New York philanthropist (see "The Astor Disaster," page 7). Whether you are choosing a trustee for your living trust or an agent to handle your power of attorney, select someone you trust absolutely. If you don't have an obvious

The Astor Disaster

Unless something goes wrong, courts generally do not supervise either powers of attorney or revocable trusts, because they are considered private arrangements. And while abuses are rare, they can be dramatic.

A notable example involved Brooke Astor, the New York philanthropist, who lived to be 105. Astor had a strained relationship with her son, Anthony D. Marshall, yet she gave him her power of attorney and entrusted him with supervising her care in old age. As Astor became incapacitated with Alzheimer's, friends complained that Marshall and his wife were diverting Astor's money for their own uses. One of Marshall's sons, Philip, filed a lawsuit in July 2006, basically accusing his father, who was 82, of elder abuse.

After several months of legal wrangling, the parties called a truce. The court appointed Annette de la Renta, a close friend of Astor's, as her guardian and put JPMorgan Chase in charge of her money. Astor died in August 2007 with an estimated net worth of $131 million.

Separately, after a six-month criminal trial in New York, in October 2009 a jury convicted Marshall of stealing tens of millions of dollars from his mother. Some of the most serious charges involved abusing the power of attorney. In the same trial, Francis X. Morrissey, Jr., one of Marshall's lawyers and co-executor of Astor's will, was convicted of conspiring with Marshall to take advantage of Astor's diminished capacity and forging an amendment to the will. Marshall was sentenced to a one-to-three-year jail term, was released in 2013 after only three months for health reasons and died a year later.

family member to choose, make a list of everyone you know and then whittle it down to trusted friends – preferably ones who are not your contemporaries. Other possibilities include an individual adviser (for instance, a lawyer or accountant) or a corporate fiduciary, like a bank or trust company. To guard against an Astor-style disaster, think about creating a system of checks and balances by naming joint agents for a power of attorney or co-trustees of a living trust.

Depending on how you set things up, the power of attorney and the revocable trust may remain inactive until you become incapacitated. Therefore, it is important to choose someone not involved in your financial affairs to decide when you have reached that state.

Traditionally, this has required a medical opinion. If that is your preference, you will need to provide the doctors of your choice the authorization to talk with your family members or advisers. Otherwise, the federal Health Insurance Portability and Accountability Act, or HIPAA, may prevent them from discussing your mental or physical condition (see "Reasons to Sign a HIPAA Release," page 9). Without this kind of authorization, your family or advisers might need a court order to get the medical records necessary to implement a power of attorney or trigger a trustee provision.

Another reasonable approach that leaves out the medical community is to name a committee of trusted family members, friends or advisers to come to a consensus about incapacity.

How to Organize Financial Records

Just as important as creating an estate plan is making key records and financial information available in case of your mental decline or for after you have passed away. Start with all the information someone would need to manage your finances. Then think about the best place and format for storing the documents and data.

Your records should enable loved ones to pay your bills and save them the sleuth work of locating all your assets, including those that exist only in cyberspace (more about that below and in the next chapter). Be sure to include:

❧ A list of all the financial institutions where you have accounts (don't forget bank CDs), including the account numbers and the type of account (for example, checking, savings or retirement). This may inspire you to consolidate your investments

❧ Serial numbers and denominations of any savings bonds that you own

❧ A beneficiary designation form for each retirement account

Reasons to Sign a HIPAA Release

Have you ever called a hospital to inquire about the condition of a friend or family member who is a patient there? If so, you may have been stymied by HIPAA. The federal Health Insurance Portability and Accountability Act, designed to protect medical privacy, prohibits doctors and hospitals from sharing medical information without the patient's permission (note, too, that this can apply to information about your own children once they reach age 18). If you want concerned friends and relatives to be privy to the details, list them in a HIPAA release.

You can also include lawyers, accountants and financial advisers who may need to stay current about your situation – for example, so they can find out whether you lack capacity. Indicate in the power of attorney or the living trust that the person in charge of finding out has the rights of a personal representative under HIPAA. According to the law, the personal representative has the same rights to medical information as the patient does. Back this up by signing a HIPAA release, authorizing doctors to disclose health information to the people you have listed, and store that with your other legal papers.

❧ Account numbers of credit cards
❧ A list of monthly, quarterly, bi-annual or yearly bills that you pay. Indicate how you receive notification of the bill (for example, by mail, e-mail or text message) and which of these are recurring bills that are automatically debited from your bank account
❧ For financial accounts managed online or bills paid electronically (such as utility bills, credit card, mortgage and car payments), all the information necessary to access those accounts, including your user name, password and answers to secret questions
❧ Paperwork for all debts, including car loans or leases
❧ The title to your car
❧ The deed to your cemetery plot, if you have bought one
❧ Insurance policies

- ❧ A list of copyrights, patents and trademarks, indicating whether you control them directly or through a trust
- ❧ Copies of all trusts that involve you: those you have created, those of which you are a beneficiary and those in which you serve as an individual trustee
- ❧ A copy of documents creating any family limited partnership or limited liability company in which you have an interest
- ❧ If you have a family business, a copy of the succession plan and buy-sell agreement for that company
- ❧ Tax returns
- ❧ Records of accounts for which you are the custodian of investments for minor children (for example, savings bonds, brokerage accounts and college accounts)

All of the documents listed above can be kept in your home in a file cabinet or safe that is fireproof and reasonably secure, or with a trusted adviser. Originals of documents that are difficult to replace belong in a safe deposit box. These include:

- ❧ Property deeds
- ❧ Birth certificate
- ❧ Social Security card
- ❧ Marriage certificate (this is more than a sentimental document – your spouse may need it to qualify for Social Security benefits)
- ❧ Savings bonds and other securities not held by a financial institution

Note that your will and the deed to your cemetery plot, if you have bought one, should not go in your safe deposit box. Why not? Unless a family member has access to it (you must not only give that person a key, but also sign a form at the bank authorizing that designee to open it), the box could be sealed when you die, and it might take court action by your heirs to get it opened. Instead, keep one original copy of your will at home, along with any supporting documents your state requires (such as an affidavit of witnesses). Ask your lawyer or other trusted adviser to keep another copy. Be sure to leave contact information so family members know who the person is.

How to Manage Digital Footprints

In recent years, a whole new set of issues has developed that estate planning needs to address. It involves what are called "digital assets." Definitions vary, but basically this refers to the footprints that we leave behind in our lives online. Unless you're a total Luddite, chances are you have digital assets in the form of e-mails, family photos or social media accounts. You may also shop online, manage your finances online or pay most of your bills electronically.

Many of these so-called assets can't be transferred. (Those that can be are covered in the following chapter.) That includes your iTunes account, which you can't take with you or leave to your heirs. Whoever inherits your devices can use whatever you've already downloaded, such as music, e-books and audiobooks. But if the material is protected by copyright (as most things are), neither your heirs nor the person administering your estate can copy or distribute those files.

Some lawyers have suggested that a way around the problem is to have a trust buy such items and hold them for the beneficiaries. This seems overly complicated, may not work legally and assumes that the trust beneficiaries will share your interest in e-books and audiobooks, for example.

In addition, most often the crucial issue is not ownership but whether you can lawfully give other people access to the accounts so they can stand in your shoes, if you become disabled or when you die. Under the law of most states the trusted people whom you appoint, known as fiduciaries, ought to have access to these accounts. But user agreements tend to prohibit that (Google is a notable exception) because companies are afraid of violating federal privacy laws. A growing number of states are passing laws to get around this problem.

The best way to avoid hassles is to put provisions in estate planning documents authorizing fiduciaries to access the accounts and allowing service providers to disclose account contents to fiduciaries. This wording should go into your will, living trust, if you have one, and in a durable power of attorney. But again, this won't help you if the service contract prohibits others from accessing the account.

Having access to the account enables the fiduciary to delete or download the content. Rather than leave this person guessing about what you want done with the material you generated or accumulated, leave instructions. If it includes potentially embarrassing items, like pornographic photos and videos, you might prefer to have them deleted, not downloaded.

If your data is financially or sentimentally valuable, make regular, redundant backups. Don't just store all those adorable baby pictures, vacation photos and family videos on a photo-sharing Web site or social media site, for example. Facebook offers a one-click option from the account settings page for downloading data to your hard drive; on Google+ it's called "data liberation." Here are other ways to help fiduciaries and heirs trace your digital footprints.

Passwords. These are the keys to your electronic kingdom. Without them, your agent under a durable power of attorney can't pay your bills or keep watch on those being automatically charged to a credit card or debited from a bank account. Nor could that trusted friend or adviser manage your investments or shut down your social media accounts.

Technology experts will tell you to start by using a different secure password for each account, though few mortals seem to follow that advice. And just to further inconvenience you, for security reasons, a growing number of institutions automatically block your access unless you change your passwords periodically. It's hard to be vigilant about keeping an up-to-date list.

And where should you put this list? The answer will depend on your technological fluency and how much you trust online security systems. Remember, too, that you want to make things easy for those who step into your shoes. Whatever storage method you are considering, don't choose one that leaves you (or them) feeling technologically challenged. Some people find it's easiest to simply write down passwords on paper and put the list (perhaps in a loose-leaf binder) in a secure place.

Here are various storage methods that rely on technology. Some can be combined with one another to create a multilevel locker.

⚜ *Create an encrypted Word document.* One step up from a handwritten list is to keep your passwords in a Word document – but not one that a hacker or a housebreaker can find and read on your computer. That means encrypting the document using Word or other software – popular ones include 7-Zip, WinZip and WinRar. Then give your agent a printout or a password for the encrypted file and tell them how to access the document.

❧ *Put it in the cloud.* These are generic online storage services that allow you to access all types of files remotely, including the list of passwords that you create. To tap into them, your family or agent would need to know your password. (Also supply them with the name of the document, but don't make it something obvious that hackers could easily discover.) If you lead a very mobile life, cloud computing can be a huge convenience, but here, too, you must trust the technology. Experts will tell you to encrypt any confidential information before uploading it to cloud storage.

❧ *Back up onto a USB flash drive.* You can make this little device, also known as a thumb drive, into a mini encrypted vault with a password of its own. The drawbacks: It's more cumbersome than the cloud to keep updated, and you must find some-place secure to store it.

> ## Did You Know?
>
> Julia Child, the culinary grande dame, was 86 when she moved into a retirement community that she and her husband had picked 20 years earlier. They had spent winters nearby. But Child did not relocate until after her husband had died.

❧ *Use an electronic password manager.* A number of services, like LastPass.com and Dashlane.com (both free), allow you to enter all your passwords in a single database and lock them up with a master electronic key. You (or your agent) need to remember only one password to access the list.

In this age of hackers and data breaches, relying on such a system might require a leap of faith. If you use a wireless connection for a home network or to access the Internet, make sure that connection is well encrypted. (Look for "https:" in your Web browser's address bar – the "s" stands for secure.) This prevents interception while the data is being transmitted.

❧ *Rely on a digital gatekeeper.* New services, aimed at people who are doing estate planning, charge a monthly or yearly fee to store the digital data that you enter, and release it according to your instructions. They can check up on you periodically via e-mail, assume you've kicked the bucket if you don't reply, and contact your heirs (most are focused on death, rather than incapacity). Trouble is, these entrepreneurial ventures themselves tend to be short-lived, and are at least as vulnerable to security breaches as more established companies. So buyer beware.

❧ *Use an old-fashioned lock box.* In combination with other methods, a fireproof safe at home or a bank safe deposit box can play an auxiliary role. Perhaps it is the ultimate depository of the paper list, flash drive or a CD with all your vital information. Or maybe this is where you put your master password, with the name of your electronic password manager.

If you don't want to put all your eggs in one basket, you can mix and match various methods to create a system that you're comfortable with and can remember. For example, you might use a password manager for the pesky sign-on information you need for practically everything these days (especially if you shop online), but create a Word file with information about your most valuable and vulnerable accounts, tuck a printout into a favorite or appropriately named book (*Great Expectations*, maybe?) and put a backup in your bank safe deposit box in case the house burns down.

> # Did You Know?
>
> John Updike sold some real estate inherited from his mother and invested the proceeds in an account for his four children. In his will, he let them know that they could find the investment records "in the office file labeled MOM-MOM-MONEY (tall gray filing cabinet)."

Computers and smartphones. The equipment is considered tangible personal property. Unless you specify in your will or living trust what should happen with the data, it generally belongs to whomever gets the hardware. So it's best to make clear in the estate planning documents whether you want the person charged with administering your estate to make copies of any of the data and distribute it to specific people before turning over the machine to the next owner.

14

E-mail. If you have your own Internet domain name, you can control every aspect of the e-mail accounts that run through it. But if, like many people, you rely on free e-mail providers, the click-through agreement that you might not have read closely (or at all) when setting up the account probably says that it's not transferable. And providers are squeamish about giving heirs access because they don't want to run afoul of federal privacy law protecting the contents. The best strategy to deal with this problem is to indicate in your will, trust or a standalone document that you authorize the service provider to turn over the contents to your fiduciary – and hope that it works.

Online sales accounts. This is a concern if you sell merchandise online, whether through your own Web site or through one of the many platforms available, such as Amazon, Craigslist, Etsy or eBay. If so, there is a chance that an order will come in and, because of death or disability, you are unable to fill it. The purchaser's credit card or PayPal account may have already been debited, and if you or your agent don't deliver, the buyer will have a claim for breach of contract.

To prevent this from happening, leave instructions so that someone can step in to complete the transaction and put a stop to future ones. The best place for these instructions is not in your will but in a side letter to family members. And don't forget to let them know how you are being notified of the sale – for example, whether by text message or e-mail. Be aware, though, that except for sales through your own Web site, these accounts are generally not transferable.

Online purchasing accounts. If you shop online, you may have credit balances – for example, for returned merchandise – that may have nominal value for your heirs. More importantly, whoever is handling your estate or your finances if you become disabled will want to close these accounts to avoid unwanted charges or fraud. So it's a good idea to keep a list of them, with your username and password, so your fiduciary can swiftly and easily do what's necessary.

What Are Your Final Wishes?

Funerals may comfort survivors, but planning one can be a wrenching task for your grief-stricken loved ones. It also leaves them vulnerable to a predatory industry with protocols that encourage consumers to spend a lot of money in a hurry. You will ease the burden if you let them know, orally or in a letter, how plain or fancy your funeral should be and whether you have any special requests – about burial or cremation; organ donation; or the text of your published death notice, for example.

The writer and filmmaker Nora Ephron left instructions in a folder marked "Exit." During a prolonged illness that preceded her death in 2012, she planned an invitation-only event for about 800, to be held at Alice Tully Hall in New York's Lincoln Center and followed by a champagne reception. Ephron indicated who should speak, in what order and for how long. She even mapped out seating and arranged for each person attending to get a copy of one of her recipes.

The comedian Joan Rivers, who died suddenly in 2014, expressed a desire that her funeral "be a big showbiz affair with lights, cameras, action." Her directions, printed on the program handed out at the service, said, "I want paparazzi and I want publicists making a scene! I want it to be Hollywood all the way. I don't want some rabbi rambling on."

Left to their own devices, friends of Copeland Marks, who wrote cookbooks about exotic cuisines and died in 1999, organized a very meaningful, more low-key memorial. It consisted of a potluck dinner with each guest preparing one of Marks's recipes, and many sharing stories about their adventures with this fun-loving man.

Whatever your preferences, keep in mind that cash flow may be an issue. Expenses can be reimbursed from the estate, but someone must pay them upfront. Funeral directors would be delighted to have you foot the bill in advance. But another option is to enter into a contract for whatever goods and services you want, then leave funds in a funeral trust set up to pay that bill when the time comes.

To-Do List

Create A Road Map

If an emergency puts you out of commission, could your family or advisers pick up where you left off? That's the question you should ask yourself in planning for the future. Here are steps to take.

❧ Give a copy of your health care proxy to the person you have designated to make health care decisions, as well as to your primary care physician and a trusted adviser. Keep a copy in your files, too.

❧ Sign a durable power of attorney, and either give it to your designated agent or make provisions for that person to access it when necessary.

❧ If you have a revocable trust, also put assets into the trust.

❧ Ask your lawyer or other trusted adviser to keep the original of your will and any supporting documentation that state law requires.

❧ Consolidate investments and make a complete list of all your assets and liabilities, including those that exist only in cyberspace.

❧ Organize all your other financial records and keep them in a safe place.

❧ Choose a system for managing your passwords and making them available to someone you trust in case of emergency.

❧ Provide family members with names and contact information for the financial advisers with whom you have relationships, including your lawyer, accountant, broker or financial planner, if any.

❧ If you have a safe deposit box, leave a note about where it is, along with the box number and a key, with your other important papers.

❧ Make sure that your will and the deed to your cemetery plot, if you have bought one, are not in this safe deposit box.

❧ Tell loved ones what your final wishes are and leave instructions in a place where they can be easily found.

Chapter 2

Who Gets What – And How Much Is Enough?

Read this chapter if you want to provide for specific people, charities or pets in your estate plan.

Thinking about how to parcel out everything you leave behind might seem like a morbid chore, more so than any other aspect of estate planning. But consider what would happen if you did not make your wishes known.

If you die without a will or living trust ("intestate," in legalese), state law will determine how most of your belongings are distributed, and the result may not be what you would want. These laws establish a ranking of inheritors. Some newer laws say everything will go first to the spouse, then to children, parents and siblings. However, plenty of state laws still divide an estate between the surviving spouse and children in preset proportions (to check the law in your state, see www.mystatewill.com/specific_states.htm). That division can lead to an assortment of awkward situations, such as when a spouse ends up short of funds even as she is the guardian of a young child's inheritance. Whatever her needs, the money belongs to the child, who is entitled to it when she reaches the age specified by state law (typically 18, 19 or 21, depending on the state).

In This Chapter...

- Dividing the Pie
- Basic Legal Documents
- Non-Probate Assets
- Special Legacies
- Who Implements Your Wishes

With an estate plan, you have much more control over who gets what. Remember, though, that you send powerful messages in the way you distribute your assets – or fail to specify what you'd like. Deciding what you want means coming to grips with both emotional baggage and a sense of finality. But it's worth doing.

Dividing the Pie

Whether you are doing an estate plan for the first time or updating an existing one, the best way to start is by making a list of everything you own. This includes: your house and personal property (you can lump them together in a single estimate or identify the most valuable possessions separately); all your investments, whether in the form of bank or brokerage accounts, retirement plans, real estate or alternative investments, and any interests you hold in a family business or partnership. For each asset, note whether you are the sole owner or own it jointly with another person.

Think of these assets, which make up your estate, as a pie that may be divided into three parts. If the total is more than $5.43 million and you are not married, 40 cents of every dollar above that amount – except for what you leave to charity – could go to federal estate taxes. The rest can be divided among family and friends according to the details you provide in your estate plan.

How much goes to family? Many spouses start by leaving everything to each other. But whether you are married or single, you should consider all the contingencies. For each person whom you want to benefit from your estate plan – a spouse, a child, another relative or a friend – you must ask, and answer, this question: "If this person dies before me, what next?"

Thinking about these issues is especially important in second marriages when there are children from the first one. For example, you may want to arrange things, in case you die before your current spouse, so that your assets will at some point go to your own children rather than ultimately passing to his (see Chapter 4).

Within a family, most people structure their estate plans to shift inheritances down a generation when one beneficiary dies rather than distributing that person's share among the other members of the same generation. Let's say you have three grown children – Harry, Sam and Molly – whom you want to benefit equally in your will. If Harry dies before Molly and Sam, most people would give Harry's portion to his children, if he has any, rather than dividing it between Sam and Molly.

How family members are treated in an estate plan, and whether some feel they were dealt an unfair hand, is a common source of discord. To deter lawsuits, many estate plans include a no-contest, or in terrorem, clause, which provides that anyone who formally challenges the plan gets nothing.

With or without such a clause, if a will is found to be invalid, assets are distributed according to the terms of a previous will or state law, depending on the circumstances. With a no-contest clause, those who lose a case to have the will thrown out, or bring a suit on lesser grounds, forfeit what they otherwise would have received.

The entertainer Michael Jackson, who died in 2009, reportedly included such a clause in his living trust, a private document that he used to dispose of most of his assets. After his death, questions arose about whether his mother, Katherine Jackson, would lose her 40 percent share of trust assets if she opposed the executors in his will. She asked the California Superior Court to rule on this issue, as state law permits, and the court found she could challenge the executors' authority without running afoul of the no-contest clause.

Did You Know?

Explaining estate planning to young children can be challenging, but they absorb more than we think. I was at the wheel one day when my son, then 10, inquired from the backseat of the car, "Will I inherit your Apple stock when you and Dad are done using it?"

Tempting as it may be to tailor your plan to the personalities, abilities and needs of individual family members, remember that disparate treatment, particularly of children, can rekindle old rivalries or ignite new ones. Whatever your justification, you might leave children thinking, "Why did she do that? Mom didn't love me as much." By treating all your children (if not all your descendants) equally, you improve the chances that they will peacefully coexist.

That said, it is reasonable to take note in your planning of children's career decisions, choice of a spouse and all the unforeseeable events that a parent witnesses in a child's life. If you encouraged your son to follow his heart and become a schoolteacher, are you penalizing him by leaving him the same size inheritance as his younger sister, who made a fortune when she sold her company?

Assuming you choose to treat everyone equally, you may want your estate plan to even out certain disparities that have arisen during your

Personal Possessions: A Lightning Rod for Conflict

Unlike financial assets, which can generally be divided easily among heirs, personal possessions – called tangible personal property – are unique.

If there are only one or two valuable possessions, your estate plan might direct the executor of the will or the trustee of a living trust to sell the diamond or the painting, for example, and divide the proceeds among the heirs. If one of them really wants a particular item (like Grandma's engagement ring) and has the funds, he or she could buy it from the estate for the fair market value. Another approach, if only one person asks for certain expensive pieces, is to honor those wishes and reduce the heir's share of other assets. To steer clear of conflicts, designate an independent third party to divide the assets or to referee.

If you want certain items to go to specific people, say so in your estate planning documents. For instance, in her will, Jacqueline Kennedy Onassis directed that most of her personal property go to her children, but she gave a handful of items to other people. She left her longtime companion, Maurice Tempelsman, a Greek alabaster head of a woman; her lawyer a copy of John F. Kennedy's inaugural address signed by Robert Frost; and a close friend a couple of Indian miniatures.

The question is what to do about everything else. One possibility is to direct your heirs to divide belongings in substantially equal shares, and if they sell anything, to use the cash to equalize things. Another is to map out a very specific rotation of choice – for instance, by birth order – so that everyone gets a turn at having first dibs on an item.

life. For instance, if you lent money to one child for a business venture and were never repaid, you could leave that child proportionately less. If one of your children never married or had children, and you have set aside college funds for grandchildren, you could give a larger inheritance to the child who is not a parent (though you should note, and hope all parties recognize, that children who are parents and have college costs need more funds).

Some parents, especially those who have created their wealth rather than inherited it, are concerned about the corrosive effect an inheritance might have on their children's work ethic, and act accordingly when they plan their estates. Unfortunately, there is no easy answer to the question, "How much is enough?"

While some people come up with an arbitrary number, others use a more nuanced approach. For example, you can identify the basics you want to provide for your children (say, education, health insurance and a house), give them enough to cover those expenses and have the rest go to charity.

Rather than leaving your children (or grandchildren) guessing about the motives behind all these difficult decisions or feeling slighted, you may want to spell out your reasoning in your estate planning documents. Having a frank discussion beforehand takes a lot of courage, but it gives all the affected parties a chance to be heard and can clear up misunderstandings – yours and theirs. The downside, of course, is that it doesn't tend to bring out the best in human nature, and you may be the target of the residual anger.

How you handle this delicate issue will depend on the dynamics of your family and your level of comfort in talking about financial topics.

How much goes to charity? Some people deliberately structure their estate plans to benefit charity and make their wishes clear. Many more think of charity as a sort of default beneficiary. For example, a charity might receive a bequest only if a person has no living relatives when he or she dies. In other cases, people who are afraid of spoiling their children structure their estate plans to benefit family up to a certain amount and leave the excess to charity. Warren Buffett and Bill Gates are two self-made businessmen who have been outspoken about their intentions to give most of their assets to charity rather than to their children.

Many people with smaller balance sheets also feel an obligation to give back to their community. For them, a crucial question is how much to donate during life and what to leave in an estate plan. Gifts made during your lifetime – if you can afford them – give you the pleasure of seeing the good works that may result from your generosity, and they can be much more tax-efficient: you are able to take an income tax deduction for the year in which the gift was made. For people with more than $5.43 million in assets whose estates may therefore be subject to the 40 percent estate tax, a donation made during life (called a "lifetime gift") reduces their net worth, leaving less to tax. In contrast, if you make a gift in your will, your estate can take a charitable deduction against only the estate tax – there is no income tax write-off. Because of the advantages of lifetime gifts, it is a good idea to give the person who holds your durable power of attorney (see Chapter 1) the power to pre-pay charitable bequests. (Chapter 16 outlines a variety of tools for charitable giving, both during life and through an estate plan.)

Still, for all the advantages of giving while you are alive, some people prefer charitable bequests to lifetime donations because they want to be sure they have enough for a comfortable retirement. For them, a key estate planning issue is how to structure the gift so that it will not shortchange family.

The basic choice is whether to describe your bequest as a preset dollar amount or as a fixed percentage of your estate. Unless you are relatively sure what your net worth will be when you die (and

> ## *Did You Know?*
>
> Today using "last will and testament" is like wearing a belt and suspenders, but it wasn't always so. Historically, a will was used to pass along real estate to heirs, while a testament covered personal property. The distinction no longer applies, although the phrase lives on.

few people have that degree of certainty), there is a potential pitfall: If your net worth declines – for example, if your investments do poorly – your family may not get as much as you intended them to have.

One alternative, if you want to describe your bequest in percentage terms (for instance, "50 percent to my wife, 20 percent to each of my two children and 10 percent to charity"), is to require that family members get at least a certain amount that you specify before anything goes to charity. For example, you could say, "50 percent of my estate but no less than $500,000 to my wife; 20 percent of my estate but no less than $100,000 to each of my children," with the balance of the estate split according to the percentage formula. Another possibility is to provide for charity to get a fixed amount but include a circuit breaker, so that it does not exceed a certain percentage of your estate. Any fixed amounts you include can be subject to an inflation adjustment.

Disclaimants Beware

Writing a will so that heirs can implement strategies through disclaimers is only half the battle. Anyone disclaiming an inheritance needs to be aware of the potential pitfalls that surround the process. Under federal tax law, your heirs must make their disclaimer within nine months of your death.

Generally a disclaimant may not have accepted an interest in the asset or any of its benefits. (There are special rules for surviving spouses.) Innocent mistakes, like depositing a dividend check in one's own account, could preclude someone from making a disclaimer.

State laws may impose additional requirements, such as giving notice of the disclaimer to the executor (called the personal representative in some states), to estate beneficiaries and to the surrogate's court or its functional equivalent.

Maximizing flexibility. When your finances or the economic environment are uncertain, build as much flexibility into your estate plan as possible, to allow your heirs to make adjustments in how the pie is divided. The primary way of doing that is with an estate planning technique known as a disclaimer.

Basically, a disclaimer involves saying "no thanks" to an inheritance. People making disclaimers, known as disclaimants, are generally treated as if they had died before the person from whom they are inheriting. Disclaimers can help your heirs implement a variety of tax strategies. They can also be used to give heirs some choices about charitable giving. If you are not prepared to make significant charitable bequests through your estate plan because you are not sure if your heirs will need the money, you can give them the option of shifting assets to a charity through a disclaimer.

In some contexts it does not matter whether your estate plan mentions the possibility of disclaiming. The law gives heirs a right to disclaim, so you don't have to provide for it in your will. But most often there is a person who would be next in line. If you want your heirs to be able to disclaim to charity instead, your will must mention this option and name the specific charity or charities that will receive any assets that are disclaimed – the choice of the charity is not up to the people who would otherwise inherit the assets. Example: "To my daughter Sally, but if she disclaims, to our town public library." The charities you name can include charitable trusts, your own private foundation or a donor-advised fund (see Chapter 16).

Restricting access. When giving away money and other assets through your estate plan, you have a choice between leaving it to your heirs outright or in trust. Outright transfers give recipients immediate control over their inheritance. Trusts put a person or company in charge of managing the assets and distributing them according to your wishes, and thus play a key role in preserving an inheritance. Trusts are widely used in a second marriage for people who want to leave assets to children from an earlier marriage (see Chapters 3 and 4).

A trust can shield assets from two key risks. One is the prospect that heirs who are spendthrifts or inexperienced at dealing with money will fritter away the assets or be vulnerable to financial scams; the other is the growing possibility in our litigious society that funds will be eroded by creditors, such as ex-spouses or someone who wins a lawsuit against your heirs (see Chapter 17).

The downside, of course, is that trusts restrict your heirs' access to the funds. And by locking up everything in trust, you may undermine the self-confidence of adult children. Without the opportunity to make their own mistakes, struggle and ultimately succeed, children might get the impression that "Dad never thought I was going to amount to anything, and that's why he kept such tight controls over this money." A combination of outright access to some of their inheritance and protection afforded by some assets left in trust can balance the goals of autonomy and your desire to preserve what you leave behind.

Here, too, disclaimers can preserve flexibility for your heirs. Let's say you would ordinarily leave an outright inheritance to your children or siblings but want to protect the assets from potential creditors. In that case, you can provide for an outright bequest but give your heirs the option to disclaim into a trust. The trust must be set up before you die, and the money must never touch the inheritor's hands. By disclaiming into this trust, the inheritor gives up control over the assets forever but can generally keep them out of the hands of creditors.

Some people try using trusts to influence their descendants' behavior. Consider the incentive trust, which makes distributions for specific achievements (such as graduating from college) or withholds funds in case of certain undesirable events (like being convicted for drug use).

These trusts can be hugely troublesome. One difficulty is that it is easier to punish people when they go astray than it is to reward them when they do good. And although parents want to inspire their children to do great things, achievement can be hard to define. For example, the so-called "investment banker clause," which provides for payouts from a trust based on how much money a beneficiary earns, seems to penalize the son who decides to teach high school or the daughter who wants to do charitable work.

History includes some notable examples of people who tried to use trusts as a way to control their heirs – even from the grave. One was Leona Helmsley, the billionaire real estate developer and hotel operator, who died in 2007. In her will, she specifically disinherited two of her grandchildren, Craig Panzirer and Meegan Panzirer Wesolko, "for reasons which are known to them" but which were not spelled out. She left two other grandchildren, David and Walter Panzirer, $10 million apiece.

Half of the sum was in a trust with substantial strings attached: In order to receive annual distributions from the trust for the rest of his life, each grandson was required to visit the grave of their father (Helmsley's son, Jay Panzirer, who died in 1982) every year on the anniversary of his death. The only exception to this requirement was if the grandson had a physical or mental disability that in the trustees' opinion made it impossible to visit.

To prove they visited, each grandson had to sign the register kept at the mausoleum where their father was buried (this, too, was described in Helmsley's will). And if they missed a single visit, they would not receive any payouts from the trust in the future.

Basic Legal Documents

The paperwork required to pass assets to your heirs can depend on a variety of factors, including what the assets are, the type of account they are in, how they are titled and which estate planning documents mention them. These documents are the foundation for most plans:

Will or living trust. There is widespread confusion about the differences between these two documents, and when you need one rather than the

Providing for Fido

Although you cannot give assets directly to pets, you can leave money and instructions to provide for them after you are gone. There are a couple of ways to do this, which can be used separately or in combination with each other.

Set up a trust. A famous example is the $12 million trust Leona Helmsley created to benefit her dog, Trouble. After Helmsley died, in 2007, two of her grandchildren, whom she had disinherited, challenged the arrangement. They persuaded the court to reduce the trust to $2 million and walked away with $3 million apiece. The other $4 million went to a charitable trust that Helmsley and her husband Harry had set up. (Trouble died in 2011.)

Pet trusts (funded with much smaller sums) have become increasingly popular, and can take effect while you are still alive if you are no longer able to care for your pet. Such a trust should identify the caregiver (and alternates) and indicate what should happen to the trust funds after your pet dies.

Choose a pet guardian. You can designate in your will the person to care for your pet. Lauren Bacall, for example, who died in 2014, left her dog, Sophie, to her son Sam Robards, along with $10,000 to take care of her. This raises two potential pitfalls: there's no legal mechanism for making sure things go as you planned or any guarantee that the person will want your pet or be able to care for it when the time comes.

A growing number of pet guardian programs have sprung up, providing animal care after an owner's death. These programs are terrific for people who don't have a specific person in mind or need to name an alternate on their pet trust if the caregivers they have listed are unable or unwilling to serve. Or you can combine the two concepts, and put the animal care organization in charge of your pet's care, while naming the trustee to oversee it and control the money.

In addition to expressing your wishes in estate planning documents, communicate them to friends, family and financial advisers. Otherwise, by the time they locate the relevant documents, it may already be too late to save Fido.

other. A common misconception is a living trust (also called a revocable trust) avoids avoid estate taxes, which is not true. Both a will and a living trust can be used to transfer assets, but each has unique uses (see chart on page 31). For example, only a will can be used to appoint a guardian for a child.

In some states, living trusts are also used to eliminate probate. Whether probate is costly or burdensome will depend on the state. Still, there are times when you might want to use a living trust to limit how much of your estate goes through probate or to avoid it altogether. For example, if you are concerned about publicity over your net worth or the identity of your beneficiaries, you might transfer assets through a trust – which, unlike a will, is not a public document. Someone with a domestic partner might use a revocable trust, because it is harder for family members to challenge a trust than a will.

Did You Know?

People are more likely to have a will as they get older, but many of all ages still don't. Among people 50 and older, more than half have a will, according to FindLaw.com. Between ages 25 and 34, about a quarter do; among 18-to-24s, less than 10 percent have a will.

A living trust is also useful if you own real estate in a state that is not your primary residence. Real estate is governed by the probate rules of the state in which it is situated. Unless the property is in a living trust, an Illinois resident who has a home in Florida, for instance, would need to probate the property separately there.

If your goal is to avoid probate totally, keep this in mind: Using a living trust for this purpose works only for assets put into the trust, and inevitably something gets left out. So you should still have a will that can cover everything else, whether or not you listed it. And, of course, this will must be probated.

Personal property memorandum. This indicates whom you want to receive jewelry, art and other personal possessions that are not described in the will. You should keep these two documents together.

Why might you want to use a personal property memorandum rather than a will? The main reason is privacy. Your will, which is a public record,

Will or Living Trust?

Both a will and a living trust can be used to transfer assets, but each also has other unique uses.

	Will	**Living Trust**
Uses besides transferring assets	Name guardians for children who are minors, create trust that takes effect after death	Hold assets for your benefit while you are alive – for example, in case of dementia
When it takes effect	Not until death	During life or at death
Privacy	None: It's a public record	Private
Procedure for creating and amending	Must be signed with certain formalities, which vary from state to state (for example, requirements for witnesses, and whether it can be handwritten)	Signature usually is sufficient; depending on state law, may be desirable to have it notarized
Steps necessary after death	Must be submitted for probate – court's approval	Probate usually not necessary
Who distributes property	Executor or personal representative	Trustee

identifies who got what, for all to see. With a personal property memorandum, strangers don't need to know that you left your Picasso to your sister or your collection of autographed guitars to your high school buddy, for instance. And if you have a change of heart, you can modify this document without the formalities needed to amend a will.

Still, there's a catch: Depending on where you live, your executor – the person or institution you appoint to put your will into action – may not be required to follow the wishes you express in an independent document. In some states, these memos are considered binding on the executor. Elsewhere, they are treated only as guidance, meaning your executor can consider your stated preferences – but need not follow them unless you make the personal property memorandum part of the will, which largely defeats the purpose.

Non-Probate Assets

It's crucial to understand the difference between assets that pass under a will or living trust, and those that usually do not. Those that pass by contract or by operation of law are, in effect, will substitutes. These include retirement assets, life insurance, medical savings accounts and savings bonds, as well as jointly titled bank accounts, brokerage accounts and real estate. For many people, these non-probate assets, as they are called, represent a large part of what they leave behind. It's important to coordinate them with the rest of your estate plan.

Misunderstandings about who is entitled to non-probate assets can lead to unintended consequences. A common example involves an aging parent with several adult children who depends on one of them as the primary caregiver. To facilitate bill-paying, the parent may open a bank account making that child the co-owner, not realizing that he will automatically receive all the money in this account when the parent dies.

That child has no obligation to share the money with his siblings. If he wants to, it's considered a gift, and the limits on yearly and lifetime tax-free gifts apply (see Chapter 3). To avoid this situation, a parent should give the child a power of attorney (see Chapter 1) over the account instead of making him an owner.

Another issue that gets neglected is who should pay expenses. Even if federal estate taxes are no longer an issue, heirs incur many costs, including state estate or inheritance taxes (in 19 states and the District of Columbia), professional fees and funeral charges. These typically come out of the pot of money covered by a will or living trust. When most of an estate passes outside of probate, there may not be enough funds allocated for expenses.

To steer clear of these and other mishaps, consider the following issues with respect to each of your assets:

Joint accounts. With bank and brokerage accounts, the most frequent form of joint ownership is joint tenancy with rights of survivorship. It appears on some account statements abbreviated JTWROS, and on others by naming the owner as one person or the other (for instance, Lucy or Ricky Ricardo). Both owners have access to the assets during life, and when one joint tenant dies, everything goes to the survivor. This form of ownership, though usually

> ## Did You Know?
>
> Warren Burger, former Chief Justice of the United States, flubbed it in his 69-word, do-it-yourself will: He made no provision for estate taxes and failed to list executors' powers. That cost the estate thousands and required a court to approve the sale of Burger's real estate.

appropriate for spouses and domestic partners, poses many pitfalls for other people. One risk is that either person can withdraw all the money without the other's consent. Another is that unless the joint tenant is a spouse, there may be gift-tax costs of adding someone's name to an account, and joint title could expose each co-owner to the other's potential liabilities (see Chapter 17).

In many states, married couples may be able to use a form of joint ownership called tenancy by the entirety to protect these assets as well as real estate. (Some states allow it only for real estate.) With this form of ownership, only the couple's joint creditors will have access to the asset. However, if the non-debtor spouse dies first, the creditors of the debtor spouse can reach it.

Co-owned real estate. Many issues that apply to bank accounts also affect real estate held as joint tenants with rights of survivorship. Another concern that can be difficult to navigate is that joint owners must agree before the property can be sold.

Assets payable (or transferable) on death. Although many people use these terms interchangeably, the exact wording may depend on state law and the type of asset. For example, you can make savings bonds "payable

Tie Up Loose Ends

Charles Kuralt, the CBS News correspondent and anchor who died in 1997, could have saved his loved ones a lot of heartache and legal expenses if he had used a will or living trust to transfer certain property to Patricia Elizabeth Shannon, his secret, intimate companion for 29 years.

Among other things, that might have avoided or at least curtailed a six-year, public court battle between Shannon and Kuralt's family. Shannon claimed Kuralt had left her 90 acres and a renovated schoolhouse near the Montana fishing retreat where they spent time together; his will left everything to his family.

During the course of the lawsuit, details of the relationship, said to be a surprise to Kuralt's wife, Suzanne Baird Kuralt, who lived in New York, and her daughters spilled into court papers. Kuralt posthumously became the subject of scandal and talk show banter.

The outcome of the case turned on a court's interpretation of a handwritten note that Kuralt sent Shannon several weeks before he died, saying he would arrange to give her the land. The court ruled in Shannon's favor, though it remained unclear whether the note was a valid amendment to Kuralt's 1994 will or simply a promise to revise the document that Kuralt never carried out.

After the court awarded Shannon the property, valued at $600,000, several more rounds of legal battles followed over who was responsible for paying the federal estate taxes on it. The Montana Supreme Court ruled in 2003 that the taxes should come out of the daughters' share. Kuralt's wife died in 1999 while the dispute was pending.

on death" to the person you name, while brokerage accounts are labeled "transfer on death." The net effect is the same. When the owner dies, the person named can promptly collect the money by presenting the death certificate and filling out any paperwork the institution requires. In contrast with joint ownership, the named people have no access to the money while the account owner is alive.

A common trap goes something like this: A mother wants to provide equally for her three children. Shares in General Electric constitute a third of her estate. So she leaves the stock to one child in a transfer on death account and names the other two as the beneficiaries of her IRA. Several months before she dies, she sells the stock. The child who was supposed to get it receives nothing.

Beneficiary designation. This is a document given to an insurance company or financial institution, indicating who should inherit certain assets that do not pass under a will or trust – such as the proceeds of a life insurance policy and retirement accounts. Note that with an IRA, you can readily name any beneficiaries you want, but for a 401(k) or other workplace plan, you must get your spouse's written permission to leave it to anyone who is not your spouse.

It's critical that you keep these forms up to date. To change a beneficiary – for example, if you get married or divorced, or your spouse dies – make sure to file an amended form.

Special Legacies

In the course of pursuing our dreams, passions or talents, some of us leave behind legacies that uniquely express who we were, and these may have significant monetary value. Whether your heirs want to continue them, or simply cash out, your estate plan should provide them with the tools and freedom to make those choices. Here are steps to take with respect to particular assets.

The family business. Company founders often want to pass along the enterprise to family members who are running it, while those who don't work in the business favor cashing out. It is hard to apportion things so that everyone comes out equally, or, if not equally, at least feeling they were treated fairly.

One way to address the issue is to find out whether any of your children want to continue in the business. If none does, your estate plan can reflect the expectation that the company will be sold. If one or more children want to continue in the business, you can look for ways the children who will not be involved might receive other, comparably valued, assets, such as stocks, bonds and real estate, or the proceeds of a life insurance policy.

Summer and vacation homes. Before leaving these assets to more than one person jointly, find out whether they want them and how they might continue using them. Various legal vehicles are available for sharing and running these homes, financing their operation and buying out people who do not want to participate (see Chapter 11).

Art and collectibles. Whether or not your heirs share your taste in these items, if you are getting on in years, the tax law gives you a strong incentive to hold on to any art or collectibles that have appreciated in value. At your death the basis of your treasures is stepped-up to their current market value – meaning heirs can sell immediately without owing capital gains tax. Conversely, if an item is now worth less than you paid for it, sell it yourself, since you, but not your heirs, can claim a capital loss, provided you qualify as an investor (rather than a hobbyist) in the eyes of the IRS.

Items not left to particular people will be distributed according to the standard clauses of your will or living trust – meaning they might be up for grabs or sold to benefit everyone. Still, without guidance from you, heirs might have no idea what they've got and may end up unloading your treasures at fire-sale prices. So keep records of what everything is, including: the purchase date; what it cost; the name of the seller and ownership history (provenance); and any proof of authenticity. Make a note of why you bought it, if that is integral to its value. (For example, "This fits well in the evolution of Gibson guitars.") If possible, leave heirs the name of an expert, such as a museum curator who specializes in your area of interest or a reputable dealer, who can help them to sell.

Intellectual property. The work of successful writers, artists, photographers and musicians continues to generate revenue long after

36

the creator has passed away. Michael Jackson, Charles Schulz and John Lennon are among the top-earning dead celebrities, for example. So it's important that you make provisions not only for the transfer of any copyrights and trademarks you own, but also for the businesslike management of this legacy.

Intellectual property law is complicated, and if you've been prolific, protecting and building on this inheritance can be a full-time job. Family harmony is another factor to consider. Without a structure that heirs can use to manage the intellectual property, including a mechanism for decision making, they could disagree about everything from licensing rights to renegotiating old contracts.

Therefore, think carefully about a succession plan, starting with whom you initially put in charge. For instance, when John Updike died, in 2009, the author left all the literary rights and property, including his manuscripts, papers and letters, to a literary trust that he had set up more than 30 years earlier. Until he died he was co-trustee with his wife,

> ## *Did You Know*❓
>
> Retirement accounts are not normally covered by a will. Instead, the funds go to inheritors according to beneficiary designation forms. You fill out the form when you open an account but can later amend it. The form notifies the bank or financial institution about who will inherit the account.

Martha, and Judith Jones, his editor at Knopf. After Updike's death they retained a literary agent for the estate who, among other things, negotiated the sale of his archives to the Houghton Library of Harvard University, for $3 million.

Digital assets. Definitions vary for this new category of assets that emerged with the Internet age. From an estate planning perspective a key issue is whether what we leave behind is purely a digital footprint, or something that we can transfer through a will or trust. The previous chapter covered the thorny issue of giving other people access to online accounts, even if they have little or no monetary value. Here are steps to take with other digital assets, which may be far more valuable.

❧ *Domain names.* These are the words and letters that make up an Internet address. The most valuable names are those of a recognized business or a keyword that people might search for to find a particular item, business or service. Since they are leased for a certain length of time, typically expressed as a number of years, it's important not to let the lease lapse, because somebody can register it as soon as it lapses. Make a list of your domain names and Web hosts, along with their annual renewal dates, and express your wishes about whether they should be transferred to your heirs, sold or allowed to lapse.

❧ *Web pages and blogs.* This content can't be transferred unless you own the copyright to the material; you probably don't if it was created in the course of your employment. If you do own the content, your fiduciary should be able to capture the material, pass it on to anyone who is interested and then shut it down. Either way, though, you should have a physical backup (for example, on a thumb drive or CD) in case there's a catastrophic problem with the hosting service.

Did You Know?

Facebook allows users to designate a "legacy contact," who can manage the account posthumously or have it deleted. To set your preferences, go to "Settings," then "Security." Directions under "Memorialized Accounts" explain how to contact Facebook after someone dies.

❧ *Bitcoin.* If you were tech-savvy and forward-thinking enough to mine this virtual currency in 2010 or 2011, you've had a taste of its volatility and appreciation. Congratulations. Taxwise, you would be smart to donate it to charity during your life or share it with your loved ones later.

Here's why: The IRS takes the position that Bitcoin, which does not exist in a physical form, is property (not cash). Therefore, when you exchange it for goods or services worth more than its initial cost, the difference gets taxed as capital gain. Since public charities are tax-exempt, there's no tax when they exchange Bitcoin for cash. (Meanwhile, you can take a tax deduction for the fair market value of your donation.) And, as with other appreciated assets, your heirs don't pay capital gains tax if there's been no appreciation between the time they inherit it and when they sell it.

Still, without the private key (password) to the digital wallet in which you store your Bitcoin, it's worthless to any of you. And, unlike other passwords, this one can't be recovered if you lose it. In an online account, it can get hacked. So if you own a lot of Bitcoin, it's best to create a paper version of your password that you keep off-line – in what security experts call "cold storage." You can transfer your Bitcoin through your will or living trust. In a separate side letter, leave instructions about where to find the digital wallet that contains your private Bitcoin passwords.

Frequent-flyer miles and hotel points. Whether you've been a road warrior or have itchy feet, these may be worth thousands, or even tens of thousands, of dollars, so don't let them go to waste.

As with digital assets, company policies generally trump anything you might say in your will. Here, too, the rules keep changing. Some companies let your spouse inherit your points; others say they can go to anyone at the same street address. And even when points are officially "non-transferable," heirs may be able to negotiate an exception – if they know about the accounts.

Best practice: Mention in your will or living trust that these accounts exist, but leave a list of them in a separate document. If you're not vigilant about it, your fiduciary can hire a service, called WebCease, to track down these accounts (and digital assets) for a nominal fee, but they won't necessarily find everything.

Who Implements Your Wishes

Your estate plan expresses your wishes, and you entrust your executor to carry them out. This is the person or institution that administers your estate after you die and remains in charge until it is legally closed. Before that happens, the will must be admitted to probate. Any creditors need to be paid; the taxes, if any, need to be paid, and the beneficiaries named in your will should receive their share of what is left. If there is an estate tax audit or a will contest, the executor will oversee that process, too.

Mapping Out the Executor's Role

A will is a road map to the responsibilities of the executor or personal representative, and you need to tailor it to your particular circumstances. Typically the personal representative is expected to:

🍃 Gather the assets and take title to them – the personal representative is the legal owner of the property until it is distributed to the beneficiaries named in the will

🍃 Inventory the assets and determine what they are worth (some states require that these lists be filed with a local court), getting appraisals as necessary

🍃 Safeguard the assets by prudently managing and investing them

🍃 Collect any debts owed to the estate

🍃 Pay medical bills and present claims to the insurance company for reimbursement

🍃 Respond to any other creditors' claims that may be filed

🍃 File your final income tax return and pay any taxes owed

🍃 File the estate tax return and submit any taxes that are due

Other powers may relate to the specific assets you own or the dynamics of your family. For example, to prevent family feuds you might want the will to include guidelines about how the personal representative should divide tangible personal property (see "Personal Possessions: A Lightning Rod for Conflict," page 23). Some people include the power to borrow and lend money. Business owners might authorize a personal representative to operate, sell or make changes in the company. And if you own significant real estate, you might want the personal representative to be able to sell, lease or mortgage it.

Being an executor is a huge responsibility. Depending on the complexity of the estate and subsequent events, the job might last for a couple of years, and sometimes many more. Whom you choose as executor or executrix (a woman who serves this role) can make the difference between an estate that is settled harmoniously and efficiently, and one that gets bogged down in a legal and financial quagmire.

The best executor is honest, efficient, has sound financial judgment and gets along well with people. Estate administration can get complex, and executors should know enough to call the experts when their own knowledge falls short.

An executor, called a personal representative in some states (the terms are used interchangeably here), is a fiduciary, which means that certain legal obligations automatically apply. These include a duty to act always in the best interests of the beneficiaries and to avoid conflicts of interest when handling the estate. Specific functions need to be outlined in the will (see "Mapping Out the Executor's Role," page 40). If you do not name a personal representative and an alternate, and your first choice is not able to serve, a local court will appoint one instead.

Did You Know?

Widows and widowers can now carry over the estate tax exemption of their most recently deceased spouse. To use this break, the executor must file an estate tax return, even if no tax is owed. This return is due nine months after death with a six-month extension allowed.

Choosing family. Most people think first of naming a family member, especially a spouse or child, as executor. The advantage of this is that your next of kin presumably understands your intentions better than anybody else and can readily find the assets that need to be inventoried.

This can also save the family money. Many states set caps on the fees that executors may charge, but they vary widely. While some are framed simply in terms of what's reasonable, others are based on a percentage of the estate value. For a large estate, the executor's fee can get expensive. When family members who are also beneficiaries serve as executors, they often waive the fees. Other times, families are happy to have this money go to one of their own rather than paying an outside executor. In that case, those who find the paperwork and complications overwhelming can hire professionals to guide them through the process.

But putting family members in charge has several drawbacks. When they are also beneficiaries, as is typically the case, conflicts of interest can arise and be difficult to navigate. What's more, mishandling a potential conflict or a particular task with financial implications can lead to ill will among beneficiaries. Ultimately they may hold the executor liable for a wide variety of missteps.

In an effort to be fair, some people name all their children as co-executors. When that happens, sibling rivalry and trouble reaching a consensus can make it hard to get things done. Likewise, naming a spouse along with children from a previous marriage, or even those children alone, can lead to friction. Making the right choice in a particular situation is a matter of knowing the individuals and how they would react.

> ## Did You Know?
>
> Co-executors and co-trustees may have logistical problems getting all the necessary signatures on various documents. A practical solution is for them to stipulate that once they have agreed on something, a signature by one constitutes signature by all.

Reaching outside the family. For all these reasons, it may be helpful to name a professional who knows the ropes either as the sole executor or co-executor with family members or a trusted friend. The options include an individual adviser or a corporate fiduciary, such as a bank or trust company. If you choose an individual, designate at least a couple of alternates in case that person is unwilling or unable to serve when the time comes. You do not have that concern with a corporate fiduciary, which provides institutional longevity. It is also more likely to carry enough insurance to cover any potential liability.

Either way, meet the professionals you have in mind to be sure they are able to provide the services you require. Inquire about their experience with similar matters and ask about fees – subject to the maximums set by state law, they are typically based on the size and complexity of the estate.

To-Do List

Prelude to Planning

The estate planning process starts with complex personal choices. Before meeting with a lawyer, give some thought to the following.

❧ Whom do you want to benefit through your estate plan?

❧ Are you concerned that once your heirs receive their inheritance, they will no longer have an incentive to work?

❧ Do you want your estate plan to treat all your children equally?

❧ If you have a family business, and only some children are involved in the company, how do you want to address this in your estate plan?

❧ Do you prefer that heirs receive their inheritances outright, or should some of your assets be left in trust?

❧ For assets left in trust, at what ages do you want beneficiaries to receive distributions?

❧ Have you coordinated assets that pass through beneficiary designation forms or "payable on death" and "transfer on death" provisions with the rest of your estate plan?

❧ If you have a summer or vacation home, do you want to keep it in the family?

❧ Are there charitable organizations that you would like to mention in your estate plan?

❧ Whom do you trust to serve the following roles: make medical decisions if you cannot act for yourself; act as your attorney under a power of attorney; be the trustee of a living trust; serve as executor of your will.

Chapter 3

Understand
The Tax System

*Read this chapter even if
you think taxes won't
affect your heirs.*

R ecent tax law changes are turning traditional estate planning on its head. Indeed, moves long considered savvy – for example, aggressively shifting wealth to younger generations while senior family members are still alive, or leaving assets to a "bypass" trust – may no longer be necessary to save estate tax and could now leave many families paying income tax they wouldn't otherwise owe.

The big rethink was set in motion by the legislative deal Congress passed in 2013. It made permanent the most generous exclusion from estate and gift tax, in real dollars, since the birth of the death tax in 1916 and raised the top income tax rate on long-term capital gains to its highest level since 1997. Including a new 3.8 percent net investment income tax that took effect as a part of ObamaCare, the top rate on long-term capital gains from stocks is now 23.8 percent, up from 15 percent in 2012.

In This Chapter...

- ❧ *Spouses Are Special*
- ❧ *Income Tax Issues*
- ❧ *New Wrinkles for Bypass Trusts*
- ❧ *Planning for State Estate Tax*
- ❧ *Gift-Tax Basics*

At the same time, many folks no longer need to worry about the federal estate tax. Currently we can each transfer $5.43 million during life or at death, before a transfer tax of 40 percent kicks in. Not only will that so-called "applicable exclusion" rise with inflation, but spouses can now share each other's exclusions. AB Bernstein projects that in 10 years a couple will be able to pass on a combined $13.64 million, and in 20 years $18.72 million. Read on for some basic rules and strategies to help you navigate the new terrain.

Spouses Are Special

The changing tax landscape has huge implications for spouses. Widows and widowers can now carry over any unused exclusion of the spouse who died most recently and add it to their own, a feature that tax geeks dubbed "portability." The tax law refers to the sum carried over as the "deceased spousal unused exclusion amount." In common parlance it has become known by the shorthand "DSUE amount."

Portability doesn't change the fact that you can give an unlimited amount to your spouse, during life or through your estate, provided she or he is a U.S. citizen, with no tax applied – this is the unlimited marital deduction. (If your spouse is not a U.S. citizen, see "What If You Married an Alien?" page 51.) But before portability, if the first spouse to die left everything to the survivor simply through an "I love you" will, the dead spouse's estate tax exclusion was lost.

To avoid that problem, you either had to leave assets, up to your exclusion amount, to someone other than your spouse, or set up a special kind of trust, known as a bypass, or credit-shelter, trust. It works like this: At the death of the first spouse, an amount up to his exemption goes into a trust for the kids. The surviving spouse can have access to the earnings (and in most cases principal) of the trust, but the money isn't hers outright and bypasses her estate when she dies. Now it's possible to rely on portability instead. Both the marital deduction and portability apply to same-sex married couples.

Still, portability is not automatic. The executor handling the estate of the spouse who died will need to transfer the unused exclusion to the survivor, who can then use it to make lifetime gifts or pass assets through his or her estate. The transfer is made by filing an estate tax return when the first spouse dies, even if no tax is owed. This return is due nine months after death, with a six-month extension allowed. If the executor doesn't file the return or misses the deadline, the spouse loses the right to portability. Spouses should see that the return is filed even if they're not wealthy today, because who knows what the future holds? Winning the lottery, inheriting a lot of money, or getting a large settlement or judgment in a lawsuit could all leave a surviving spouse with much more money than she now has.

Income Tax Issues

For more than two decades, a key strategy for people concerned about estate taxes has been to give away assets during life and leave less for the government to tax later. The theory was that anything transferred through lifetime gifts, whether shares of stock, a vacation home or an interest in a family-owned business, wouldn't count as part of the donor's estate. Therefore, both the gift and any future appreciation on it would avoid estate tax.

FAQs About the $10.86 Million per

Federal law now allows widows and widowers to add the unused estate tax exemption of the spouse who died most recently to their own, and together give away $10.86 million during life or through an estate plan. (The amount will be adjusted for inflation.) Portability, as this new provision is called, takes us into uncharted waters. Here are answers to some frequently asked questions.

Does this provision help me if my spouse died years ago? No. It applies only to deaths after Dec. 31, 2010.

Does portability apply to lifetime gifts as well as assets that pass through an estate plan? Yes.

Is portability automatic? No. The executor handling the estate of the spouse who died will need to file an estate tax return transferring the "deceased spousal unused exclusion" (DSUE) amount to the survivor.

Does the executor have a duty to elect portability? Not under the law, but you can create such an obligation with a provision in your will. For stepparents in a second marriage, this might be a subject to cover in the prenuptial agreement.

Is the DSUE amount adjusted for inflation? No. The value remains the same as it was when the first spouse died.

You still might have good reasons to want to help family and friends financially. But now, if you're giving them anything other than cash, consider whether they would be better off inheriting it in order to reap income tax savings from the step-up in basis.

Step-up? When you sell an asset such as stock, you owe capital gains tax on the difference between what you paid for it (your cost basis) and what you get for it. But if you inherit certain assets, you can step-up their tax basis to whatever they were worth at your benefactor's death. That means highly appreciated inherited property can be sold immediately with no capital gains, or later, with all the gains before you inherited it disregarded. By

Couple Federal Estate Tax Break

What happens if you remarry? That depends on who dies first – you or your new spouse. For example, let's assume Harry has an unused exemption amount of $2 million when he dies (say, because he left $3.43 million to his children outright). His widow, Sally, has a $5.43 million exemption amount of her own. As the executor of Harry's estate, Sally files a return, transferring Harry's unused exemption, so that she will then be able to pass $7.43 million tax-free (her own $5.43 million exemption plus Harry's $2 million unused exemption). Then she marries Joe.

If Joe dies before Sally, she can no longer use Harry's unused exemption amount – only Joe's. If Joe's unused exemption is less than Harry's (or if he has no unused exemption at all), Sally is out of luck.

On the other hand, what if Sally dies first? She came into the marriage with a $7.43 million exemption amount, including the $2 million unused exemption from Harry. Assume that she leaves $3.43 million to the children she and Harry had together. In that case, Joe can use the remaining $4 million exemption, along with his own. However, under the law the amount carried over can never be more than $5.43 million.

Can I use my exclusion instead to provide for children from a previous marriage? Yes. You can do this with just part of your exclusion amount – or the whole thing – by leaving assets to them outright or in a trust.

contrast, if you receive property from a living donor, you take on his tax basis when the time comes to calculate capital gains. (You can neither inherit nor be given capital losses.)

Step-up isn't new but has now become more significant to wealth-transfer planning for many families, including some still likely to have taxable estates. Depending on where you and your intended beneficiaries live, the income tax savings from the step-up in basis may be greater than the transfer tax cost, if any.

For example, in California, which has no state estate tax but levies a 13.3 percent state income tax on income above $1 million, heirs would pay a combined state and federal top rate on gains from the sale of a Mark Rothko painting that exceeds the top estate tax rate of 40 percent. But families in Washington State, which has no income tax but levies a top estate tax of 20 percent, would still find estate tax more onerous. This suggests that Californians should be much more passive in their estate plans, choosing more often than not to simply die with their assets, than Washington residents.

> ## Did You Know?
>
> When tallying up the value of your assets to see if your estate will be subject to tax, your heirs can use either the value on the date of death, or an alternate date six months later if it would reduce the tax. But whatever date the heirs choose must apply to everything in the estate.

Note that not all assets benefit from the step-up in basis, so factor that into decisions about what, if anything, to give away during life. Low-basis stock and intellectual property, such as copyrights, trademarks and patents, all benefit. So do art, gold and collectibles, which are particularly good items to hang on to, since gains on these are taxed at 28 percent (plus the 3.8 percent ObamaCare tax and any state tax). Fully depreciated investment real estate is another keeper; if you sell or give it away while you're alive, depreciation you've claimed will be "recaptured" at a 25 percent rate (plus, again, 3.8 percent and any state tax).

There's no step-up benefit to leaving your heirs cash or variable annuities, whose payouts are taxed as ordinary income. As for pre-tax IRAs and 401(k)s, while heirs can stretch out withdrawals, thus benefiting from tax

What If You Married an Alien?

If your spouse is not a U.S. citizen, you don't have the benefit of portability, and your ability to use the marital deduction is much more limited. Congress was concerned that foreigners married to U.S. citizens would take inherited assets out of the country and never pay estate tax on them. So, in 1988, it passed a law to prevent that from happening. This law applies even if your spouse has a green card and is a permanent resident.

You can still use your estate tax exclusion and leave your spouse $5.43 million tax-free. But anything above that gets taxed immediately unless it goes into a special kind of trust, called a qualified domestic trust, or QDOT. Any time this trust distributes principal, it must withhold estate tax – at the rate that was in effect when you died.

How does this put aliens at a disadvantage? First, the marital deduction applies only if assets are in a trust (with citizens it applies to outright inheritances as well), and for all their advantages (see Chapter 6), trusts can be cumbersome. In addition, while a surviving spouse who is a U.S. citizen can postpone estate tax until he or she dies, a noncitizen could be forced to pay it earlier. Of course, if the spouse dies without ever receiving principal, the estate tax is delayed until then.

To be a QDOT, the trust must include certain features. The most important is that your spouse can't be the only trustee. At least one trustee must be a U.S. citizen or company. (For information on choosing a trustee, see Chapter 6.) Ideally, you should set up a QDOT while you are alive, even if nothing goes into it until after you die. You can even leave it up to your spouse to decide, based on financial circumstances at the time, which assets to put into this trust.

All is not lost if you neglect to set up a QDOT. Your spouse can rescue the situation in one of two ways. The best strategy is to become a U.S. citizen before your estate tax return is due (nine months after you die), though it may be hard to navigate the government bureaucracy that quickly. Alternatively, within the same time frame, your survivor can set up a QDOT and fund it with anything that doesn't fit within the exclusion amount.

deferral, all the dollars they eventually take out will be taxed at high ordinary income tax rates. (But a Roth IRA is one of the best assets to inherit, since heirs can stretch out income-tax-free growth and withdrawals. For advice on Roths, see Chapter 7.)

New Wrinkles for Bypass Trusts

Now that portability makes it unnecessary in most cases for spouses to use a bypass trust solely to preserve the federal exclusion amount, relying on portability might make more sense, particularly if your assets are comfortably under $10 million and you live in one of the 31 states without its own estate or inheritance tax. These are issues to weigh.

Other goals. In certain situations, using this old standby might be preferable, for example, to:

- ❧ Protect against disgruntled spouses, creditors and others who may sue your heirs
- ❧ Prevent the evil stepmother or stepfather from cutting your children out
- ❧ Prevent the evil stepmother or stepfather from saddling your children with the bill if estate tax is possible. That could happen if this spouse, after surviving you, uses the DSUE amount for his or her own property and family, and leaves your children to pay any tax due with what comes out of the marital trust
- ❧ Preserve the exclusion, in a remarriage, in case the new spouse dies first
- ❧ Make your grandchildren rich. Portability does not apply to the generation-skipping transfer (GST) tax that is levied, on top of any estate tax, to transfers to grandchildren or more remote descendants of more than $5.43 million (see Chapter 14). You can apply all or part of your exclusion from that tax to the bypass trust and include grandchildren as beneficiaries
- ❧ Reduce state estate tax if you live in a state that has one. Nineteen states and the District of Columbia have a separate estate tax, and so far only two (Hawaii and Delaware) have portability provisions. (Many states are reviewing their systems based on revenue concerns.)

Income taxation of trusts. Aside from the hassle factor of a trust, the "tax drag" of having assets in a trust is now greater than before. Assets in a bypass trust won't get a step-up in basis at the death of the second spouse. In addition, unless trust income is distributed, the income tax penalty can be huge. That's because a trust hits the highest income tax bracket once it has more than $12,301 of taxable income. In contrast, a single individual doesn't hit this bracket until his taxable income is more than $413,200.

There are various ways to minimize the tax damage from existing trusts and adapt future trusts to avoid expensive income tax consequences. One possibility, for widows and widowers already stuck with bypass trusts, is for the trustee to distribute assets out of the trust (assuming the trust terms allow this) to the surviving

Did You Know?

If the surviving spouse will have a power of appointment over assets in a bypass trust, consider whether it should be limited. Some lawyers prefer not to give the surviving spouse the power if it could be used to cut out children of a previous marriage.

spouse. Obviously, this wouldn't be the responsible thing to do if there is an evil stepparent in the picture.

Trusts can also minimize the negative income tax effect by giving a trust beneficiary what's called a power of appointment – the right to decide who will get the assets after he or she dies. This makes it count as part of the beneficiary's estate so it qualifies for the basis step-up.

Another tactic involves living donors who made irrevocable transfers to what are called grantor trusts – those in which the person who sets it up retains certain powers and therefore is able to pay the trust's income tax. All the annual income in these trusts goes on the donor's income tax return, so that's not a problem, but the loss of step-up could be. So donors might want to shuffle assets, swapping low-basis assets out of their trust (and into their taxable estates) and property that won't benefit from step-up into the trust. The stated trust powers must allow for this, but typically, with a grantor trust, they do.

A hybrid approach. Whether or not taxes are a concern, you might want to keep your options open, especially if your estate is in the range of $5 million to $10 million, or higher. When the first spouse dies, you can do what's best based on all the sands that may have shifted since the estate planning documents were written, including:

- ❧ The age and health of the survivor
- ❧ The children's financial needs
- ❧ Current income- and estate-tax rates
- ❧ Tax rates in the states where the surviving spouse and beneficiaries live
- ❧ Growth potential of the assets

One way to do that is to give the spouse the option to disclaim (or turn down) some assets and funnel them into the bypass trust to make use of the deceased spouse's estate tax exemption. If need be, the survivor can still receive income or principal from the trust, but whatever remains in it bypasses the survivor's estate.

Another possible approach is more complicated. It involves an additional trust, called a contingent qualified terminable interest property (QTIP) trust or Clayton QTIP, and leaves open the possibility of shifting assets between two pots after the first spouse dies.

Traditionally, QTIP trusts have been used to preserve assets for the children in case the spouse remarries. Here's how they work: Instead of leaving your spouse's share of the estate to him or her outright, you put it in this special type of marital trust. The trust must require the trustee to pay all income to the surviving spouse for life (the trustee can sometimes make distributions of principal as well) and not permit distributions to anyone other than the spouse while he or she is alive.

> ## *Did You Know?*
>
> Joe Robbie, an entrepreneur and lawyer who owned the Miami Dolphins, didn't plan for a $47 million estate tax bill. To cover it, his family had to sell the team and its stadium in 1994 and missed out on the huge surge in the value of pro football teams in recent years.

When that spouse dies, however, the trust reserves whatever is left for children or whomever you specify in the trust. Only then is the property in the QTIP trust subject to estate tax.

To apply the marital deduction to the QTIP, a formality must be observed: Your executor, who signs the federal estate tax return, Form 706, must elect to treat the trust property as if it has passed to the surviving spouse. This is called a QTIP election. There have been plenty of malpractice lawsuits against executors, as well as the lawyers and accountants they hired to prepare the estate tax return, who neglected this detail.

Did You Know?

If you are filing an estate tax return (Form 706) solely to elect portability, there is a simplified procedure for valuing assets: You can estimate, rounding to the nearest $250,000. Note that there's no box to check electing portability – just filing the form is enough.

A Clayton QTIP – named for the 1992 Fifth Circuit U.S. Court of Appeals case *Clayton v. Commissioner* and also the subject of Treasury Regulations (see Treas. Reg. § 20.2056(b)-7(d) and 7(h)) – is a variation on this theme. It has been used in the past to deal with uncertainty about estate tax rates by postponing the decision about how to allocate the estate between the bypass trust and the marital share until the first spouse died. Now lawyers are recommending that the same strategy be employed with respect to portability. In other words: Postpone the decision about how to divide assets between the QTIP trust, to which portability would be applied, and the bypass trust, which would use at least some of the exemption amount of the spouse who just died.

In terms of the legal documents required, there are at least a couple of ways to set things up. You can start out with two trusts, or just a single trust that can be split into two after the QTIP election has been made.

Who decides how the pie gets divided? There is one potential pitfall if the executor making a QTIP election is the surviving spouse. Shifting what otherwise would have been his or her right to receive distributions from the trust may be considered a taxable gift. (The law on this point isn't entirely clear.) So the conservative approach is to give the power to make a QTIP election to a co-executor or, if the spouse is the sole executor, to an independent party.

Planning for State Estate Tax

If you live in a state that has a separate estate or inheritance tax (at last count 19 states and the District of Columbia) or own real estate in one of those states, you need to consider the effect of this additional tax. In most states the state exemption is less than the federal one. This poses a dilemma for spouses who have divided their estates between a bypass trust and a marital share, a classic estate planning tool discussed more in the next chapter.

For example, in Massachusetts, where the state exemption is only $1 million, fully funding the bypass trust in order to take advantage of the federal exemption would leave your estate to pay state tax, when you die, on the $4.43 million that is not covered by the state exemption.

Did You Know?

In her will, Joan Rivers stated that she was a resident of New York (which has an estate tax) but intended "to reside indefinitely on a permanent basis" in California (which doesn't). Her actions may speak louder than these words if New York tries to tax her estate.

This situation poses a tough choice. If you allocate more to the marital share, your estate avoids both federal and state estate tax when you die but could get stuck paying more federal tax (if the assets appreciate), as well as the state tax, when your spouse dies. If you put more in the bypass trust, there's no federal tax on this sum when you die but your heirs must immediately pay state estate tax.

Because the federal tax rates are higher than the state ones, in most situations it will be best to make sure that as much property as possible is not subject to federal estate tax – either at the first or second death – even if that means paying some state tax.

But you don't need to decide now. Instead, you can postpone the decision about how to allocate the estate between the bypass trust and the marital share until the first spouse has died. This is where portability is a real benefit. If the state-only QTIP is not available, the strategy would be to allocate the state exemption amount to the bypass trust and elect portability for the remaining federal exclusion so it is not lost.

There are several ways to do that. Here, too, you could give your spouse the option to disclaim into the bypass trust. Other approaches rely on the QTIP election, which (for reasons noted above) should not be done by your spouse.

Some states, including Massachusetts, Rhode Island and Washington, offer an easy way for married people to address the problem. In these states, it's possible to make a separate state QTIP election when the first spouse dies. This enables the first spouse to preserve his or her entire federal exclusion and delay the state estate tax that would otherwise apply to some funds in the bypass trust until after the second spouse dies.

For instance, if the state exemption is $1 million, as in Massachusetts, and the bypass trust is funded up to the federal exclusion of $5.43 million, the executor could make a state QTIP election for $4.43 million ($5.43 million minus $1 million) of the funds in the bypass trust. As a result, that part of the estate would be exempt from federal estate tax and would not be subject to state estate tax until the second spouse dies.

Elsewhere, you can use the same strategy that you might use if you weren't sure you would need a bypass trust: Fund the bypass trust with the full federal exclusion but give the executor the option of making the QTIP election over some of these funds when the first spouse dies.

Gift-Tax Basics

Without any limits on lifetime gifts, it would be very easy to avoid estate tax. To prevent that, the law imposes a gift tax of 40 percent once you have passed a certain point.

You can give up to $14,000 each year to as many recipients as you would like without incurring a gift tax. Spouses can combine this annual exclusion to jointly give $28,000 to as many people as they want tax-free. You can make these gifts outright to individuals or put the funds into certain trusts for their benefit (see Chapter 6). Annual exclusion gifts do not count against the $5.43 million limit on transfers during life or through your estate plan.

Over time, these gifts can really add up. Consider a married couple with two adult children, both of them married, and four grandchildren. If the grandparents together make annual exclusion gifts of $28,000 to each child, each child's spouse and each grandchild (a total of eight people), they can reduce their taxable estate by $224,000 a year.

There are also strategies that benefit family without using your annual exclusion, and, in effect, reduce the size of your taxable estate. They include paying for tuition, dental and medical expenses (see Chapter 9), and converting traditional retirement accounts to Roth accounts (Chapter 7).

Gifts that exceed the annual exclusion (which is indexed for inflation) count against the $5.43 million lifetime gift-tax exclusion, and gift tax applies once you have passed the limit. When you die, the estate tax exclusion available to you is reduced by the amount of the gift-tax exemption you have used.

Other chapters will cover the many ways to use the annual exclusion and the lifetime gift-tax exemption. Some, like subsidizing family members who are less fortunate (see Chapter 10), paying life insurance premiums (Chapter 8) and funding college savings accounts (Chapter 9), can be very simple and require little, if any, involvement by a lawyer. Other, more complex tools enable you to leverage the limits to make them go further (Chapter 15). Because of the transaction fees needed to implement them, these sophisticated techniques tend to be used primarily by people with a net worth of at least $10 million or by prescient business owners or investors who think they are about to strike it rich.

With all estate tax strategies, it's best to start with the least complicated approach that will achieve your goals. You can accomplish a great deal while keeping it simple.

To-Do List

Plan for Today's Tax Breaks

The estate tax plan that Congress made permanent in 2013 is far more generous than anything we have had in the past. That poses potential traps and creates planning opportunities. Consider the following issues.

❧ If you don't have a will, tackle this subject for the first time.

❧ Make sure your estate planning documents do not result in any unintended consequences. For example, some people who had their estate plans prepared many years ago may have left the full exclusion amount directly to their children, or the full GST exemption amount directly to trusts for their grandchildren. With the current $5.43 million exclusion, that may result in their entire estate being transferred that way.

❧ Discuss with financial advisers whether your plan should include a bypass trust.

❧ If you live or own real estate in a state with an estate tax, find out how much is exempt in that state. Then ask advisers to coordinate strategies for minimizing that tax with your federal estate tax planning.

❧ Review ownership of assets to determine whether, for estate planning purposes, any property should be transferred from one spouse or partner to the other, or out of joint ownership into the name of one of you individually.

❧ If you are married, leave your spouse a note in the same file as your will and other important papers, with this reminder: In order to carry over any unused estate tax exclusion amount, the executor needs to file an estate tax return within nine months of death, even if no estate tax is due.

❧ Let your adviser know if your spouse is not a U.S. citizen.

Chapter 4

Protect Your Spouse Or Partner

Read this chapter if you are involved in any committed relationship.

For most people involved in a committed relationship, leaving a spouse or partner well provided for is the No. 1 goal in estate planning.

Married couples have more built-in protections than unmarried ones. For example, provided both are U.S. citizens, they can leave each other at death (or transfer to each other while alive) an unlimited amount of property without worrying about estate or gift taxes.

Same-sex spouses now get the same federal tax breaks and

In This Chapter...

- ☙ "A/B Planning" Explained
- ☙ Planning for Gay Couples
- ☙ Sources of Cash
- ☙ What to Do About the Roof Overhead
- ☙ Transferring Retirement Assets
- ☙ Providing for Children of a Previous Relationship

other rights that heterosexual spouses rely on in estate planning. State estate or inheritance taxes, in states that have them, remain a separate concern, in states where same-sex marriage is not legal. The U.S. Supreme Court may resolve the problem in a case that was pending as this book went to press.

If you have been divorced and are planning to re-wed, discuss estate plans before you tie the knot. Especially when there are children from a previous relationship, do you want to leave everything to the kids instead of to each other? If you want to benefit them in addition to your current spouse, consider various ways to do that. Whatever you decide, spell it out in a prenuptial agreement. What a surviving spouse receives is often tied to the length of that marriage.

"A/B Planning" Explained

For decades, some of the most important planning for couples revolved around preserving each person's estate tax exemption. That was especially true when the tax-free amount was significantly lower than it is today. For example, in 2001 the total gift and estate tax exemption was only $675,000.

Then, as now, you could give an unlimited amount to your spouse, during life or through your estate plan (provided she or he is a U.S. citizen) with no tax applied – this is the unlimited marital deduction. But until portability (discussed in the previous chapter) became part of the law, without proper planning, when the second spouse died, anything above the exempt amount not going to charity would be taxed. There's no equivalent of the marital deduction for single people and unmarried couples.

Note, however, that the marital deduction doesn't avoid estate tax; it just postpones it. If assets inherited from a spouse remain when the survivor dies (say the wife inherited money from her husband and never spent it), those assets count as part of her own estate and could be taxed at that time if she doesn't have enough exclusion to cover it (including what she carried over with portability). By delaying the tax on these assets, the spouse is left more to live on. And, of course, any or all of this money spent before your surviving spouse dies escapes tax altogether.

Until portability, A/B planning was the most popular method for using both spouses' exclusion amount, and some lawyers still favor it. Here are issues to consider.

Keep assets in your own name. Unromantic as it may sound, this approach starts with each of you holding at least $5.43 million worth of assets (or as much of that as you can afford) in your own name (see "For Richer or Poorer," page 66).

After that, it works like this. In your will (each spouse needs to have one of her own) or living trust (again, you need one of your own unless you live in a community property state), divide your estate into two parts. When the first of you dies, an amount up to the federal exclusion goes into the bypass or credit-shelter trust. It can distribute income and principal to family members (which may be just the surviving spouse but more often includes other family members such as children and grandchildren) for as long as that individual is alive. After that, whatever is left goes to the people you designate (for example, your children).

Because funds in the bypass trust (often labeled the family trust) are covered by the exclusion amount, they will not be taxed when you die, no matter how large the trust grows. Putting them in trust, rather than leaving them to your spouse outright, ensures that they will not be considered part of her estate, either. Therefore, they are not subject to estate tax when she dies. Neither is any increase in the value of the funds after they go into the trust.

Allocate the marital share. The rest of your estate can be distributed any way you like. For married couples, whatever goes to your spouse, called the marital share, is covered by the unlimited deduction, so long as it goes to your spouse outright or in a special kind of trust. While a trust creates more paperwork and gives your spouse less control over the funds, it can also protect the assets from creditors (see Chapter 17), prevent a spouse with unwise spending habits from disbursing everything too quickly and preserve the funds for your children in case your spouse remarries.

The marital deduction doesn't apply to all trusts but only if you take one of two approaches to make it apply. Which of them you use will depend on your answer to this question: "Do you want your spouse to decide who gets the trust assets next?" (Remember, she might choose a future spouse rather than the children you had together.)

- *You don't want your spouse to decide.* Use a qualified terminable interest property, or QTIP, trust. This trust must require the trustee to pay all income to the surviving spouse for life (the trustee can also make distributions of principal) and not permit distributions to anyone other than the spouse while she is alive. After that, the assets can go to whomever you specify in the trust.

- *It's okay for your spouse to decide.* In that case, you could give your spouse a general power of appointment – the right to leave the assets after she dies to anyone she chooses. Or you can restrict to whom your spouse can leave the assets by giving her what's called a limited power of appointment – in this case, over assets in a QTIP. For example, you could let your surviving spouse decide which of your children should receive the funds when she dies, and whether they should receive them outright or in further trust.

Bogie's Legacy to Bacall

Humphrey Bogart was 25 years older than Lauren Bacall, and his will, signed eight months before he died, in 1957, anticipated that she would enjoy a long life after that. (She did, in fact, outlive him by 57 years.) It created a classic A/B estate plan with the flexibility for trustees to make tax-savvy financial choices during the years ahead.

Bogart left all his personal possessions to Bacall outright, and provided that, after gifts to two of his servants, half of the rest of his estate would go into a marital trust. Taxes would come out of the other half, and whatever remained after that would go into a separate trust for the couple's two children, Stephen, who was 8 when his father died, and Leslie, who was 4. Bacall was co-trustee of both trusts, along with A. Morgan Maree, Jr., a prominent Hollywood money manager.

At the time, there was no provision in the Internal Revenue Code for QTIP trusts, and the marital deduction was 50 percent of the adjusted gross estate. However, the trust for Bacall did not qualify for that deduction since her right to the trust income was not absolute. Instead, recognizing "her high earning potential" and the associated income tax, Bogart gave Maree absolute discretion about whether to make both payments of income and distributions of principal. (Perhaps Bogart didn't care that as a result he was forfeiting an estate tax benefit.) Any income not distributed would be added to principal.

With a handwritten amendment to his will, initialed in the margin, Bogart noted that Bacall could not make distribution decisions – a wise move to render the trust funds unreachable by her creditors.

In contrast, a power of appointment in the marital trust gave Bacall free rein. When Bacall died, in 2014, she exercised it to benefit not only the two children she had with Bogart, but also Sam Robards, her son with Jason Robards, Jr., from whom she divorced in 1969. Her will provided that all the remaining principal and any undistributed income from this trust that Bogart created would be distributed to them in equal shares.

For Richer or Poorer

To use the estate tax exclusion to make direct transfers or fund a bypass trust, you must have assets of your own. Jointly held property (for example, those bank accounts titled joint tenants with right of survivorship) doesn't count, because when one owner dies, ownership automatically passes to the other.

What can couples do if one is richer than the other, and they don't each have enough in their own name to use the exclusion amount fully? The simplest solution is for the wealthier person to transfer assets to the other. If spouses don't want to make an outright gift, they can put the assets in a qualified terminable interest property, or QTIP, trust (explained on page 67) that they set up during life. That way you can be sure the assets will ultimately go to your children but still use your spouse's exclusion.

Unfortunately, this strategy doesn't apply to retirement accounts – you can't give them away while you are alive.

Another consideration: shifting assets may require you to pay gift tax if the recipient is not your spouse or if your spouse is not a U.S. citizen. How much you can give away without using your $5.43 million lifetime gift-tax exemption will depend on your marital status and, if you're married, the citizenship of your spouse. These are the rules.

Marital status	Amount of annual tax-free gift
Married couple, both citizens	Unlimited
Married couple, poorer spouse not a citizen	$147,000 (indexed for inflation)
Married couple, richer spouse not a citizen	Unlimited
Unmarried couple	$14,000 (indexed for inflation)

Assuming your spouse doesn't spend all the money, what remains of the marital share will be taxed when she dies if it's more than the tax-free amount.

Decide how to fund the bypass trust. To get the full benefit of A/B planning, you must fund the family trust with the entire $5.43 million exclusion amount. But that doesn't work for everyone. It might result in a large portion of your spouse or partner's inheritance being locked up in trust. (In smaller estates it could eat up the entire inheritance.) And unless the trust provides that she can receive distributions liberally for broad purposes, the trust arrangement could limit her access to the funds. Not knowing what you will be worth when you die can make it unwieldy to put such a plan in place.

There are a variety of ways to address these uncertainties. In the process, you need to answer some difficult questions:

How much should go into it? One possibility is to put a cap on the amount going into the bypass trust. For instance, you can limit it to a specific sum or a certain percentage of your estate. Although this might forgo part of the exclusion amount, the welfare of your spouse or partner is, presumably, more important.

Spouses can put a more flexible plan in place that builds upon the QTIP. Fund the bypass trust with the full federal exclusion but give the executor the option of making the QTIP election (see page 55) over some of these funds when the first spouse dies. To make this strategy possible, the bypass trust must be "QTIP-able," meaning it provides (or could provide, as the result of the election) that the spouse will get all the income and that nobody else is entitled to any distributions from the QTIP portion of the trust. Depending on the election, the executor can turn the entire bypass trust, or just a portion of it, into a QTIP trust.

This is sometimes called a one-lung trust, because instead of setting up both a marital trust to provide for the spouse and a separate bypass trust, as described in Chapter 3, your estate plan starts with just a single trust. After the QTIP election has been made, the trust can be divided into two separate trusts – one for the portion over which there has been a QTIP election and a separate trust for the rest.

There is one potential pitfall if the executor making a QTIP election is the surviving spouse. Shifting what otherwise would have been her right to receive distributions from the trust may be considered a taxable gift. (The law on this point isn't entirely clear.) You can avoid that risk by giving the power to make a QTIP election to a co-executor or, if the spouse is the sole executor, to an independent third-party appointed as a special executor, with authority to make the QTIP election. (For this purpose, a trustee of a revocable trust may, in some cases, be treated as the "executor.")

Another approach for spouses, which also relies on the QTIP election to make the necessary adjustments after the first spouse dies, is to start by funding a marital trust with a specific amount that you expect will provide adequately for the surviving spouse, and creating a bypass trust that can be funded with anything more than that, up to the exclusion amount. Here, too, you would give the executor the option of making the QTIP election over only a portion of the assets, and then putting the rest into the bypass trust if it was not already fully funded. This strategy takes care of the spouse first and relies on a bypass trust to shelter any excess. (Again, the person making the election should generally not be the surviving spouse.)

A more controversial option that looks much simpler on paper is to leave everything to your spouse or partner outright but give her the right to disclaim (turn down) all or part of the inheritance and have it go into a bypass trust. When it comes to disclaimers, the world of estate planning lawyers is divided into two camps: those who like the flexibility a disclaimer affords, and those who think there are so many ways to mess up a disclaimer that it should be avoided.

Did You Know?

Carroll Rosenbloom, who owned the Los Angeles Rams football team, groomed his son Steve as his successor. By leaving 70 percent of the ownership to his wife, Georgia Frontiere, Rosenbloom gave her free rein. Within months of his death she fired her stepson.

If you use a disclaimer, your will should incorporate several important caveats – not for legal reasons but to educate your survivors. One is that your spouse must take this step within nine months of your death. Another, trickier, rule is that the Internal Revenue Code prohibits someone who disclaims, known as a disclaimant, from accepting an interest in the asset or any of its benefits. Heirs have fouled up by making such innocent mistakes as depositing a dividend check in their own account, changing the way an IRA is invested or collecting life insurance proceeds. One exception to this rule applies to surviving spouses. A spouse is allowed to receive income and principal from property disclaimed into a bypass trust.

Although a spouse can be a beneficiary of a trust funded by disclaimer, federal regulations, which say disclaimants can't have control over the property, bind her hands in two other ways. If she is the trustee, she must follow specific or ascertainable standards in making distributions rather than having total discretion. And she can't be given a power of appointment. If the tax efficiency of your estate plan depends on your spouse exercising the power to disclaim, make sure someone else has the power to disclaim on her behalf if she becomes mentally incapacitated (see Chapter 1).

Finally, keep in mind that as useful as disclaimers can be in this context and others (see Chapter 16), estate planners joke about the five-word lie spouses routinely tell each other: "Honey, I promise to disclaim."

Will my spouse have as much cash as she needs? Assuming you want to set up a bypass trust, or at least leave open the possibility, you can arrange things so the spigot can be turned on and off, but you must think about this issue in advance. (For basic information about how trusts work and why flexibility is desirable, see Chapter 6.) Here are some issues to ponder before you have a lawyer prepare a bypass trust.

❧ Does income have to be distributed to the surviving spouse, or are payments at the trustee's discretion?
❧ Should the trustee be able to distribute principal?
❧ If so, should that power be completely discretionary, or subject to preset standards included in the trust?
❧ Should the surviving spouse be the only current beneficiary, or should children be, as well?
❧ Should the surviving spouse have a power of appointment? This power should not be included if the trust might be funded through disclaimer: A disclaimer isn't valid if the asset being disclaimed is still subject to the individual's direction about how it passes at death.
❧ If the spouse will have a power of appointment, how should that power be limited? (Some lawyers prefer not to give the surviving spouse the power if it could be used to cut out children of a previous marriage.)
❧ Should the surviving spouse or partner have the power to remove and replace trustees? If so, should it be exercisable by the spouse alone, or only by the spouse and the children acting together?

Which assets should be used to fund the trust? The ideal assets are cash, bonds or marketable securities. But for many people, their home and retirement accounts are their most valuable assets or the only ones available to fully fund a bypass trust. Each presents its own challenges because of special rules that apply.

If you use retirement assets to fund a bypass trust, you may lose certain income tax benefits (see Chapter 7). Therefore, you need to weigh the potential estate tax savings and creditor protection against the income tax cost.

Using a home to fund a bypass trust is also problematic. The way to do this with a jointly owned home is for the surviving spouse to disclaim the one-half interest in the property she has inherited. That part of the house then becomes a bypass trust asset, although the spouse could buy it out of the trust and replace it with cash, either all at once or over time.

There are several problems with this approach. It takes away the survivor's sense of ownership. Depending on the arrangement, the trust may need to share the cost of maintenance and repairs, and it can't deduct property taxes. And depending on the state, the home may also lose protection from creditors.

Planning for Gay Couples

Until recently same-sex spouses did not get the federal tax breaks and other rights that heterosexual spouses rely on in estate planning. That changed as a result of the 2013 Supreme Court decision in *United States v. Windsor*, invalidating a provision of the 1996 Defense of Marriage Act that defined marriage as between a man and a woman, and spouses as heterosexual.

Two months after the ruling, the Internal Revenue Service issued Revenue Ruling 2013-17, saying that same-sex couples who legally married in the U.S. or in a foreign country will get the same federal tax breaks no matter where they ultimately live – including states that do not allow same-sex marriage. This decision includes all the benefits related to income tax, IRA inheritances, gift and estate tax. So, for example, if you married in New York, the IRS will consider you married even if you retire to Tennessee – a state that does not allow same-sex marriage and where there is strong sentiment against it.

So far the Supreme Court has stopped short of meddling with state regulation of marriage, or expressing any opinion about what happens to anything other than federal rights when same-sex spouses cross state lines. Since the decision in *Windsor,* the number of states permitting same-sex marriage has nearly doubled, though. As the fourth edition of this book went to press, same-sex marriage was legal in 36 states and the District of Columbia. But the Court could undo much of that progress with *DeBoer v. Snyder,* another crucial case that was pending. It raises two key questions involving the 14th Amendment: whether states must license a marriage between a same-sex couple; and whether a state must recognize a marriage between a same-sex couple that was lawfully performed in another state.

In states that don't honor these marriages, same-sex married couples are still on the same footing as unmarried partners. Therefore, it is harder for them to save on state taxes, including income tax, estate or inheritance taxes, in states that have them. Typically, they must continue to rely on estate planning tools that are not limited to spouses. At least for now, their filing status for federal and state income taxes (if any) will also be different. This will make tax preparation more cumbersome and time-consuming, and perhaps create more possibilities for errors.

> ## Did You Know?
>
> Rock Hudson, a leading man in Hollywood, was gay – and his death from AIDS, at age 59, raised awareness of the disease. In his will, he originally left his tangible personal property to a longtime companion, Tom Clark. But months before Hudson died, he struck Clark from the will.

They must be especially vigilant, too, about signing the necessary documents to provide for each other. Without a will or living trust, for example, they cannot inherit from each other under state law. Don't forget beneficiary designations for retirement accounts and other non-probate assets (see Chapter 2).

And unless they have signed a health care proxy, even legally married same-sex couples from out of state may have trouble being treated as spouses in case of emergency. As an extra precaution when traveling to these states, they ought to carry a health care proxy, living will and HIPAA release on a thumb drive, or put these documents in the cloud (for example, in Dropbox), where they are easily accessible. Another very practical approach: Send yourself an e-mail with the key documents attached as PDFs and save it in an e-mail folder on your cellphone. In an emergency, you can simply forward that e-mail to hospital administrators.

If this rapidly evolving area of the law affects you, register at this book's Web site, www.estateplanningsmarts.com, to receive updates.

Sources of Cash

The death of a key breadwinner can leave heirs strapped for funds to meet current expenses, including funeral costs. To avoid the need to liquidate assets, perhaps at fire-sale prices, consider these steps.

Buy life insurance. Using life insurance as a source of cash could be even more important for partners than it is for spouses. They don't have the benefit of the unlimited marital deduction, which permits the tax-free transfer of assets to a spouse who is a U.S. citizen (for the rules on non-citizen spouses, see Chapter 3), so that the money is not counted for tax purposes until the second spouse dies. In contrast, a person in an unmarried relationship can get saddled with immediate estate tax when the total assets that he or she inherits from the other partner are worth more than $5.43 million.

Another advantage of life insurance for non-spouses has nothing to do with taxes but rather with confidentiality. Life insurance passes outside your will. Therefore, nobody but the beneficiary, the insurance company and the Internal Revenue Service need to know about it.

No matter what your reason for wanting life insurance, beware a common pitfall: If you are both the insured and the policy owner, the proceeds will be considered part of your estate. If your spouse is the beneficiary, there would be no tax when you die because of the unlimited marital deduction, though what remains in a large estate could be taxed when the surviving spouse dies if there is not enough exclusion amount to cover it. But if your partner is the beneficiary and your total assets, including the life insurance proceeds, are worth more than $5.43 million, the 40 percent estate tax could immediately eat into the inheritance, leaving less for him to live on. The best way to avoid the tax in both cases is to set up an irrevocable life insurance trust, which can buy the policy and, when you die, hold the proceeds for whomever you have named as beneficiary (see Chapter 8).

Create a grantor retained income trust, or GRIT. This is one of the few estate planning tools that a spouse and close family members cannot use. But it's great for other couples (and can also work well with nieces and nephews). With a GRIT, you put assets into an irrevocable trust and retain the right to get income from the trust for a specific number of years. When that term expires, all the trust assets, including any appreciation, go tax-free to the remainder beneficiaries you've named. To maximize what they get, you can invest the GRIT in property or other assets that you expect to grow in value.

> ## Did You Know?
>
> When you die, your spouse or partner will probably not have immediate access to your individual bank accounts. So every couple should keep a reserve fund in a joint account, designated for day-to-day emergencies. The surviving partner would have instant access to this money.

For gift-tax purposes, you've made a taxable gift when you set up the trust, but the value of that gift is discounted. The discount reflects the value of the right to get the assets a certain number of years from now, reduced to reflect the probability that you will live that long. The chief drawback of a GRIT is that if you don't survive the trust term, the entire property is included in your estate.

When setting up the trust, you should also consider the possibility of a breakup in your relationship. Since the trust is irrevocable, you can't retain the right to change the beneficiary. However, the trust can stipulate that if you are no longer living together (unless, perhaps, one of you needs to go into a nursing home or relocate for work), the remainder interest goes to another person named in the trust document.

Keep money in the bank. If, like many couples, your assets are divided into "yours," "mine" and "ours," make sure there is enough money to cover immediate expenses. These reserve funds can be held in each of your separate accounts or in a joint one. Just be aware that when you die, your spouse or partner will probably not have access to your individual account right away, and you will each need the discipline to keep the reserve fund flush. A better approach is to maintain a joint account designated for emergencies that can also be available for this purpose.

How should that account be titled? This is just one of various contexts in which titling is relevant to estate planning. Title affects how rapidly assets become available to your heirs, how those assets are taxed and whether they are protected from creditors' claims. Each option has pros and cons, and the best choice for one purpose might not be the best choice for another. (This subject is also discussed in Chapters 2 and 17.)

Did You Know?

Your state's law governing what happens to your assets if you die without a will may differ from what you would want done. In most states, parents share the estate with a surviving, childless spouse; in some, siblings and more distant relatives have a claim on separately titled assets, too.

With bank and brokerage accounts, the most frequent form of joint ownership is joint tenancy with right of survivorship. It is available to any two people who want to own assets together. Both owners have access to the assets during life, and when one joint tenant dies, the survivor immediately becomes the sole owner of the whole property, regardless of what the will says, or whether there is a will.

Immediate access provides secure funds in case there is a will contest, as often happens with gay couples. Let's say one partner wants to leave the entire estate to his partner and his family members are likely to challenge the will. He wouldn't want his partner to be short of funds should a battle drag on. So he might set aside a certain amount in a bank account, naming his partner as joint tenant with right of survivorship.

Joint tenancy has serious drawbacks, though. Either owner can withdraw everything in the account. It also exposes each owner to the other's liabilities (see Chapter 17). Unmarried couples also need to be aware that state laws on joint tenancy for non-spouses may vary. Consult a lawyer who is familiar with the rules of the state where you live.

What to Do About the Roof Overhead

Renters should be sure they each have the right to retain the lease. If you own a home together, you must determine the best way to hold title to it. Again, your choice can affect taxes and creditor protection.

Joint tenants with right of survivorship. The advantage of this form of ownership is that a co-owner automatically inherits the whole property when the other owner dies, so his right to live in the house is secure. However, it could be used to satisfy a judgment against either of you unless you live in a state with a homestead law that protects a personal residence from creditors' claims (see Chapter 17).

You also need to consider taxes. For spouses, half the property is automatically included in the estate of the first to die but is covered by the unlimited marital deduction. Non-spouses get less favorable treatment. For them, the tax law presumes that the entire property is included in the estate of the first to die, which could trigger immediate estate tax on the whole property. You can avoid that result by showing in an estate tax audit how much the survivor contributed to buying the home. In that case, the portion allocated to the estate would be reduced.

Tenancy in common avoids some of these problems. With this form of title, you own just part of the property, known as an undivided interest. Typically your share would equal whatever you kicked in, though if someone gave you the asset – say an interest in land – as a gift or bequest, it would equal whatever percentage of the property you received. As a rule, creditors have access only to the portion owned by the person who owes them money rather than to the whole thing. When one owner dies, just that person's share gets included in his or her estate; if you want that share to pass to your spouse or partner, you should provide for it in your estate plan. This form of title may interest spouses who want to fund a bypass trust with their home (see page 70).

In 26 states, spouses – but not other couples – also have the option of holding real estate in tenancy by the entirety. As with joint tenants, each spouse automatically inherits the other's share. As noted in Chapter 17, the key advantage of tenancy by the entirety is that, at least in non-community property states, only the couple's joint creditors have access to the asset. Creditors of just one spouse cannot collect on their lien unless there is a divorce or the non-debtor spouse dies. (Here, too, homestead laws offer protection in some states.)

What if you live in a home that only one of you owns – for example, you bought the house before the start of the relationship? If both spouses are U.S. citizens or the spouse who does not own the home is, a half-ownership interest can be transferred tax-free (see Chapter 3). Everyone else must consider the gift-tax rules that would apply to the transfer. You can give up to $14,000 each year (adjusted for inflation in $1,000 increments) to your partner – and as many other recipients as you like – without incurring gift tax. Any gift that's more than this annual exclusion counts against the lifetime gift and estate tax exclusion – what each individual can give away during life without triggering gift tax or increasing future estate taxes. Once you have passed the limit, which is $5.43 million, a gift tax of up to 40 percent applies.

> ## Did You Know?
>
> If you get married or enter into a committed relationship, you need to change not only your will or living trust to provide for your mate, but also beneficiary designation forms for assets that pass outside of probate such as retirement accounts and life insurance policies.

The simplest way to fit more into each of these amounts is to transfer partial interests in the home to your partner. Whether you do this all at once or by successive gifts over time, you can reduce the value of each interest substantially (see Chapter 11).

But beware of potential complications. Each time you make a gift, you will need to have that partial interest appraised. You will want your partner to be a beneficiary of your homeowners' policy. If you're dealing with a co-op apartment, you may need approval from the board of directors. (With condominium properties, this is not a concern.) And whenever there's an existing mortgage, you will probably need the lender's permission. Also check the fine print to be sure the transfer of a partial interest doesn't give the bank the right to cancel the loan and require you to pay up.

For spouses, there are times when a smart tax strategy might be for just one of you, rather than both of you, to own the house. One scenario is when you want to use it to fund a bypass trust (though, as noted on page 70, this has pros and cons). The other involves the sad situation when, because of health issues or a significant difference in ages, you are fairly certain which of you will die first. In that case, when the home has appreciated significantly in value, it might make sense to have it owned solely by the spouse whose death will occur sooner.

This strategy could result in a substantial income tax savings for the surviving spouse. Here's why: Inherited assets are entitled to an adjustment in basis to their value on the date of death. If the property has appreciated, there will be a step-up in the cost basis, which could reduce or eliminate the capital gains tax your heirs have to pay if the property is sold.

One important condition applies: If your spouse transfers the assets, you die within a year and your spouse inherits the same assets back, there is no step-up. This provision in the Internal Revenue Code, which applies to non-spouses, too, prevents a healthy spouse from transferring everything to a dying spouse (with no gift tax) and getting it back with a basis step-up (and no estate tax). (For a further discussion of estate planning when bad health is a factor, see Chapter 18.)

Transferring Retirement Assets

Money in individual retirement accounts or employer-sponsored retirement plans, such as 401(k)s and 403(b)s, cannot be covered by a will. Instead, the money is distributed according to beneficiary designation forms that you fill out when you open the accounts or later amend. With

How Community Property Affects Your Estate Plan

Most states leave it up to married couples to separate their assets into "yours," "mine" and "ours." The law imposes a framework for spouses in these nine community property states: Arizona, California, Idaho, Louisiana, Nevada, New Mexico, Texas, Washington and Wisconsin. Two other states, Alaska and Tennessee, also have community property, but you have to "opt in" to it, and in Tennessee it must be held in trust.

If you are domiciled in one of these states, meaning that you call it home, you are subject to the rules of community property: Anything you have going into the marriage, or individually receive by gift or inheritance during the marriage, is considered separate property. Most of what you acquire once you are married and living in a community property state is community property, and you are each considered a one-half owner. That includes your house, regardless of how it is titled, your salary and your IRA. Commingling separate and community property often results in the entire property being treated as community property. The law in most community property states allows you and your mate to agree – either before or after you're married – that certain property that would otherwise be considered community property is separate property, and the reverse.

The distinction between community and separate property affects how you calculate your federal income tax, the degree to which your assets are protected from creditors and how they are divided in divorce. IRS publication 555, "Community Property," provides a primer and can be downloaded at www.irs.gov.

For estate planning purposes, keep in mind a couple of things. One is that the total value of your assets when you die includes both your separate property and half the value of any community property. There's also a huge tax advantage associated with community property: When the first spouse dies, both halves of the property get a step-up in basis. This enables you to minimize capital gains tax if the surviving spouse sells the property – such as a house.

an IRA, you can readily name any beneficiaries you want, including friends, family members, a trust or charity. For a 401(k) or other workplace plan, you must get your spouse's written permission to leave it to anyone else. To change a beneficiary – for example, if you get divorced or your spouse dies – make sure to file an amended form. It's extremely important that you complete these forms and keep them up to date, and have your lawyer co-ordinate them with the rest of your estate plan. (For a detailed discussion of estate planning with retirement assets, see Chapter 7.)

Providing for Children of a Previous Relationship

In a functional relationship, spouses and partners share a common interest in their children's well-being. In second marriages or partnerships, this dynamic is hard – often impossible – to replicate, and sometimes with good reason. For example, there might be residual anger from a messy divorce that children witnessed, grief for a parent lost or concern that the surviving parent's new, sometimes much younger, spouse will inherit everything. If you want to benefit children from a previous marriage and your current spouse, decide whether the kids should receive an immediate inheritance or be forced to wait for the death of the surviving spouse.

> ## Did You Know?
>
> In most states, when couples are jointly represented, everything you tell the lawyer is not confidential from your spouse. It's better to have separate lawyers in second marriages when there are kids from a previous one; a marriage is troubled; or when one spouse has skeletons in the closet.

Either way, it's best to make arrangements for your children that don't require any help or cooperation from your new mate. Similarly, don't create a plan that your new spouse could foil. For example, don't make your children's inheritance dependent on your spouse's disclaimer into a bypass trust for their benefit or the ongoing payment of insurance premiums.

(This could come up with a second-to-die life insurance policy that names the children as beneficiaries when the surviving spouse is responsible for paying the premiums.)

There are a number of ways to structure your children's inheritance. You can leave them specific sums or a percentage of your estate, subject to inflation adjustments. You can make them the remainder beneficiaries of your QTIP and beneficiaries of various trusts, including a bypass trust.

It also pays to discuss these issues frankly with your spouse or partner. When the stakes are high, some people cover them in a prenuptial or postnuptial agreement that specifies not only what happens in the event of divorce, but also how assets will be divided if the couple is still married when one of them dies.

Did You Know?

State elective share laws prevent spouses from disinheriting each other. Instead, they are entitled to a minimum portion of each other's estate. But they can waive that right in a prenuptial agreement that specifies how assets will be distributed if the couple is married when one of them dies.

That's what Peter Jennings, the ABC News anchorman, did when he married Katherine Freed, his fourth wife, in 1997. A 21-page prenup, which pegged the size of Freed's inheritance to how long they were married, provided that once they reached the eight-year mark, her share of the marital estate would double, from 25 percent to 50 percent. Most of the rest would go to Jennings's two children from his third marriage. Freed gave up her right as spouse to claim an elective share of Jennings's estate, a minimum portion spouses are entitled to under state law (in New York it's one-third when there are children; one-half when there aren't).

Jennings's 10-page will, signed three months before he died of lung cancer, in 2005, not only incorporated the prenup, but also stipulated that no matter when he died, the couple would be deemed to have been married for more than eight years. It was fortunate for Freed that Jennings took that step, as he passed away several months short of their eighth anniversary. According to Jennings's estate tax return filed in New York Surrogate's Court, Freed received more than $21 million, including the couple's Manhattan co-op apartment, valued at $10.5 million.

80

To-Do List

Providing for the financial security of your spouse or partner requires you to do much more than have your lawyer prepare the standard legal documents. Here are some other steps to take.

❧ Keep enough funds in joint accounts to cover immediate expenses.

❧ Based on all relevant factors, determine the best way to hold title to your other assets, especially your home.

❧ Figure out whether you have enough assets apart from your home and retirement accounts to use at least part of the $5.43 million federal estate tax exclusion.

❧ Check the latest rules on estate or inheritance tax in your state and plan for it.

❧ If you have children from a previous marriage, discuss how they will factor into your estate plan.

❧ If you and your spouse are a same-sex married couple, consider whether you need to update your estate plan to reflect the 2013 Supreme Court decision in *United States v. Windsor*.

❧ Make sure you are not the owner of a life insurance policy that names you as an insured. If you are, the proceeds could be subject to estate tax. (For ways to remedy this situation, see Chapter 8.)

❧ Fill out beneficiary designation forms for all retirement accounts and other non-probate assets and ask your lawyer to coordinate them with the rest of your estate plan.

Chapter 5

What if? Provide for Young or Disabled Children

*Read this chapter so you can
anticipate their needs and
make sure they will be nurtured.*

W ho would raise your children if something happened to you?

For most people, few prospects are more wrenching. Often, parents put off writing a will because this particular thought is unbearable. Some assume – incorrectly – that it is enough just to ask a relative or trusted friend to step in if the need arises.

But not formalizing the arrangements and doing some estate planning along the way could leave your children in a vacuum. For example, if you are a single or surviving parent and do not have a written document outlining your wishes, a court usually decides who will fill your shoes. And without financial planning, there may not be enough money for your child's support.

In This Chapter...

- ⚜ *Choose a Guardian to Care for Your Child*
- ⚜ *Beware the Implications of Adoption*
- ⚜ *Leave Sufficient Funds*
- ⚜ *Provide for Children with Special Needs*
- ⚜ *Put the Money in Good Hands*

In families where a child has special physical, emotional or cognitive needs, the issues are even more complicated. In the past, special needs children frequently might not have outlived their parents. Now, medical advances have greatly extended their life expectancies. So it is essential for parents to make provisions for their care, custody and financial needs.

Addressing this issue requires that you talk openly about the subject, something not so often done a generation ago. Lawyers have learned to ask if there are special needs children because clients might not mention them otherwise.

Choose a Guardian to Care for Your Child

A guardian's responsibilities range from the mundane to the monumental: everything from tying shoelaces and drying tears to selecting schools and medical care. You should designate more than one person, so if your top choice is not available, your second preference is clear. Depending on the financial arrangements you make, the person in charge of caring for your child may not be the same person who controls the child's assets – as discussed on page 95, there are good reasons for assigning each role to a different person. In some states, if you have not made arrangements for both functions, the court will appoint a separate person to deal with the child's money.

When choosing a guardian in case their child is orphaned, people typically look first to relatives, starting with their own siblings – the child's aunts and uncles. Especially if these siblings already have children of their own, the idea is that your children would be raised with their first cousins. A second choice for some people is their own parents, if they are young enough. When there is a big age gap between children (for instance, if a parent has been married more than once and has offspring from both unions), older siblings sometimes serve as guardians for younger ones. How well this works depends on the family dynamics.

Even if certain family members seem like obvious candidates, take into account all the factors involved. For example, it may not be good for a child who has lost his parents to suddenly have to relocate, losing contact with friends and the world he lives in. Put some thought into the lifestyle and values, as well as the location, of the person you're thinking of choosing.

You should consider, too, whether the prospective guardians can incorporate your children into their households. If they have their own children, can they handle more? If they have none, are they prepared to accept a ready-made family? For many parents, an important goal is keeping their children together. Think back to when you became a parent and how it changed your world; would you want someone who has never played that role to start with your child?

Ideally, couples should agree on the choice of guardian to care for their children, and each of their wills should appoint the same person. But disagreements often delay planning, or lead to unusual compromises. Consider Beastie Boy Adam Yauch, who died of cancer in 2012 at

Factors to Weigh in Choosing a Guardian

Appointing a guardian for your children is an agonizing decision, and few parents find someone who meets all their criteria. More often, the choice involves a process of elimination or deciding which qualities are most important. Here are some questions to ask.

❧ Do I have a relative or close friend who would be willing to take on the role?

❧ Would that person love my child and provide the attention that he or she would need?

❧ Am I comfortable with the individual's lifestyle and values?

❧ Does the person have children about the same age as mine?

❧ Can the prospective guardian incorporate my children into his or her household?

❧ If I have more than one child, would the guardian be able to keep them together?

❧ Does my child already have a relationship and a good rapport with the person?

❧ Would my child have to relocate?

❧ Can the person handle any special needs, including medical or behavioral issues, my child may have?

the age of 47. Yauch's 2001 will suggests that he and his wife, Dechen, disagreed about who would raise their children if they both died – say, in an auto accident. (Their daughter, Tenzin Losel, was born in 1998.)

The will, which is a public document, provides that if Yauch died in a year with an even number, he appointed his parents, Noel and Frances Yauch, as the guardians, with his wife's parents, Sonam and Chuki Gangdu, as the backup if his own parents were unable to play that role. On the other hand, if he died in an odd-numbered year, the arrangement would be reversed, with her parents stepping in as guardians, and his serving as the backup.

Unmarried couples take note: If you are not both biologically related to the child, it is especially important for your estate planning documents to cover all the issues. The rules on adoption of children by unmarried couples vary enormously from state to state, and though the law is evolving, it lags behind current practices. If you and your partner have a child, it's important to consult a lawyer who is familiar with the rules of your state, and to revisit the subject if you move to a different one.

You will want to have heart-to-heart talks with the people you have in mind before you name them as guardians. You can discuss your goals and theories of parenting in as much detail as you like, but including these specifics in the will is shortsighted. It might feel right to say, "I want you to live in the Northeast and send the child to private school," but circumstances change. You don't want to tie the hands of the person whom you are trusting with your child's future.

Instead, you can supplement the will with a letter or memo outlining your wishes (for one example, see "The Mummy Manual," page 89). This might cover everything from your preferences about religion, education and allowance to the name of your pediatrician. It could also ask the guardian to consult

Did You Know?

The person in charge of caring for your child may not be the same person who controls the child's assets – ideally, they should be different. You can name a separate guardian for the money, or put the funds in a trust, which gives you much more say over how they are spent.

with specific friends or family members who know your children well but who, for whatever reason, would not be appropriate as guardians.

Though not binding the way a will is, this document provides the guardian with a clear, written record of your preferences. It also sends a message to your children about how much you cared.

Still, try not to micromanage or create a moral obligation for the guardian to follow very precise instructions. Sometimes it's better to express broad goals rather than precise tactics – for example, to help build your child's independence and confidence, encourage her to pursue interests that come naturally and to maintain relationships with family and friends. Being a parent is full of surprises, and requires constant judgment calls and adaptation. Try as you might to cover all the bases, ultimately you need to choose the people whom you really trust to do the right thing, and hope for the best.

Given the complexities of providing for minor children, you should review your arrangements at least once every five years. Revisit the subject sooner if something changes – say, your aging parents suddenly cannot handle a rambunctious toddler, or the sister you've named as guardian relocates.

If you have a special needs child who will require a guardian on a continuing basis, you will want to put a more long-lasting plan in place. You should name an alternate guardian, in case the original one becomes unable to play that role, and create a backup plan for choosing successors.

Beware the Implications of Adoption

From an estate planning perspective, adoption brings potential pitfalls, as well as benefits. For example, while it is possible to become entitled to an inheritance through adoption, quirks in the law could also cause adoption to wipe one out.

With the growing number of blended, or non-traditional, families, these issues arise more frequently, but the law has not kept up. Some states still do not allow same-sex marriage; that may change as the result of a Supreme Court case that was pending as this edition went to press. (See Chapter 4.) These laws can have an enormous effect on the inheritance rights of out-of-marriage children.

Being aware of the rules, which vary from state to state, can help you steer clear of the pitfalls and take advantage of the opportunities. Here are five different adoption scenarios that could affect inheritance rights. A will or trust could change any of the results described below by including or excluding specific individuals or categories of people. For example, some people cut off inheritance rights of individuals who are older than a certain age when they are adopted – primarily as a deterrent to adults adopting each other.

A single person adopts a child. The child can inherit directly from this parent, and receive the parent's share of assets left by others – for example, if the child is next in line for all or part of the parent's inheritance under a will or trust (see Chapters 2 and 6).

'The Mummy Manual'

After she was diagnosed with incurable breast cancer, Helen Harcombe began to prepare her family for the inevitable. One of her chief concerns was how her husband, Anthony, a builder, would raise their daughter, Ffion, who was 7 at the time.

Harcombe, a consumer advocate in South Wales who died in 2004 at the age of 28, left behind a three-page, handwritten list that the British press dubbed "the Mummy Manual." The main focus is near term – the sort of detailed information, complete with shorthand wording and abbreviations, that a mother might compile before embarking on a lengthy business trip. Some items are mundane, like instructions about eating fresh, rather than processed, foods, how often to change the bedding and checking her daughter's hair for lice. It covers school, with reminders to rummage through her daughter's book bag for notices, attend parent-teacher conferences and look out for signs of bullying by classmates. There are also suggestions for Christmas stocking fillers and back-to-school shopping.

In the most moving part of the manual, Harcombe projects into the future and imagines a world without her. As her daughter matures, there will be a need for a lock on the bathroom door, she notes. And without elaborating, she includes a reference to her husband taking down her photos. She simply asks that he put them away for Ffion.

The list concludes with an effort to leave her family laughing – Harcombe clearly understood that death is hardest for those who are left behind. She asks her husband to keep in touch with her own friends, her parents and Ffion's godparents. And she threatens to haunt him if he doesn't.

(At the time of this book's publication, the full text of "the Mummy Manual" was available at http://bit.ly/dEtGrs.)

A married couple adopts a child. The child has all the same inheritance rights as those of a child of a single parent, only those rights derive from both parents. So if you are the beneficiary of a trust set up by your own parents that makes payouts to you while you are alive, and then to your own children, adopting a child would give her the right to receive distributions when you die.

In a second marriage, one spouse adopts the other's child from a previous marriage. Here, too, the child can inherit from both these parents. But what about the former spouse who was the child's other biological parent? Whether adoption extinguishes that right will depend on state law.

Let's say Jill marries Jack, the heir to a software fortune, and they have a child named Brandon before Jack tragically dies. Then Jill remarries and her new husband wants to adopt Brandon, who is still a minor. In this situation, Brandon may no longer be considered Jack's descendant. Depending on state law and how Jack's parents set up their own estate plans, Brandon could lose his right to inherit part of the software fortune.

One partner in an unmarried couple adopts the other partner's biological child. It's important to determine whether, under state law, the adoption will cut off inheritance rights that stemmed from the biological parent. If so, the parent could still make provisions for the child in her own estate plan, but if the child is not considered her descendant, any associated inheritance rights would be cut off.

An unmarried couple wants to adopt a child who is not biologically related to either of them. As in the example above, the result would depend on state law.

Leave Sufficient Funds

Except for the wealthy, raising a child is a pay-as-you-go proposition. You may gradually set aside money for large future expenses, such as college, but most funds for day-to-day costs come from current earnings. A premature death ends that income stream. Unless the person you are naming to care for your child is willing and able to pay for raising him, you need to leave enough money to cover everything your child will need.

As discussed on page 95, you can name a guardian for the money, or put the funds in a trust and designate a trustee to spend the money on your child's behalf. While financial guardianships are a matter of state law and require court supervision in some states, trusts are a private matter. A trust also gives you much more say over how the funds are spent (see Chapter 6)

Lessons From Philip Seymour Hoffman's Will

By not updating his will to cover all his children, the actor Philip Seymour Hoffman left their grieving mother in a conundrum.

Hoffman's will was signed in October 2004. At the time, he had only one child – a son, Cooper, who was 11 when Hoffman died of a drug overdose, in 2014, at age 46. He never amended that will to include his daughters, Tallulah and Willa, who were born later. The will left everything to his longtime companion, Marianne O'Donnell, who is the children's mother.

Hoffman's estimated net worth at the time of his death was $35 million. Because he and O'Donnell weren't married, she doesn't get any of the estate tax breaks available to spouses (see Chapters 3 and 4). All totaled, Hoffman's estate would owe combined estate tax of more than $15.1 million, AB Bernstein estimated for Forbes. Any assets that remain when O'Donnell dies could get taxed again.

The will left open a possible strategy to avoid the double tax. O'Donnell could disclaim (turn down) all or part of her inheritance and have it go into a trust, which could soak up some or all of Hoffman's exemption ($5.34 million at the time). But the trust referred to in the will mentions only Cooper, not his sisters. It provides that he'll get half the trust principal when he reaches age 25, and the other half when he turns 30.

This is an example of what's called the "after born child" problem. In most states, including New York, where Hoffman lived, the law protects children from disinheritance if a parent forgets to update the will. The Surrogate's Court appointed a guardian ad litem (on behalf of the children) to establish that Hoffman was the father of all three. That would enable them to share equally in the trust.

The guardian interviewed Hoffman's accountant, who advised him about estate planning, and the lawyer who drafted the will. Both said Hoffman told them that he didn't like the idea of setting up a trust for his children and that O'Donnell would take care of them. Since O'Donnell did not disclaim, the trust referred to in the will was not funded. Only time will tell whether a disclaimer would have saved taxes.

and a chance to address lifestyle differences between the guardian's family and your own. Say the people caring for your child have more limited means than you do. You could give them permission to move into your house, or leave money in trust for a larger house – perhaps to ensure that your child has her own room – and set aside funds for maintenance and repairs. To avoid situations where your children have privileges the guardians can't afford for their own children, you can authorize payments from the trust to cover certain extras for all the children.

Life insurance is the obvious vehicle to supplement whatever assets you have accumulated. Just do not make the mistake (as many people do) of owning a policy that insures your life. If you do, the entire sum could be taxable as part of your estate even though you have named your children as beneficiaries. The alternative is to set up a life insurance trust that buys the policy, owns it, and, when you die, holds the proceeds for whomever you've named as beneficiary.

Special considerations apply when making provisions for a child with special needs. To qualify for Supplemental Security Income (a welfare program) and Medicaid, which they may someday need, disabled people cannot have more than $2,000 ($1,600 in some states) of assets in their own names. This affects the way you set up and fund life insurance trusts (see Chapter 8), as well as other strategies for covering the child's future expenses.

Many people wind up disqualified for these benefits because well-intentioned parents and grandparents did not know the rules. For example, putting money in a custodial account for the child under the Uniform Transfers to Minors Act can easily disqualify the recipient. Potentially, so can Section 529 college savings plans, which allow you to set up for each child a separate account earmarked for higher education (see Chapter 9).

Provide for Children With Special Needs

A common misconception is that planning for children with special needs requires families to disinherit them so they will qualify for public assistance. A much more attractive alternative is to set up a special needs, or supplemental needs, trust to provide for each such child. As long as the trust meets certain federal requirements, the child can still be eligible for public assistance upon reaching age 18, or sooner in certain cases, such as when the family is indigent.

This is desirable not only for the Supplemental Security Income (SSI) benefit, which is $733 per month, but also to help the child qualify for Medicaid. Medicaid picks up many health care expenses, pays for supervision in a group home and foots the bill for job training.

Although some very wealthy people choose to cover all these expenses themselves, those who do lose access to various public services, including case management, which can be hugely beneficial to disabled people and their families. Instead, most families use their own funds to supplement what is available through public assistance. Like other trusts, special needs trusts also protect assets from claims of creditors (see Chapter 17) and people who may prey on the beneficiary.

Depending on your circumstances, you should consider two basic types of special needs trusts. The most common is what is known as a third-party trust, set up and funded by someone who is not a beneficiary – typically a parent or grandparent. These tend to be put in place while the older generation is still alive but not funded until those elders die. For instance, the trust may be named as the beneficiary of a will, a retirement plan or a life insurance policy.

The Secret Son

When Arthur Miller, the playwright, died in 2005, most newspaper obituaries did not mention his son Daniel, who has Down syndrome, and was then 39. Daniel had spent most of his life in state-run institutions and programs in Connecticut, while his father kept his existence a secret. Shortly before Miller died, he revised his estate plan and made Daniel an heir through a trust of 25 percent of the estate, equal to the shares left to each of Miller's other three children, according to published reports about the family.

The inheritance made Daniel wealthy and disqualified him for government aid. It also resulted in a reimbursement claim by the state, resolved privately, for the care he had received. There were ways to avoid that, but Miller did not take advantage of them.

The second trust to consider is an OBRA '93 trust (a reference to the Omnibus Budget and Reconciliation Act of 1993 that permits it). These are generally self-funded trusts created for people younger than 65 to shift assets out of their control so they will qualify for public assistance. Often, OBRA '93 trusts are funded with inheritances, or recoveries from personal injury or medical malpractice lawsuits.

OBRA '93 trusts can also be useful for elderly parents or grandparents who have a disabled family member and want to qualify for Medicaid themselves. Normally, moving property out of the parent's name would not make the parent eligible for Medicaid. But the 1993 law enables parents to transfer all their assets to an OBRA '93 trust to benefit the disabled person. In this limited context, both parties could then receive Medicaid. Although this technique is rarely used right now, as the longevity of children with disabilities increases, more people may want to consider it in the future.

While third-party trusts may not have money to spend right away, OBRA '93 trusts sometimes start out with millions of dollars in funding. And these assets can be spent even while the parents are still alive. For example, they have been used to build houses and swimming pools, install an elevator in an existing home, redo kitchens to make them wheelchair accessible and buy vans.

Under federal law, all OBRA '93 trusts must include a payback provision, giving the state or states that have been providing Medicaid services to the individual the right to get reimbursed, after the beneficiary dies, for any expenditures made on her behalf. The payback requirement applies only when you are dealing with the beneficiary's own money – not funds in third-party trusts. With third-party trusts, when the disabled beneficiary dies, whatever is left goes to any other beneficiaries designated in the trust document.

Some families have both a third-party trust and an OBRA '93 trust. When that is the case, it is best to deplete the OBRA '93 trust first, since only this trust has a payback provision.

Another restriction to be aware of is the monthly limit on earned income for people who may be eligible for Social Security Disability. Unlike Supplemental Security Income, which is a welfare program, Social Security Disability is an insurance program for disabled workers who can no longer work and their family members. There are no asset or unearned income limits for receiving Social Security Disability, but the benefit is limited based on earnings. Eligibility rules are technical, but an individual may earn approximately $1,040 a month ($1,740 a month if blind) without losing Social Security Disability benefits.

On top of the federal rules, a crazy quilt of state laws can affect the forma-
tion and administration of special needs trusts. Since Medicaid is a federal-
state program, states have the power to regulate these trusts, and inevitably
there are differences from state to state. State laws can affect trust terms,
administration and how they are funded.

For both special needs trusts and OBRA '93 trusts, rules on how the money can be spent are roughly the same. Ideally, the trust shouldn't be used for
food, clothing or shelter – the purpose is to supplement, rather than to sup-
plant, public benefits. If the trust is used for the necessities, the beneficiary
could lose up to one-third of the Supplemental Security Income benefit.

Within these parameters, it is possible to greatly improve the beneficiary's lifestyle. These trusts have paid for cable TV, computers, telephones,
vacations, medical benefits that Medicaid doesn't cover, or a higher quality
of care, like a dentist or psychotherapist, of the beneficiary's choice.

Generally speaking, the trustee – the person or institution in charge of the
trust – should have full discretion about how much to distribute and when to
make those payouts. And the funds should be sent directly to the provider of
the goods or services, such as a travel agent, a home health agency or a store.
Distributions to the beneficiary, even for pocket money, would be considered
unearned income and could reduce the Supplemental Security Income benefit.

Starting in 2015, it's also possible to set up tax-advantaged savings accounts for people with disabilities. Called ABLE (the acronym stands for
"Achieving a Better Life Experience"), or 529A accounts, they resemble the
529 accounts used to save for college but will not disqualify the beneficiary for
Medicaid or SSI. For more about ABLE accounts, see Chapter 10.

Put the Money in Good Hands

J ust as your will should appoint guardian, it is vital that you leave
instructions about who should manage the assets you leave.

As noted earlier, setting up a trust that requires a trustee to follow your
instructions is much better than a financial guardianship arrangement,
even one in which you have handpicked the guardian. Worse yet, if you
do not name a specific person for the guardian's role, the court takes over
supervision of any money left to children. This includes not just the assets

that pass under the will – such as stocks, bonds and the family home – but also payments from life insurance policies, retirement accounts and custodial accounts. The person caring for your child may have to go through an onerous process to get any expenditures approved.

To avoid various undesirable financial consequences, you should use a trust in conjunction with life insurance policies and when leaving funds for children with special needs. Other times, you may be tempted to rely on much simpler and less expensive custodial accounts, which name an adult to oversee the funds until the child reaches age 18, 19 or 21, depending on the state.

Did You Know?

If you are setting up a special needs trust for a child with a disability, let other relatives know. That way, if a grandparent wants to help, she can indicate in her will that the trust should receive the inheritance. Money left outright to the child could disqualify him from public assistance.

Custodial accounts, however, have a number of disadvantages (see Chapter 9). One is that children are legally entitled to the money when they reach the specified age, even if they lack the maturity or experience to manage it. Another drawback, when you are providing for the support of a child who is still a minor, is that you have much less say over how the money will be spent.

In contrast, by putting assets in trust for minor children, you can direct that income and principal be paid any way you like. Until your children reach a certain age (say 25), you might leave distributions entirely up to the trustee. After that, you may select two or three ages at which portions of the principal will be distributed (for instance, one-third at 25, another third at 30 and the balance at 35).

Compared with the emotionally charged issue of choosing someone to care for your child, deciding who will manage her money may seem relatively easy. But proceed with caution. Much as you would like to believe, "If I'm going to trust someone with my child, I might as well trust him with her money," it's much better to keep the two functions discrete and select another person or financial institution to manage the money (see Chapter 6).

To-Do List

Coordinate Elements of an Estate Plan

When parents die prematurely, a lot of loose ends can be left behind. The following precautions can help avoid potential legal and economic pitfalls.

❦ *Review all accounts for which you are a custodian for your child.* Include those at banks, mutual fund companies or brokerage houses, as well as 529 college savings plans; verify that there is an alternate custodian. You should not be the custodian of an account that you set up.

❦ *Determine whether children are named as primary or backup beneficiaries of retirement accounts, such as IRAs and 401(k)s – either your own or accounts set up by the child's grandparents.* Discuss with financial advisers the possibility of creating a trust to receive the child's share (see Chapters 6 and 7).

❦ *For a child with special needs, do not create custodial accounts or 529 college savings plans for that child if she may become dependent on public benefits.* If you or a relative have already set up such an account, spend the funds on your child before she will be eligible for public assistance. If a 529 plan is in place, consider changing the beneficiary to another family member in the same generation.

❦ *Make sure life insurance policies are owned by a trust and that it is named as the beneficiary of the policy (the child, in turn, is a beneficiary of the trust).* This should be a special needs trust if your child has a disability that would ultimately qualify him or her for public assistance.

❦ *Examine any existing trusts that name your child as a beneficiary.* If you have a special needs child, the trust should not give him or her a Crummey power – the right for a limited time, usually 30 or 60 days, to withdraw from the trust the contribution to the trust during the current year (see Chapter 6).

❦ *Keep plans up to date.* It may be necessary for you or your relatives to amend wills and trusts to cover children born after those documents were signed.

Trusts: Not Just for The Wealthy

Read this chapter even if you think you don't need these useful tools.

Y ou may think trusts are just for the super-rich. In fact, they are enormously useful – and sometimes essential – for people of more modest means. There are numerous situations when a trust is the best way to achieve your goals.

A trust can safeguard your assets and provide for your own care should you become unable to handle your affairs.

> ## In This Chapter...
>
> ⚜ *What Is a Trust?*
>
> ⚜ *How Do You Create a Trust?*
>
> ⚜ *What Are the Key Issues to Consider?*
>
> ⚜ *Whom Should You Choose as Trustee?*
>
> ⚜ *What Checks and Balances Are Available for Long-Term Trusts?*
>
> ⚜ *What Does It Cost to Set Up And Use a Trust?*

A trust can prevent payouts from life insurance policies being subject to estate tax.

A trust can avoid tax on an inheritance when one spouse is a U.S. citizen and the other isn't.

A trust can provide for children from a previous marriage.

A trust can hold money for minors and ensure that they can't spend it all the minute they reach majority.

A trust can prevent funds from being eroded by family members whom you consider spendthrifts.

A trust can protect assets from creditors and former spouses, whether your own or those of your heirs.

A trust can save estate taxes on both assets put into the trust during your life and on any future appreciation of those assets.

A trust can help you avoid or minimize generation-skipping transfer taxes on money destined for grandchildren or future generations.

A trust can benefit family and charity through one tax-efficient vehicle.

What Is a Trust?

One thing that makes trusts hard to conceptualize is that you can't see them or touch them. They are an invisible legal wrapper for holding assets, such as cash, copyrights, patents, real estate, an insurance policy, shares in a closely held company or publicly traded securities. A trust is created by a document that looks like a contract and is called the trust instrument. The person who sets up the trust and funds it is known as the grantor or the settlor. Briefly, here's what happens next.

Step 1: Title to any assets you put into the trust passes to the trustee. This is the person or company that you have chosen to carry out your wishes. You can have one trustee or several.

Step 2: The trustees manage the assets, either by themselves or by hiring investment managers. Legally, a trustee is a fiduciary, which means the trustee has a duty to always put the beneficiaries' welfare first.

Step 3: Following your directions in the trust instrument, the trustees make distributions, or payouts, to the people or charities you have named as beneficiaries.

How Do You Create a Trust?

You can set up a trust during your lifetime (an inter vivos trust) or with your will (a testamentary trust). Lifetime trusts may be either irrevocable, meaning that you can't change them or undo them, or revocable, meaning that you can. Unfortunately, trusts set up to save estate taxes usually have to be irrevocable. You will need a lawyer's help with the paperwork, which might run 20 pages or more.

What Are the Key Issues to Consider?

One advantage of a trust is that it can designate someone to fulfill your goals when you are no longer around. The more clearly you spell out those goals, the easier it will be for the trustee or trustees to follow your wishes. These are some issues to sort out.

Who are the beneficiaries? A trust can benefit one person or many – known as a pot trust. Often they have both current beneficiaries, who are entitled to assets immediately, and future (remainder) beneficiaries, who will not receive distributions until some event occurs – such as when they reach a certain age or the current beneficiary dies.

Trusts that pay income to current beneficiaries and preserve principal for future ones pit one set of interests against the other. Legally, trustees must be impartial, but in real life they can get caught in the middle of the two sets of beneficiaries. Lifetime beneficiaries generally want the largest possible payout, while future beneficiaries prefer trust assets to accumulate and increase in value. These conflicting priorities are affected both by the choice of investments and by decisions about when to make distributions.

What is the timetable for distributions? Often trusts start making payouts at specific ages – for example, with income to people in their 20s, and distributions of principal staggered at ages 30, 35 and 40, to encompass the high-spending years when many people are getting married, starting families and buying homes.

What are the trustee's responsibilities? Traditionally, the primary obligations are to:
- Interpret the trust document
- Make distributions of income or principal and keep records of these payouts
- Invest and maintain investments in an ever-changing market
- Send annual Crummey notices, when required (see "Crummey Fundamentals," page 103)
- Prepare the trust tax return

Depending on the purpose of the trust and who the beneficiaries are, trustees may serve a variety of related functions. Some people rely on

---

Crummey Fundamentals

A popular way of funding many types of trusts is to use the annual exclusion – the $14,000 ($28,000 for spouses who make joint gifts, a process known as gift-splitting) that you can give each year to as many people as you would like without having to pay gift tax. One condition for the annual exclusion is that the gift must be a present interest, meaning something the recipient can use right away, rather than a future one.

The most common way to satisfy this requirement is to give beneficiaries Crummey powers: the right for a limited time, usually 30 or 60 days, to withdraw from the trust the yearly gift attributable to that beneficiary. Each year, the trustees must send a notice, called a Crummey notice, to the beneficiaries (or the parents, if the beneficiaries are minors), letting them know about their right to withdraw their portion of the annual gift to the trust.

Although there's nothing difficult about preparing these notices – some lawyers will even give you a template – many people neglect to send them and to keep copies with the trust documents. This could come back to bite your heirs later if your estate is audited. In the worst-case scenario, they could get stuck paying gift taxes for the money you put in the trust.

---

trustees to help educate younger generations about financial matters. When trusts are set up for minors, the trustee may step into the shoes of a parent who dies prematurely and become the child's financial guardian (see Chapter 5).

How should the trust assets be invested? Without specific directions to do otherwise, trustees have a legal obligation to invest in a diversified portfolio – in other words, not put all the eggs in one basket. The precise asset allocation should reflect the needs of beneficiaries. That will determine if the portfolio is invested for growth or value, or to generate income, for example.

Will the trustee have broad or narrow powers to make distributions?
With narrow powers, the trustee can pay out income, and occasionally
principal, for only very specific reasons, such as "health, education, maintenance or support," "college education" or "medical emergencies." Narrow powers are commonly used in situations in which the creator of the
trust wants to control and tightly define the use of trust property.

Broad powers to make distributions – with or without a specific standard – allow for more subjective decisions. These trusts call for the trustee to exercise independent judgment to "maintain reasonable comfort" of
a beneficiary, to preserve the person's "accustomed manner of living" or
"for any purpose." Often these powers show up in trusts for the benefit of
a surviving spouse or children where the grantor is comfortable that the
trustee won't abuse the broad guidelines.

Giving a trustee broad powers is a good idea if you want the trust to last for
multiple generations. The more flexibility the trustees have, the better they will
be able to react to unanticipated situations. Some people even make the trust
fully discretionary – giving trustees the last word over payouts. That's all the
more reason to explain your intentions as clearly as possible in the trust document – and to be sure that you are comfortable with the trustees you designate.

Should beneficiaries be able to remove and replace trustees? More and
more trusts include this power. For example, in a marital trust, which initially
benefits the surviving spouse, that individual – assume it is the wife – might
have the power to remove a corporate trustee unilaterally if she is not satisfied with its services. In longer-term trusts, the document could designate as
trustee one person, a group of people (such as a committee of family members or beneficiaries) or a business (such as a bank or law firm) to appoint
the successor. If you plan to include powers to remove and replace trustees,
the trust document should clearly define the circumstances under which
removal may occur and the type of successor trustee you prefer.

How long should the trust last? Trusts can last for a finite term or, in
states that permit dynasty trusts, continue for many generations. Some
trusts are set up to end at the time of a specific event, such as when an
income beneficiary dies or reaches a certain age. But in our litigious society, having a trust continue for longer offers this distinct advantage: It can
protect a beneficiary's assets from someone who wins a lawsuit against the
beneficiary (see Chapter 17).

Whom Should You Choose as Trustee?

The ideal trustee is objective, a careful record-keeper and either experienced with taxes and investing or capable of retaining others who are. You will want a fiduciary who is able to give your trust as much attention as it requires, over a prolonged period, if necessary. These are the options.

Family, friends and business colleagues. One attraction of such trustees is that they presumably understand the family dynamics and can balance the needs of various beneficiaries when making decisions about distributions. But even assuming they have the background, training and objectivity, these individuals, who often serve as trustees without compensation or for a nominal charge, may not have time to handle a trustee's numerous responsibilities.

Another consideration is the potential legal liability. A fiduciary can be found liable for negligence, as well as for intentional misdeeds. If they mishandle trust investments or distributions, trustees could be the target of a lawsuit by disgruntled beneficiaries. They may not have the financial resources and insurance protection to cover their errors or the desire to put themselves in this position.

> ## *Did You Know?*
>
> Paul Newman, who died in 2008, flourished in the spotlight but kept his estate plan offstage. His will directed that "airplanes and all race cars" be sold and most tangible property go to his wife, Joanne Woodward. Everything else went into a trust, a private document.

Professional advisers (such as lawyers and accountants). A key concern is whether they are equipped to field the day-to-day questions that can come up. When acting as fiduciary, they may not have the resources, the time or the knowledge base of a large organization. So you had better question them closely on these issues before designating them. They typically charge their standard hourly fee for the service (in some states, a maximum is set by law).

Corporate trustees. Institutional services are available through banks, trust companies and some law firms. On the whole, corporate trustees have a depth of experience that most individuals can't match. They are more likely to keep up with changes in the law that affect investment returns or the tax efficiency of the trust. And they understand the complexities and potential pitfalls of certain types of trusts. Corporate fiduciaries also provide continuity through multiple generations and an institutional memory, which is especially helpful in long-term trusts.

A common criticism of corporate trustees is that they are rigid and bureaucratic. Not all corporate fiduciaries operate this way, but you do need to perform due diligence (see "Interviewing Corporate Trustees," page 107). Because distribution decisions are often made by committee, you want to be sure it meets frequently enough to implement the trust terms.

A combination of individual and corporate trustees. Some people find the most flexible arrangement is to appoint co-trustees: an individual who knows the family well and a corporate fiduciary with extensive experience in trust administration. This might be appropriate when something comparable to parental authority is necessary to protect the interests of children or grandchildren. In that case, you might want to limit the individual's role to making the kind of decisions that would normally fall to a parent, such as deciding how much money to distribute to the beneficiaries. As co-trustee, the corporate fiduciary could have sole responsibility for asset management and legal compliance.

In recent years, it has become increasingly popular to appoint beneficiaries as co-trustees for their own trusts, which are primarily overseen by a corporate fiduciary. This fosters a sense of involvement that beneficiaries might not feel when all the control resides elsewhere, and this structure can be a tool for educating the next generation about money.

One potential pitfall, however, is that giving beneficiaries of the trust authority over discretionary distributions could have adverse consequences, such as causing the property to be included in their estates or exposing it to their creditors. It is much more common – and sensible – to have family co-trustees participate only in decisions that do not involve distributions to themselves.

Many long-term trusts that start out with individual trustees ultimately end up with corporate fiduciaries, which are more enduring. Over time, corporate trustees may be better suited to deal with events and people that you cannot anticipate when establishing the trust.

Interviewing Corporate Trustees

If you are considering a corporate trustee, look for an organization with decades of experience in the business, a track record for integrity and a presence in your community. Here are some questions to ask.

❧ What do you charge? (If they are managing an investment portfolio, their fees will be higher than if they are simply making distribution decisions.)

❧ Do you require the trust to have at least a certain monetary value before you will serve as trustee?

❧ How do you plan to invest the assets?

❧ Will you be delegating investment decisions? (If so, to whom?)

❧ If the trust has unique assets (such as art, copyrights, patents, real estate, water rights, oil and gas interests, or shares in a family-owned business), how will they be managed?

❧ If you do not have expertise in managing these kinds of assets, what process will you use to hire the right experts?

❧ Who will have custody of the assets?

❧ How will you balance the interests of current and future beneficiaries?

❧ What process do you use to make decisions about discretionary distributions?

❧ If beneficiaries live in different geographic areas, how do you plan to communicate with them?

❧ Do you have offices in various locations?

Especially when individual trustees are involved, it is essential that your document include a succession plan – so a mechanism is in place for choosing subsequent trustees if the initial ones become unwilling or unable to serve. Some grantors allow individual trustees to choose their successors. Others provide that when a trustee's tenure ends, for whatever reason, that power shifts to a successor, perhaps a corporate fiduciary.

What Checks and Balances Are Available For Long-Term Trusts?

One challenge when setting up long-term irrevocable trusts is to come up with a framework that will achieve your goals many years in the future. Problem is, neither a family's needs nor the state and federal tax laws are constants. Will those angelic toddlers grow up to be black sheep? Another hugely important factor is whether the law may change.

The rules that govern a trust depend on its situs (location), and state laws are evolving. Among the key areas currently in flux are the extent of creditor protection for certain trusts, whether a trust can be a dynasty trust that continues forever, and whether it is possible to decant the trust – that is, to pay out funds from one trust to another. State laws that allow decanting essentially permit amendment of irrevocable trusts. Over time, it might be desirable to change the situs of a trust so that it can take advantage of strategies in states where the beneficiaries live or the corporate trustees are situated.

To address these issues and others, a growing number of people are designating a trust protector, sometimes called a special trustee or trust adviser. This is someone, independent of the trustee, whom you assign to make certain key decisions and adapt various trust terms as circumstances change. Choices for the role include friends, personal advisers who know the family, business associates or family members who are not beneficiaries.

Although trust protectors have been common in other countries for decades, they're something of a recent phenomenon in the United States. American lawyers first started using protectors 50 or more years ago in offshore trusts aimed at asset protection (see Chapter 17). More recently, trust protectors have shown up in domestic trusts. Though most common in irrevocable trusts, they also can be useful to oversee the trustees of revocable, or living, trusts set up to safeguard assets for those who no longer have the faculties to manage funds themselves (see Chapter 1).

Trust protectors are especially helpful with two other kinds of trusts. One is a trust that will not be funded until the grantor dies. With the grantor gone, someone must be entrusted with tough personal decisions. Professional trustees may prefer not to make judgment calls about when to accelerate payments of principal, for instance.

Trust protectors can also perform a key function with irrevocable trusts funded during life in order to get property out of the grantor's estate. Much as the grantor might like to be able to add beneficiaries, for example, doing so would cause the trust property to be included in her estate for federal tax purposes. But let's say the grantor has named her brother as protector. The brother may be able to take that action instead.

The flexibility a protector provides can be useful for other reasons. Given all the recent mergers and changes at financial institutions, you may want the freedom to switch trustees after familiar trust officers have been replaced. A protector can be given the power to remove and replace a corporate trustee if you have not given that power to the trust beneficiaries.

A trust protector's powers can be broad or limited. Initially, grantors gave protectors only the power to remove or replace trustees or to veto distributions – for instance, in a trust authorizing fiduciaries to make discretionary payouts to beneficiaries. More recently, the menu of options has expanded. Some trusts authorize the protector to veto or direct investment decisions, to split a pot trust into multiple trusts, so that each beneficiary has his or her own trust, and even to end the trust and distribute the assets.

Increasingly, lawyers recommend that protectors be able to change the situs of the trust to implement various tax strategies. For example, you might give the protector the power, when appropriate, to switch a trust to a state that's more favorable for creditor protection or that permits dynasty trusts.

The more expansive a protector's powers, the greater the potential for problems. For certain kinds of trusts, the protector needs to be careful that exercising his or her power doesn't ruin the tax advantages that go with that trust. For example, with a Crummey trust (see "Crummey Fundamentals," page 103), denying the holder of a Crummey power the right to make withdrawals during the specified period each year could result in certain gifts to the trust being taxable rather than eligible for the annual exclusion.

Another issue to consider is whether you want to provide for successor protectors and a mechanism for choosing them.

What Does It Cost to Set Up and Use a Trust?

F or all the benefits and tax savings that trusts can achieve, significant costs can be incurred in establishing and overseeing them.

Set-up costs. The legal bill to prepare a trust can run from $2,500 to more than $15,000, depending on the type of trust, its complexity, where you are situated and the size of the law firm doing the work (see Chapter 18).

Trustee's fees. Fees for corporate trustees or advisers serving that function vary widely and will depend on the services they perform. If trustees are managing an investment portfolio, their charges will be higher (typically, a percentage of assets under management) than if they are simply making distribution decisions.

Income taxes. The rules that govern a trust depend on its situs (location), and state laws are evolving. Among the key areas currently in flux are the extent of creditor protection for certain trusts, whether a trust can be a dynasty trust that continues forever, and whether it is possible to decant the trust – that is, to pay out funds from one trust to another. State laws that allow decanting essentially permit amendment of irrevocable trusts. Over time, it might be desirable to change the situs of a trust so that it can take advantage of strategies in states with the most favorable laws. Generally you need some connection with a state to locate a trust there. Often, but not always, it's enough to have a trustee (such as a corporate trustee) in the state.

One strategy to address the problem is to make the trust a grantor trust – one in which the person creating the trust retains certain powers. In that case, the grantor, rather than the trust, pays the income tax while she is alive, leaving more for beneficiaries. Attractive as this may be in some cases, you must be able to afford that tax bill annually (see Chapter 15).

Tax preparation. The trust needs to file an annual income tax return, whether or not it owes income tax, and submit tax information to beneficiaries. Expect an accountant to charge at least $1,000 for this service.

To-Do List

Look Before You Leap

Trusts can achieve a variety of goals, and other chapters of this book include details about trusts created for particular purposes. The tradeoff is that trusts can also create complications for you and the people you hope to benefit. So before you go feet first into a trust, discuss all the ramifications with your lawyer and tax adviser. Here are some important questions to ask.

✤ What's the profile of the person who typically sets up this type of trust? (Then ask yourself: "Does it make sense for me?")

✤ Is there a simpler or less expensive way to achieve my goals?

✤ From a tax perspective, what are the best assets to put into the trust? (Then ask yourself: "Am I willing to part with any of these assets?")

✤ Is it possible to contribute these assets without paying gift tax?

✤ What are the income tax consequences of the trust?

✤ What is the best situs (home state) for the trust?

✤ Will the trust save more than it will cost to create and operate?

✤ Will the trust tie my hands or restrain the beneficiaries in ways that are undesirable?

✤ Is there a way to undo or alter any aspects of the trust should I change my mind?

✤ Do the individuals or institutions I plan to name as trustees or the people I plan to name as beneficiaries live in high-tax states? If so, how will that affect the trust's effectiveness?

Chapter 7

Preserve
Retirement
Accounts

*Read this chapter if you have
your own retirement account or
have inherited one.*

F or many people, money in individual retirement accounts or employer-sponsored retirement plans, such as 401(k)s and 403(b)s, is their biggest asset. Chances are, it's also the one they least understand. This can lead to costly mistakes, oversights and missed financial opportunities.

Contrary to popular misconception, retirement accounts are not normally covered by a will. Instead, the funds go to inheritors according to beneficiary designation forms. You fill out the form when you open an account but can later amend it. The form notifies the bank or financial institution (the custodian) about who will inherit your accounts. These are your beneficiaries.

In This Chapter...

- Understand the "Stretch-Out"
- Keep Beneficiary Forms Current
- Beware of IRA Trust Traps
- Go Roth, if You Can
- Be Smart About Inheritances
- Use Retirement Assets to Benefit Charity

If your account is what's called a traditional IRA or employer-sponsored plan (as opposed to a Roth account), your heirs will be required to pay income tax each time they withdraw funds. Therefore, much of the focus in estate planning with retirement accounts involves minimizing income tax. That's true whether you're aiming to protect your heirs or you have inherited a retirement account.

Estate taxes can also shrink the pie, though that's of less concern now that the tax-free amounts have gone up. If taxes might be an issue, it's best to leave sufficient other funds to cover taxes so your heirs don't need to cash out the retirement account to pay them.

Understand the "Stretch-Out"

Generally IRA inheritors must withdraw a minimum amount each year, starting on Dec. 31 of the year after they inherit the account. The rules for spouses are more lenient (see page 118).

If they choose to, heirs can draw out these minimum required distributions over their own expected life spans. This is known as the stretch-out – a financial strategy to extend the tax advantages of an IRA. Stretching out the IRA gives the funds extra years and potentially decades of income-tax-deferred growth in a traditional IRA or tax-free growth in a Roth IRA. This is a wonderful investment opportunity.

Minimum required distributions are based on life expectancy. The longer the life expectancy, the smaller – as a percentage of the IRA balance – each payout must be. From an income tax perspective, therefore, the best designated beneficiary is a young person.

If you are dealing with a company plan, there is no automatic right to a stretch-out. Unless the spouse is the beneficiary, most businesses require inheritors to take the money out of the plan in a lump sum, often within five years or less. But if you have inherited one of these accounts, you can avoid the lump-sum payout if you roll over the funds from the company plan into an inherited IRA. This enables you to stretch out the withdrawals. Company plans are required to allow all named beneficiaries to do this.

Calculating the minimum required payout each year is fairly straightforward: Take the account balance on Dec. 31 of the previous year and divide it by the beneficiary's life expectancy, as listed in IRS tables. (These tables can be found in the Appendix of this book.) Unless the account is a Roth, you must pay income tax on this payout. (For more about rules and strategies for inheritors, see page 133.)

For better or worse, IRA owners can't control whether inheritors take maximum advantage of the stretch-out. Consider Sally, who leaves part of her IRA, worth $100,000, to her grandson, who is 21 when Sally dies, at age 69. He must begin taking distributions by Dec. 31 of the year following Sally's death but can stretch out withdrawals for the rest of his life.

Based on an account balance of $100,000, the grandson's first required distribution at age 22 is $100,000 divided by his remaining life expectancy of 61.1 years (from the IRS table), or $1,636.66. If he continues to withdraw just the minimum required distribution each year, and the investments appreciate at a steady rate of 6 percent, this inheritance can provide the grandson with a nest egg for his own retirement. At the same time, in a year in which he needs more money, he can withdraw more than the minimum without penalty. In this respect, the inherited IRA is different from one the grandson might set up for himself.

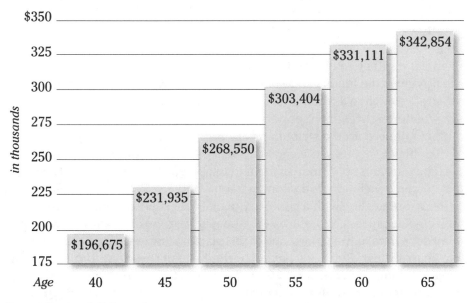

Source: Brentmark Software Inc.

But what if the self-indulgent grandson cashes the money out early because he wants to buy a BMW? Or what if he needs it to help finance the purchase of a house or a child's college education? In financial lingo this is called "blowing the stretch-out." And in real life it happens all the time. The grandson will owe ordinary income taxes, or, if it's a Roth, no taxes. But there's no "early withdrawal" penalty as there might be if he were taking money from his own IRA.

Keep a couple of other caveats in mind when leaving retirement accounts to grandchildren. One is that if they might be minors when you die, you should name an adult custodian for the assets or consider naming a trust for the grandchild's benefit as the designated beneficiary (see page 120). Another is that IRAs left to grandchildren are subject to generation-skipping transfer tax, in addition to estate tax and income tax. This is a levy of 40 percent on the amount of a grandparent's total transfers to all grandchildren that exceeds $5.43 million. As with any other asset, an IRA left to the owner's child could be subject to the generation-skipping tax if the child decides to disclaim (legalese for decline) the inheritance, passing it on to a grandchild. (For more about the generation-skipping transfer tax, see Chapter 14.)

Keep Beneficiary Forms Current

Beneficiary designations affect not only who gets the assets, but also how quickly funds must be withdrawn from the account.

If you opened the account years ago, check the designation on file to make sure it's what you intend. For example, if you or a family member married or divorced, or have had children or grandchildren, you might want to make some changes. Then get in the habit of re-viewing these forms once a year – perhaps every January, or on your birthday, or when you change the clocks in the spring or fall. Each time you change the form, send it to the financial institution that holds the account, and ask them to acknowledge receipt.

Be sure to name both primary and alternate (contingent) beneficiaries. That way, if your primary beneficiary died and you neglected to update your forms, the assets will go to the alternate.

But never name your estate as the beneficiary – a mistake even smart, highly educated people have made. That will cut short the tax benefits. Here's how. If the account is a Roth IRA, all funds must be withdrawn within five years. For a traditional IRA, the same rule applies unless the former owner was already 70½ – the age at which a traditional IRA owner must begin cashing out. In that case, the distribution rate for the heir is based on the age of the person who died.

This could also happen in a variety of other circumstances: if you forget to name a beneficiary at all, haven't named an alternate beneficiary and the first beneficiary has died, or if no one can find the beneficiary designa-tion form when the time comes.

If there's no beneficiary form on file, heirs are at the mercy of the IRA custodian's default policy. Some award an IRA first to a living spouse and then to the estate, but most send it straight to the estate. In that case, the money will pass pursuant to the terms of the will if there is one, or according to state law that determines how property passes when someone dies without a will. And, again, the tax benefits will be cut short.

Another disadvantage of having the IRA pass through an estate is that it becomes available to pay your final bills, including the income tax bill on the IRA.

For each account you have, you will need to choose beneficiaries. If you have multiple accounts at the same institution, it's best to do this with a separate form for each, even if you want to distribute all the accounts the same way.

The best way to fill out the form will depend on your goals. Here are some possibilities.

Provide for your spouse. Most married people start by naming their spouse as beneficiary of a retirement account. In fact, if the account is a qualified plan (a category under federal law that includes a defined-contribution plan, defined-benefit plan, Keogh plan for the self-employed and 401(k) – but not an IRA), the Employee Retirement Income Security Act of 1974 gives your spouse the right to be the sole primary beneficiary of the account. To name anyone else, you need your spouse's written consent.

For IRAs and qualified plans, the law gives special privileges to spouses who inherit the funds. Unlike other inheritors, who must begin making withdrawals by Dec. 31 of the year following the account owner's death, a spouse – let's assume it's the wife – who inherits an IRA or company plan has another option. She can roll the assets into her own IRA and postpone required minimum distributions until she turns 70½.

The catch is that, like other IRA owners, she may have to pay a 10 percent early-withdrawal penalty if she takes money before age 59½ from her own IRA. So a young widow should generally wait until after reaching 59½ to do the rollover. Meanwhile, she doesn't have to take out any money until her late spouse would have turned 70½.

Keep things equal. This is an issue that often comes up when leaving assets to children and grandchildren, whether they are primary or contingent beneficiaries. Let's say you want your three children to have equal shares of your IRA. On the beneficiary designation form, you would list each of them and indicate that they should get one-third of the account.

But what if one of them dies before you? Many standard beneficiary designation forms let you provide for per stirpes distributions; that's the legal term for passing inheritances down to the next generation if one beneficiary dies before the account owner rather than automatically having that beneficiary's share go to other co-beneficiaries.

Give your heirs options. Sometimes a beneficiary will want to disclaim (legalese for decline) an inheritance, typically with the intent of benefiting another person or a specific charity. People who disclaim, known as disclaimants, are generally treated as if they had died before the person from whom they are inheriting. The assets go to the person next in line, or to a specific charity. Inheritors can't disclaim to whomever they please.

Anticipate this possibility when you indicate, on the form, whom the alternate beneficiary should be. For example, you might name your spouse as primary and your children as alternates, or your children as primary and grandchildren as alternates. Your primary beneficiary then has the option of disclaiming the account, enabling it to pass to the younger alternate. In this scenario, checking the "per stirpes" box, on a form that has one, can achieve the same result.

> ## *Did You Know?*
>
> You need to choose beneficiaries for each of your retirement accounts. If you have more than one account at the same institution, it's best to do this with a separate beneficiary designation form for each, even if you want to distribute all the accounts the same way.

Once you have completed the form, ask an estate planning lawyer to review it and coordinate your retirement accounts with the rest of your estate plan. The larger your retirement account and the more complicated the estate plan, the harder it may be to cover all the bases with the custodian's boilerplate. Depending on how the standard form is set up, you may prefer to have your lawyer prepare a customized, more complex beneficiary designation form. Some lawyers will include a couple of customized beneficiary designation forms as part of the standard estate planning package. Otherwise, you will need to pay extra for that service, most likely at your lawyer's hourly rate.

Be aware, though, that using a customized beneficiary designation will most likely delay transferring assets to beneficiaries down the line, since financial institutions will need to interpret documents you've submitted rather than simply working with their own, which have been vetted and kitchen tested.

Beware of IRA Trust Traps

A 2014 Supreme Court decision rekindled the debate about whether it is better to inherit IRA assets in a trust than to receive them outright. In that case, *Clark v. Rameker*, the Court found that a woman who inherited an IRA from her mother in 2001 and filed for bankruptcy nine years later could not shield the account from her creditors. This situation could have been avoided if the mother had named a trust as the IRA beneficiary rather than leaving it directly to her daughter. The facts in the case are unusual, though. After all, how many folks with unspent inherited IRAs will go bankrupt?

Even if you don't expect an heir to file for bankruptcy, a trust can serve other purposes. It can protect the IRA assets from other creditors – the most common one is a divorcing spouse. You might also consider a trust if you want to control the cash flow to heirs you regard as imprudent. If the intended beneficiaries are minors, you can't leave property to them outright, so you have a choice between naming a custodian for the child who will inherit the IRA or creating a trust for the benefit of minors that will in turn be a beneficiary of the IRA. With a trust, you can limit these young beneficiaries' access to the money that would otherwise come under their control when they reach the age of majority (18, 19 or 21, depending on the state).

However, complex rules govern this strategy. Before you go this route, ponder the pros, cons and potential snags of making a trust the beneficiary of your IRA. Here are issues to consider.

The effect on the stretch-out. When the trust meets certain requirements set by federal regulations (more about that later), the IRS will "look through" the trust and treat its beneficiary as if he or she were directly named the IRA's beneficiary. This enables the trust to take advantage of favorable minimum-distribution rules that apply to individual beneficiaries. In trusts with multiple beneficiaries, the required yearly withdrawal will be based on the life expectancy, under IRS tables, of the oldest beneficiary.

If the trust doesn't qualify as a look-through, or see-through, trust, it will still get the money. However, it may be required to take the payout within as little as five years if the account owner hadn't reached the required beginning date for taking IRA withdrawals (April 1 of the year after the account owner reaches 70½) before he or she died.

A different payout period applies if the owner died on or after this date. In that case, a trust without designated-beneficiary status can calculate withdrawals according to the account owner's remaining life expectancy, as if he or she were alive. This would probably mean a more rapid payout than if the trust could use the life expectancy of its oldest beneficiary to calculate withdrawals.

To qualify for look-through treatment, the trust must meet four criteria outlined in 26 Code of Federal Regulations Section 1.401(a)(9)-4. The requirement that has proved most troublesome is one dictating that beneficiaries be identifiable as of the date of the IRA owner's death. The goal is to know who is the oldest beneficiary so withdrawals can be based on his or her life expectancy. As a practical matter, though, if it's possible that the oldest beneficiary might not be identifiable in certain situations, the trust could flunk the test and the IRA would be treated as if there were no beneficiary.

For example, powers of appointment, a popular device that permits beneficiaries to decide who will receive certain trust property, could cause a trust to violate the rule, because older beneficiaries could conceivably be added to the trust. For the same reason, "spray" powers, authorizing the trustees to give out principal among a class of beneficiaries when appropriate, could also cause a trust to fail this test if the trust permits older beneficiaries to be added to the trust later.

Equally problematic is the fact that the regulations define an identifiable beneficiary as a human. Trusts with a beneficiary that, however remote, is not a person, won't qualify for look-through treatment. That's true whether the beneficiary is a charity or the estate of the IRA owner. Many trusts name a charity or the estate as the contingent beneficiary that will receive the funds if all the human beneficiaries have died.

How many beneficiaries? A trust with just one beneficiary could use that person's life expectancy in figuring withdrawals. In a trust with multiple beneficiaries, the trust would take withdrawals based on the life expectancy of the oldest beneficiary. When naming multiple beneficiaries, though, there is a risk of the stretch-out being significantly shorter than the IRA owner would have liked. This could happen if there's one beneficiary – even a contingent beneficiary – who is significantly older than the others.

Spouse as beneficiary. If you name a trust for your spouse as the IRA beneficiary, you lose the major income tax benefits of leaving an IRA to a spouse outright. Normally, the spouse (assume it's the wife) can roll over the IRA into her own and defer distributions until reaching age 70½. Another advantage of doing the rollover is that, when calculating her required minimum distributions, she can use the IRS Uniform Lifetime table that applies to IRA owners rather than the so-called Single Life Expectancy table that applies to inheritors; using this table results in smaller required distributions each year. Rolling the IRA over into her own also entitles her to convert it to a Roth, which can add tremendous value to the IRA (as noted on page 124). This option is not available to non-spouse inheritors.

Did You Know?

When you pass away, money in your retirement accounts gets tallied up, along with the rest of your assets. If the total (not counting assets bequeathed to a citizen spouse or charity) is more than the exclusion amount, your heirs will need to pay estate tax.

Another drawback if the children are the ultimate beneficiaries of the trust is that the trust cannot use their life expectancies in figuring the minimum distribution that it must withdraw from the IRA each year. Instead, this calculation must be based on the age of the oldest beneficiary, who will generally be the spouse.

Existing trusts might not work. People who have set up other trusts in their estate plan, such as a bypass trust, dynasty trust or living trust, might be tempted simply to name those trusts as IRA beneficiaries rather than creating one for the purpose. Pitfalls abound. These trusts may contain boilerplate language that's fine in other contexts but detrimental when an IRA is concerned because it inadvertently limits the stretch-out.

The same goes for the qualified terminable interest property trust, or QTIP. This trust is designed to qualify for the unlimited marital deduction when the first spouse dies. It must require the trustee to pay all income to the surviving spouse for life (the trustee can also make distributions of principal) and not permit distributions to anyone other than the spouse while he or she is alive. After that, the assets can go to whomever you specify in the trust. (See Chapters 3 and 4.)

Accumulate distributions or pay them out? With a conduit trust, as its name suggests, the IRA distribution simply passes through the trust and gets paid out immediately to the beneficiary. In contrast, an "accumulation" trust permits assets to build up in the trust over time rather than requiring them to be distributed immediately. Each has its uses.

A conduit trust might appeal to doting grandparents who want the grandchildren to have some extra money without ever being able to completely cash out the IRA. Although the trustee may have discretion to distribute more than the minimum, the trust largely forces the grandchildren to use the life expectancy payout.

Some advisers are reluctant to set up conduit trusts for a minor who doesn't really need the money, but the payouts, based on the child's life expectancy, will usually be so small that it doesn't make much difference, especially if the funds are going to a custodian anyway.

Also note that conduit trusts are generally not appropriate if you want to provide for a family member with special needs. The purpose of a trust in this case is to prevent these individuals from owning assets directly because such ownership could disqualify them for public assistance.

Income taxes. As a conduit trust makes payments, those funds become vulnerable to creditors, defeating the goal of asset protection. But from an income tax perspective, these trusts do have one advantage: Since the IRA distribution gets paid out immediately, the beneficiary, rather than the trust, pays tax on the withdrawal. In contrast, with an accumulation trust, the trust pays the tax. And trusts reach the top tax bracket when their earnings exceed $12,301; individual taxpayers, on the other hand, don't reach that rate until they have income of more than $413,201. In effect, then, there is an income tax cost for the asset protection you achieve by making a trust the beneficiary of an IRA. But you do have the flexibility of deciding, on a year-by-year basis, whether to keep the required minimum distribution for that year in the trust or pay it out to beneficiaries. Another way around the problem is to convert the IRA to a Roth while you are alive. Since beneficiaries don't have to pay income tax on distributions from a Roth IRA, this eliminates the potential tax problems. (For more about Roth conversions, see page 128.)

Other costs. If you want to make a trust the beneficiary of your IRA, consult an adviser who is fluent in both the language of trusts and the intricacies of using them to hold IRA assets. Ask this professional to examine trusts already in place (or one created by your will or living trust) to see whether it meets the federal criteria, or set up a new one specifically designed to inherit the IRA. For the former, you might be able to pay by the hour; for the latter, it will cost you between $1,500 and $5,000 to create the document, depending on the size and location of the law firm. (For more about hiring a lawyer, see Chapter 18.)

When you pass along IRA assets this way, you also pass along additional costs to your heirs. These include the fees of professional trustees and investment managers, if you choose to leave them in charge. Plus, it will cost from $500 to $1,500 yearly to have the trust tax return prepared. It's hard to justify all these expenses unless the value of the IRA assets is at least $500,000. Many corporate trustees (if that's what you contemplate) won't even take on a trust unless it's worth at least that much.

Whether you decide to use an existing trust or create a standalone trust for the purpose, make sure you name it on the beneficiary designation form. Otherwise, it will not be considered the beneficiary of your IRA. Forgetting this last step is a common oversight.

Go Roth, if You Can

Roth retirement accounts are among the best tax planning tools available, and one of the most desirable assets to inherit. They are named for the late Senator William Roth (Republican of Delaware), and grew out of a congressional compromise in 1997 involving IRAs. Since then, Congress and the IRS have sanctioned new ways to create these tax-favored accounts. It's now possible to set up Roths within company plans, and in certain contexts to shift funds between those plans and IRAs to turn taxable accounts into Roths.

What makes Roth accounts so desirable? With a Roth, you generally pay tax when you put money into the account, or when you convert or roll over a traditional account to a Roth. The payoff is that, subject to certain restrictions, no income tax is assessed on distributions by you or your heirs. In other words, all future growth takes place inside a permanently tax-free wrapper. So if the investments explode in value (and/or tax rates rise later), you will have paid off the tax bill for this account at a bargain rate.

Plus, a Roth does not require that you take yearly minimum distributions once you reach age 70½. That gives you a lot of flexibility. You can take money out of the account if you need it, or let it continue compounding tax-free. This may increase the amount that your beneficiaries inherit. What's more, any withdrawals – by them or by you – don't get added to taxable income. So under current rules, it won't push either of you into a higher tax bracket that might require payment of extra Medicare premiums or the ObamaCare 3.8 percent surcharge on investment income.

In some situations, withdrawals from a Roth IRA soon after a conversion could result in income tax, a 10 percent penalty or both, so keep them in mind. You're home free if you have had a Roth account for at least five years and are 59½ or older. In that case, none of the withdrawals will be subject to income tax or a penalty. And your heirs are home free if they inherited a Roth IRA and you have had the account for at least five years. They can withdraw the money at any time without paying tax or a penalty. The table on page 130 summarizes the tax consequences of some other common scenarios.

Leaving your heirs a Roth account does not do away with potential estate tax (a common misunderstanding), but as noted in earlier chapters, saving your heirs income tax makes their inheritance more valuable. In this context, you are essentially pre-paying the income tax for them. In effect, this is an enormous gift – and one that the government will not tax. (An Obama Administration proposal, to require non-spouse heirs to deplete inherited IRAs within five years, seems unlikely to gain traction.)

Not surprisingly, the super-wealthy, who have no problem pre-paying the income tax, have amassed tax-free Roth retirement kitties worth many tens of millions of dollars. But you don't have to be rich to take advantage of this opportunity. There are various routes to a Roth. Which ones are available to you will depend on your personal circumstances. Here are some possibilities.

Convert a traditional IRA to a Roth account. Since 2010, all taxpayers, regardless of their income or filing status, can do a Roth conversion. The most painful aspect of the conversion is the price tag. When converting from a traditional IRA to a Roth, you owe income tax on the amount you convert (this can be the entire account balance or part of it). Unfortunately, if you inherit a traditional IRA, you cannot convert it to a Roth. But spouses can roll over the inherited IRA into their own IRA and then convert to a Roth.

Open or invest directly in a Roth IRA. To contribute to a Roth IRA, you must have earned income, not just income from investments. The maximum you can put into the account is $5,500 a year if you are younger than 50, and $6,500 if you are 50 or older (annual contributions to traditional IRAs and Roths together can't exceed these limits). You can make these contributions whether or not you participate in a company plan, but income limits apply.

If your income exceeds the limit, which varies from year to year, there is another route to a Roth. It starts with making the maximum contribution to a traditional, after-tax (meaning non-deductible) IRA. Money in these accounts grows tax-deferred, but there's tax, at ordinary income rates, on withdrawals. You can avoid that tax forever by converting the account to a Roth immediately after making your contribution.

Contribute to a Roth 401(k) or 403(b). Traditionally, salary deferrals into company plans have been pre-tax, enabling workers to take a tax deduction for their contribution. Money in the account grew tax-deferred, and all withdrawals were taxed as ordinary income. Roth contributions, which are made after-tax (so there's no deduction), have been permitted within company plans since 2006. Companies can choose whether to offer this option (they're not required to); studies by employee benefits firms show that about half now do. If you can afford to forgo the income tax deduction when you put money into the account, this strategy can later pay off handsomely.

Your choice of a Roth or a traditional contribution can vary from year to year – you make the election when you fund the plan. Unlike a Roth IRA, no income limits restrict your ability to fund these accounts. Here, too, though, the contribution limits are adjusted for inflation and vary from year to year.

Weighing the Options

The choice between a traditional retirement account and a Roth is not always obvious.

Can you afford to pay the associated tax?

Yes   No

Do you plan to leave at least some of your retirement assets to family?

DON'T do a Roth

Yes   No

DO a Roth

Do you assume your tax rate will be the same or higher when you retire?

Yes   No

DO a Roth

Will you be able to recoup the money you would pay in taxes to do the conversion?

Yes   No

DO a Roth   **DON'T do a Roth**

Roth Conversion Mechanics

These are the essential steps in converting a traditional IRA to a Roth.

- Take the payout for the current year – if you are required to be-cause of your age – before converting the entire IRA to a Roth.

- Transfer the funds. If you move the money to a different institu-tion, it's best to open the new Roth account at the company receiv-ing the funds and ask it to retrieve the money.

- Make sure the institution where you are doing the conversion does not withhold income tax.

- Confirm that the balance in the traditional IRA has been reduced by the amount you converted, and that a corresponding amount appears in a separate account that is clearly labeled a Roth.

- Fill out a beneficiary form for each Roth account you set up.

- Monitor investment performance. You can reverse the transaction – a process called recharacterization. You're allowed this do-over any time until Oct. 15 of the year after you do the conversion. Once a con-version of assets has been undone, the same assets cannot be con-verted again until the year following the original conversion or more than 30 days after the conversion was undone, whichever is longer.

If you can't foot the whole tax bill, you can make part of your retire-ment contribution to a Roth and the rest to a traditional account. But you should not do a Roth at all if, for budgetary reasons, it reduces what you can save for retirement. For example, if you have allocated $10,000 for a retirement contribution this year and have a choice of put-ting $7,000 after-tax dollars into a Roth 401(k) or $10,000 before-tax dol-lars into a traditional one, you should opt for the latter. Whether you have chosen tax-free or tax-deferred growth, it is better to have $10,000 in a retirement account than $7,000.

Note, however, that if you receive a company match on your contribution, IRS rules require that the match be treated like a traditional retirement account, even if you are contributing your own money to a Roth.

Do an "in-plan conversion" of a traditional 401(k) or 403(b) to a Roth account. The American Taxpayer Relief Act of 2012 makes it possible for many more people to do a conversion within these plans, as well as a government 457(b) plan. Previously, you had to be entitled to distributions from these accounts. That requirement has now been dropped, but your company plan must still offer the option to convert (federal regulations do not require it to). The money you convert can stay within the plan. In contrast to converting a traditional IRA to a Roth IRA, though, you're not allowed to undo the conversion. This option will be especially appealing to people who want to keep assets within the plan in order to protect them from creditors (see Chapter 17) or because they want to continue investing through the plan.

Did You Know?

The longer you live, the longer the IRS assumes you will live. According to life expectancy tables used to compute the minimum yearly withdrawals from your own IRA (not an inherited one) or a 401(k), a 21-year-old is expected to live until age 96.3, an 80-year-old to 98.7.

Roll over your traditional company plan into a Roth IRA. Owners of 401(k)s, whether Roth or traditional, must start taking distributions at 70½ unless they are still working for the company. But you can easily avoid this requirement once you leave the company by rolling over the account into a Roth IRA before you reach 70½, or when you retire, if you work past age 70½.

This is a strategy to consider if you are about to change jobs or are approaching retirement. At that point, you can roll the assets directly into a Roth IRA, but you must pay income tax on the account balance. The question is whether you can afford that toll charge. It is better not to pay those

Rules for Roth Withdrawals

Depending on the situation, withdrawals from a Roth IRA could result in income tax, a 10 percent penalty, or both.

	Income Tax	10 Percent Penalty
You invested directly in a Roth		
• You withdraw contributions before age 59½	No	No
• You withdraw account income before age 59½	Yes	Yes *(certain exceptions apply)*
You converted a traditional IRA to a Roth		
• You withdraw converted funds within the first five years of the conversion	No	Yes *(certain exceptions apply)*
• You withdraw account income within the first five years of the conversion	Yes	Yes *(certain exceptions apply)*
You inherited a Roth IRA		
• You withdraw converted funds within the first five years of conversion	No	No
• You withdraw account income within the first five years of when the original account owner opened any Roth IRA or converted a traditional IRA to a Roth	Yes	No
• You withdraw account income more than five years after the original account owner opened any Roth IRA or converted any traditional IRA to a Roth	No	No

Source: Barry C. Picker, CPA/PFS, CFP

130

taxes with funds withdrawn from the IRA or other retirement accounts, especially if that would generate yet more tax. And, ideally, the conversion shouldn't push you into a higher tax bracket.

Roll after-tax company plan contributions into a Roth IRA. This route to a Roth is a bit more complicated than the others and is available to fewer people. But if you are one of them, it's a windfall since, unlike other Roth conversion techniques, this one does not require you to pay tax on the conversion.

The strategy involves plans that allow employees to set aside extra for retirement by contributing after-tax money to these accounts (subject to IRS limits that vary by year), in addition to pre-tax and Roth contributions. According to Aon Hewitt, only 6.6 percent of 401(k) participants take advantage of this option when it is available. If you are one of them or would consider it in the future, read on.

Traditional after-tax contributions grow tax-deferred, but when you make withdrawals, the portion attributable to earnings (not your original contribution) is taxed at ordinary income rates. This doesn't make much sense, since Roth contributions, which are also made after-tax, have been able to grow tax-free. After years of maneuvering by tax pros to address the problem, the IRS, in Notice 2014-54, mapped out a route to a Roth. It involves separating the after-tax contribution from the growth by doing a split rollover:

❧ Your basis in the account – that is, money that was taxed before you put it into the retirement wrapper – can be rolled over into a Roth IRA. Going forward, it grows tax-free, and, as with other Roth accounts, withdrawals will not be taxed.

❧ Earnings, up to the time of the conversion, can be rolled over into a separate, traditional IRA or even to your new company's traditional 401(k). They will continue to grow tax-deferred, meaning there is no tax until the money is withdrawn from the account.

The IRS notice requires that you do both these transactions, referred to as "distributions," at the same time. You can make the split rollover when you change jobs or retire, or while still at the company if your plan allows in-service distributions.

You can essentially do the same maneuver for each pay period during which you make new, after-tax contributions (again, if your employer's plan allows "in-service" distributions). By directing the contribution to a money market fund, and immediately rolling it over into a Roth IRA, you avoid the need to separate earnings from basis each time.

Roll over an inherited company plan into a Roth IRA. People who inherit retirement assets from a traditional company plan may be better off than those who inherit a traditional IRA from anyone other than a spouse. Why? Because of a quirk in the law, non-spouse beneficiaries of an IRA cannot convert it to a Roth IRA, but those who inherit a company plan are able to do that.

Doing the rollover avoids the need to take the money out of the company plan in a lump sum, as most businesses require non-spouses to do – often within five years or less. By rolling the money into an inherited Roth and paying the income tax now, inheritors also avoid income tax on later withdrawals.

Note that when an estate is subject to federal estate tax, beneficiaries are entitled to an income tax deduction for the portion of the estate tax attributable to an inherited IRA. They can take this deduction whether or not, under the will, they are personally responsible for paying the estate tax. With a traditional IRA, heirs can use the deduction only to offset funds withdrawn in a given year. Those who roll over a company plan into a Roth IRA can take the entire deduction in the year of the conversion. This can greatly reduce the out-of-pocket cost of doing the rollover.

When doing the rollover, spouses have a choice not available to other inheritors. They can either roll the account over into an inherited IRA or into their own IRA. The difference is when they must start making withdrawals. With an inherited IRA, Roth or traditional, distributions must begin by Dec. 31 of the year following the account owner's death, unless the spouse who died was younger than 70½. In that case, distributions do not have to begin until the year the spouse would have reached age 70½. On the other hand, when you have your own Roth IRA, there is no requirement for lifetime distributions.

Non-spouses who want to do the rollover only have the option of rolling over the inherited company plan into an inherited IRA – not into their own IRA. Therefore, they must begin taking distributions by Dec. 31 of the year following the account owner's death, although they can stretch out these withdrawals over their life expectancy.

Bottom line: Because of the mandatory distribution requirements, you don't get as much benefit from converting an inherited company plan to a Roth IRA as you would from converting an IRA you had set up yourself.

Be Smart About Inheritances

Inheriting a retirement account provides more than a stash of cash. It can also be a powerful investment vehicle. But one mistake in how the beneficiary forms were filled out or how those assets were transferred from original owner to inheritors can wipe out all the growth potential. Here's how to maximize the value of your windfall.

Find out who the beneficiaries are. The beneficiary designation form must be filed with the bank or financial institution (custodian) holding the account. When there is no beneficiary for an IRA, a default policy, spelled out in the custodial agreement, applies. Most default to the estate, some let it to go first to the spouse, but very few will let it pass to children.

Check whether the owner took the last distribution. Determine whether the IRA owner, if 70½ or older, took his or her minimum distribution in the year of death. If not, the beneficiaries must withdraw it before doing anything else.

Consider a disclaimer. Beneficiaries who don't need the money or who want to do some estate planning of their own can disclaim the inheritance, permitting their shares in an IRA to pass to the next person, trust or charity in line. Whom they can disclaim to depends on the form that the account owner filled out – it's not for the beneficiaries to decide. The deadline for disclaiming is nine months after the IRA owner's death.

Roll over from a company plan. Most company plans require non-spouse beneficiaries to take the money out in a lump sum, often within a year. But beneficiaries can avoid that lump sum distribution by rolling the money over into an inherited IRA – either a traditional one or a Roth.

Maintain the IRA wrapper. Just as you can't put toothpaste back in a tube, once you remove money from an inherited IRA, there is no way to reverse that. Never combine an inherited IRA with your own IRA. And when moving funds between institutions, request a "trustee-to-trustee" transfer. Do not withdraw the money and redeposit it; if you do, the whole thing will no longer be considered an IRA, and unless it's a Roth, you will be taxed on the withdrawal.

Retitle the account. Unless they've inherited from a spouse, beneficiaries must retitle the IRA, including the original owner's name and indicating it is inherited. Sample: "Daddy Warbucks, deceased, inherited IRA for the benefit of Little Orphan Annie, beneficiary."

Split the account. If two or more people are named as co-beneficiaries on an account, they can ask the custodian to split it, giving each person the share he or she was entitled to under the beneficiary designation form. That avoids squabbles over investment strategies; it also allows beneficiaries to take distributions over their own life expectancy or, if they prefer, to cash out. The deadline for subdividing such an account is Dec. 31 of the year following the year of the owner's death. Watch this process carefully, because mistakes often occur when changing account names and moving assets.

Some custodians won't divide an account when the estate is named as beneficiary (which is not a good idea for other reasons discussed above). The alternative is to open an account someplace that's hospitable to the idea. Give it the same name as the original one. Then move the assets directly from one IRA custodian to another. Here, too, be sure to specify a "trustee-to-trustee" transfer.

Consider a spouse's options. As discussed on page 118, a spouse – let's assume it's the wife – who inherits an IRA or company plan has options not available to other inheritors. While she ponders the choices, there's no requirement to take out money until the late spouse would have turned 70½. (This rule is different than it is for other inheritors.)

Name a successor. Someone who inherits an IRA has the right to choose the person who will in turn inherit any money not distributed from the IRA when the original beneficiary dies. Although successor beneficiaries generally can't switch to their own life expectancies when they inherit, they can take distributions over the prior beneficiary's remaining life expectancy.

Naming a successor beneficiary is especially critical for a spouse who inherits an IRA and decides not to roll it over into her own, waiting to take distributions until the year her husband (the original owner) would have turned 70½. If this surviving spouse dies without naming a new beneficiary, whoever inherits the IRA from her must withdraw the money within five years.

Take the first distribution. Generally non-spousal IRA heirs must withdraw a minimum amount each year, starting by Dec. 31 of the year after they inherit an IRA – whether it's a traditional IRA or a Roth. To calculate this distribution, you take the balance on Dec. 31 of the previous year and divide it by the individual's life expectancy, as listed in the IRS' "Single Life Expectancy" table (found in the Appendix of this book). In subsequent years, simply take the number you used in the first year and reduce it by one before doing the division. If the account is a Roth, you will not owe tax on the distribution. With a traditional IRA, find out whether it was funded with non-deductible contributions. If so, this basis reduces how much tax you will owe on the distribution.

Deduct the estate tax. If there is federal estate tax due on the IRA owner's estate, the beneficiary can take an itemized deduction for the portion of this estate tax attributable to the inherited IRA. Beneficiaries can take this deduction whether or not they were personally responsible under the will for paying the estate tax. But they can use the deduction only to offset funds withdrawn from the inherited IRA in a given year. This important and often overlooked deduction can be spread out over future tax years until it is used up.

Withdraw more as needed. Although most financial strategies are framed in terms of taking the smallest possible distributions from an inherited IRA, beneficiaries can always withdraw more if they need it. And, unlike with their own IRA, taking money out before age 59½ won't subject them to a 10 percent penalty. Unless the inherited IRA is a Roth, they will have to pay taxes on the funds withdrawn. But they can use the money for big expenses like buying a car or paying a child's tuition, or just think of it as a rainy day fund.

Use Retirement Assets to Benefit Charity

Given a choice about how to divide up the assets in their estates, some philanthropically inclined people find it more tax-efficient to give retirement assets to charity and leave their heirs other property. This strategy saves both income taxes and estate taxes. A charity, which is tax-exempt, can draw the funds without paying income tax, and if the estate is subject to tax, it can take a charitable deduction for the amount left to charity.

The simplest way to make the gift is by directly naming the charity on the beneficiary designation form. You can either make the charity a 100 percent beneficiary of the account or indicate that the charity is a beneficiary of a specific percentage of the funds and have the rest go to other beneficiaries.

Lifetime gifts can be made as an "IRA charitable rollover" if they are permitted in the tax year when you want to make your donation. This on-again, off-again provision, first introduced in 2006, allows people 70½ and older to transfer as much as $100,000 per year directly from their traditional IRAs to charity. The donation can count against the minimum required distribution they would otherwise be required to take.

Note that there's no income tax deduction for these contributions, but the sum going to charity is not included in the donor's adjusted gross income. (The advantage of this is that the older donor isn't subject to percentage limitations on charitable deductions and may be able to avoid certain penalties that come with a higher AGI, such as higher Medicare premiums.)

So far, Congress has extended (sometimes retroactively) the law permitting IRA charitable rollovers for one or two tax years at a time. Often this happens late in the year, which makes it difficult to coordinate these donations with taking the minimum required distribution. If you want to use IRA funds to benefit charity, here's what you can do while waiting for the next extender: Make the donation, up to $100,000, directly from your IRA to charity. If the IRA charitable rollover is extended, you can count it as your minimum required distribution and there will be no tax on the funds you have donated. If not, you'll pay tax on the distribution, but if you itemize, you can take a charitable income tax deduction for your donation.

Funds donated while you are alive cannot be used for contributions to donor-advised funds, supporting organizations or private non-operating foundations.

To-Do List

Give Your Retirement Plan A Checkup

An annual review of your retirement plan can help you spot estate planning oversights as well as tax-saving opportunities. Consider these issues.

❧ Make sure that all beneficiary designation forms are up to date, and coordinate the transfer of retirement assets with the rest of your estate plan. The forms should include primary and alternate beneficiaries, and should not name your estate as beneficiary. If you have named minors as beneficiaries, make sure assets are left to them either in custody or in trust.

❧ If you want a trust to be the beneficiary of your IRA, ask your advisers to design one that meets various criteria contained in IRS regulations. Then make sure you name the trust on the beneficiary designation form on file with the financial institution that holds your retirement account.

❧ If you send a change-of-beneficiary form to your financial institution, use certified mail and request that it return a copy of the form acknowledging, in writing, its receipt of the change.

❧ Keep copies of all beneficiary designation forms with your will and other important papers.

❧ If you recently changed jobs or retired, decide whether to roll over your company plan into an IRA (it could save your heirs some hassles later).

❧ Check any powers of attorney you have signed to be sure they cover retirement assets (see Chapter 1). They should authorize someone to make rollovers and choose beneficiaries if you become incapacitated.

Chapter 8

Be Smart About Life Insurance

*Read this chapter whether or not
you have life insurance.*

F or most people, life insurance is a tool for income replace-
ment – to pay the mortgage or foot the bill for college
education when the primary breadwinner dies. However, its
role in an estate plan may go far beyond that. Insurance can be a tool
for making lifetime gifts to family go further, building a charitable
legacy and paying es-
tate taxes, if they are a
concern. Death benefits
are typically free of in-
come tax and, if you set
things up properly, not
subject to estate taxes.

In This Chapter...

- ❧ *Estate Planning Goals That Life Insurance Can Serve*
- ❧ *Avoiding Tax Traps*
- ❧ *Finding the Best Way to Fund The Premium*

Premiums for the
simplest form of insur-
ance – term life policies, which provide a preset death benefit when
you die – have fallen sharply in recent years. With a level-premium
policy, you're guaranteed that the cost of the plan will not increase
during the initial coverage period – for example, 10 or 15 years. When
the stated period is up, the premium may increase dramatically.

Permanent (sometimes called whole life or universal life) insurance, which combines a death benefit and an investment compo-
nent, known as the cash value, is more expensive and raises other
issues, including how you will finance it. A major selling point for
these policies is that if the cash value of the policy does well, it can
be accessed tax-free. But, of course, these investments can also do
poorly, just like any other investment. Don't buy a product that you
can't understand. If it sounds too good to be true, it probably is.

Whatever policy you own or are considering, read on for how to
avoid some potentially costly pitfalls.

Estate Planning Goals That Life Insurance Can Serve

The conventional wisdom is that once your children are out of college and your mortgage is paid off, it no longer makes financial sense to carry life insurance. The big spending years are behind you, so your expenses are lower. And if you're shopping for a new policy, it can be expensive because the premiums are so high – either because of your age or because your medical history makes it hard to qualify for the most favorable rates.

While this wisdom may be true, even older people who can afford the premiums buy large amounts of life insurance. No matter what your life stage, insurance provides a source of money for the following purposes.

Covering the family's living expenses. The death of a key provider can radically alter the financial life of a family. Heirs need cash for current expenses, and raising the necessary funds is not always easy. The estate may be left with such assets as art, restricted stock, family business interests or real estate that can't be readily liquidated. And whatever the assets, there's always the risk that market conditions may not be favorable at the time your family needs the cash. Life insurance avoids the need to liquidate assets simply to pay the bills.

Paying estate taxes. If your estate is big enough to be subject to state or federal estate tax, the tax is due nine months after you pass away. This is an issue especially for estates made up of illiquid or hard-to-sell assets. Now that the federal estate tax exclusion is $5.43 million per person ($10.86 million for couples), you might be tempted to drop coverage that no longer seems necessary. Before you do, though, consider this: Even minor medical issues that develop in the future could interfere with your ability to qualify for favorable insurance rates.

Protecting your business. The death of a business partner or key employee can be devastating to a small business. Life insurance proceeds can be used to meet payroll, fund retirement benefits or cover other expenses until the company bounces back.

Financing buy-sell agreements. Life insurance can also be used in a small business setting to finance buy-sell agreements. In these contracts, partners or co-owners decide in advance what would happen to each of their business interests should various contingencies, including death, occur. This avoids situations where a surviving owner becomes an unwilling partner with the co-owner's heirs.

Instead, partners can agree that the surviving owner has the obligation to buy out the other's share from the estate (a cross-purchase agreement) or that the shares of the owner who died will be sold back to the business (a redemption agreement). With a redemption agreement, the company buys the policy on the owner's life. With a cross-purchase agreement, the owners insure one another individually. Either way, the policy proceeds provide the resources to settle at least part of the purchase price.

Did You Know?

In an estate tax audit, the IRS often asks for annual Crummey letters – which remind trust beneficiaries of their right to withdraw certain gifts you made that year on their behalf. Without these letters, contributions that might have qualified as tax-free gifts could be subject to tax.

Equalizing inheritances. When a business interest accounts for a large portion of an owner's estate, dividing it equitably requires careful planning. Most likely, the owner will want heirs who are actively involved in the business to inherit it but will not want to shortchange other family members. If the owner doesn't have other, comparably valued assets (such as stocks, bonds or real estate) to give those who are not involved in the business, life insurance can equalize inheritances.

Financing charitable giving. You can enhance your philanthropic efforts by donating new or existing life insurance policies to charity. As with most other charitable donations, this entitles you to an income tax deduction for the fair market value of the policy. How you calculate that deduction will depend on whether the policy is new or older, whether it has cash value and whether it is paid up, meaning no further premiums remain to be paid. For tax reasons, if a policy still requires premium payments, it's best to donate funds to the charity and let it pay the premiums.

A tax-efficient way of financing the premiums is to contribute appreciated securities to the charity, which can liquidate them to pay the premiums. In this scenario, you get an income tax deduction, and you avoid the capital gains tax you would have to pay if you sold the assets and donated the proceeds.

Sometimes donors use life insurance to back up a large pledge – for instance, a gift that will be acknowledged with the naming of a building, an endowment or a school within a university. That way, if the donor dies before the pledge is fulfilled, the life insurance proceeds can be used to carry out the donor's intentions.

Funding dynasty trusts. In the growing number of states that permit dynasty trusts – which are designed to pass wealth through multiple generations without incurring estate, gift or generation-skipping transfer taxes (see Chapter 14) – life insurance proceeds can be owned by and payable to the trust, so the proceeds flow into the trust at the insured's death. Typically, the trust would pay income to current beneficiaries and allow the principal to grow tax-free for future generations.

Leveraging lifetime gifts. Currently, you can give up to $14,000 each year (indexed for inflation) to as many recipients as you would like without it counting against the $5.43 million that you can transfer during life or through your estate plan. Spouses can combine this annual exclusion to jointly give $28,000 to any person tax-free – a practice known as gift-splitting. One way to make these gifts go further is to use the money to buy life insurance. Individual family members can buy the policy directly, using your gifts to pay the premiums. Or you can make the gift to a trust, which in turn can buy the life insurance. To make such a gift to a trust qualify for the annual exclusion requires special planning and special drafting of the trust. People in a position to make larger gifts can use the lifetime gift-tax exemption of $5.43 million per person ($10.86 million for married couples).

How does life insurance leverage your gifts? Only the money you give your family or put into the trust counts against the annual and lifetime limits – the face value of the policy doesn't matter. And the rewards could be substantial. For a 55-year-old male who qualifies for the most

Update Beneficiary Forms

When Warren Hillman died in 2008 at the age of 66, his assets included a life insurance policy worth $124,558.03. For five years his ex-wife and his widow fought over that money. The U.S. Supreme Court found in 2013 that Judy Maretta, whom Hillman divorced 10 years before he died, was entitled to every penny of it.

All this because Hillman made a basic and unfortunately all too common estate planning mistake: When he divorced Maretta, he did not change the beneficiary designation for a life insurance policy.

A beneficiary designation is a document given to an insurance company or financial institution indicating who should inherit certain assets that do not pass under a will or trust, like the proceeds of a life insurance policy and retirement accounts (see Chapter 2).

Forgetting to coordinate these non-probate assets, as they are called, with the rest of your estate plan can completely thwart your objectives, as it may have done for Hillman. Paperwork designating Maretta as the beneficiary of the life insurance policy, which he got as a federal government employee, was dated 1996. The next year, Hillman started his own management consulting firm.

Perhaps he forgot about the life insurance policy. He didn't change the beneficiary, either, when he and Maretta (his second wife) divorced in 1998, or after his subsequent marriage to Jacqueline Hillman in 2002, or after being diagnosed with a rare form of leukemia from which he ultimately died.

Some states have laws protecting a subsequent spouse from such oversights. Virginia, where Hillman lived, is one of them. The law there provides that divorce or annulment revokes a beneficiary designation under a life insurance policy. But the Supreme Court found for technical reasons that it did not apply to Hillman's policy.

Words to the wise: Keep beneficiary forms up to date. To change a beneficiary – for example, if you get married or divorced, or your spouse dies – make sure to file an amended form. Even if your state has a law designed to cover oversights (or procrastination), you can't always count on it to work.

favorable rates, a 20-year term policy with a $2 million death benefit costs approximately $5,700 per year.

Avoiding Tax Traps

One mistake many people make is to buy a life insurance policy and name themselves as the owner. If you do that, the proceeds will be part of your estate. In that case, those funds are added to everything else you leave behind. If the total is more than the exclusion amount and you've left it to anyone except your spouse or a charity, it will be subject to estate tax.

Naming your spouse as the beneficiary of a policy you've bought doesn't necessarily solve the problem. True, no estate tax applies when you die because of the unlimited marital deduction – assets inherited from a spouse are not taxed. However, if the total estate, including the insurance proceeds, is worth more than the limit happens to be when the surviving spouse dies, the money could be taxable at that time. Special rules apply to spouses who are not U.S. citizens (as noted in Chapter 3).

With the federal limit now at $5.43 million ($10.86 million for married couples), that may not seem like a concern. But it could be if you live in a state that has a separate estate tax (see Chapter 3). And here, too, it's wise to hedge your bets against changes in the law and your net worth by arranging to avoid estate tax on life insurance proceeds. The best way to do that is to have the policy owned by an irrevocable trust. You must not retain any ownership over the assets or the power to change the trust terms. The type of trust used for this purpose is an irrevocable life insurance trust, or ILIT. Typically, the ILIT buys the policy and, when you die, holds the proceeds for whomever you've named as beneficiaries. These beneficiaries can be anyone you choose, including your spouse, your partner and children.

Using an ILIT has a number of advantages, in addition to saving estate taxes. It can benefit minors, who are not allowed to own the policy directly but only through a custodianship or a trust, and can protect the assets from creditors, ex-spouses and spendthrifts.

If you already own a policy, you can sell it to the trust or to family members for its fair market value.

Finding the Best Way
To Fund the Premium

The goal, especially with expensive policies, is to put enough money into the trust so it can pay the premiums while using no more gift-tax exemption than necessary. How you do this will depend on the number of beneficiaries, the annual cost and how much you have to contribute. The tax-free amount of $5.43 million gives you a lot of latitude. (From 2002 to 2010, while the lifetime exemption was $1 million, premium-financing strategies focused on avoiding gift tax.) Whether you are funding a new policy or reviewing an arrangement put in place while the exemption was lower, here are some options:

You have plenty of money and many heirs among whom you want to divide it. Oddly, the more beneficiaries you designate for your ILIT, the easier it is to fund a policy. By using the annual exclusion, you and your spouse can put in $14,000 apiece every year for each trust beneficiary.

If you plan to fund an ILIT with annual exclusion gifts, the trust must give the beneficiaries what are called Crummey powers, and the beneficiaries must receive an annual Crummey notice, sent by you or by the trustee at the time you add the gift to the trust. This gives them the right for a limited time (usually 30 or 60 days) to withdraw from the trust the yearly gift attributable to them. Without providing the beneficiaries Crummey powers, your gift to the trust would be considered a future interest (something beneficiaries can't use right away), rather than a present one, and would not qualify for the annual exclusion.

Note that when a beneficiary is disabled, the right of withdrawal – even if unexercised – may cause a reduction or loss of public benefits, because the person may have access to more money than he or she is allowed to have to qualify for state and federal assistance (as noted in Chapter 5). Therefore, when a special needs trust is the beneficiary of an irrevocable life insurance trust or when an irrevocable life insurance trust is written as a special needs trust, you should not give Crummey powers to the disabled beneficiary.

Choose the trustee carefully. It's better not to take on this responsibility yourself, even as a co-trustee, because that might look as though you still own the policy. Even while you are alive, when the main responsibilities are paying the premiums and sending Crummey notices, it is better to have professional advisers – such as lawyers, accountants or financial planners – serve as trustees (as noted in Chapter 6). If you start with an individual trustee, you might want to make provisions to involve a corporate fiduciary as co-trustee to invest the proceeds and administer the benefits after you die.

You don't have a lot of heirs, but you have plenty of cash. If the trust owns a large policy, annual exclusion gifts may not be enough to fund the premium. By using the gift-tax exemption of $5.43 million per person, you can make a large gift to the trust that will enable it to pay the premiums going forward without your making additional gifts.

Did You Know?

State insurable interest laws prohibit people from buying insurance on the lives of strangers. Most states make an exception for charities so they can insure key donors and continue their endowments. Beware of unscrupulous investment promoters who attempt to piggyback on that exemption.

Another use for the generous gift-tax exemption is to make a large enough gift to the trust that it can undo, or "roll out," a family split-dollar arrangement (described below). When the limit on lifetime gifts was lower, these deals were a way of financing costly policies without having to pay gift tax. Now your planning can be much simpler.

You don't have a lot of cash. One approach is to lend the money to the trust rather than making a gift of it. This loan must be documented, and the trust must pay interest at the applicable federal rate, set each month by the Treasury (or interest must accrue at that rate and be paid with the principal at the insured's death). If you have the cash, you can lend it directly. If you don't, you can borrow from a bank and then lend that money to the ILIT. The difference between the interest rate you pay the bank and the IRS-approved rate you get from the trust amounts to a tax-free gift to the trust.

If you have only enough cash to pay part of the premium, you may be able to get someone in the family to share the cost in a split-dollar arrangement. Split-dollar is typically used with permanent insurance. Here's how the arrangement works: you give enough money to the ILIT to pay a portion of the premium, reflecting what a term life insurance policy would cost. Then a family member pays the balance.

When you die, the trust and the family member typically share the proceeds. The family member, who gets repaid first, must get back either what was paid out or the cash value of the policy, whichever is greater. Otherwise, the arrangement would be considered an interest-free loan subject to gift tax.

You don't have a lot of cash, but your privately held business is flush. This is a common situation among entrepreneurs. In this case, your business can lend money to the trust so it can pay the premium. You can arrange the loan so that the principal is not due until your death and can be paid out of the policy proceeds. To help the ILIT finance the yearly interest payments, you can make annual gifts to the trust.

You are setting up other trusts anyway. This is a terrific opportunity to use payouts from those trusts to fund the ILIT, with the goal of making it self-sustaining. For instance, suppose you place appreciating assets, such as stocks, into an irrevocable trust and retain the right to receive an annual income for a preset period. If you're alive at the end of the period, any property left in the trust (known as a grantor retained annuity trust, or GRAT) could pass to the insurance trust. (For more about GRATs, see Chapter 15.) For technical reasons, it is not a good tax strategy to fund an ILIT that is a dynasty trust with this GRAT remainder interest.

Before using a family deal to finance costly life insurance, ask advisers whether the arrangement can be undone if your circumstances change.

Remember, too, that with any loan transaction, at the end you have to repay the debt – most likely out of the policy proceeds.

To-Do List

Review Your Life Insurance Arrangements

Tax law changes might make it necessary to rethink your life insurance needs and funding tools. Consider these issues.

❧ Is the payout on existing policies adequate for your heirs to meet current expenses, and will the policy last as long as necessary?

❧ Have you (or the trustee) been sending Crummey notices to beneficiaries of life insurance trusts funded with annual exclusion gifts each year when you make your annual gift to the trust? (You should keep copies of these notices with the trust documents.)

❧ If you are the owner of a life insurance policy that names you as an insured, what steps are necessary to transfer ownership to a trust?

❧ If you are setting up a life insurance trust, how long should the trust last, whom should you name as an independent trustee and backup trustee, and how much power should the trustee have over distributions (see Chapter 6)?

❧ If a family member is disabled, what special trust provisions are necessary to maintain the person's eligibility for public benefits?

❧ If you are buying new or additional insurance, what is the best way to finance the premium?

❧ If you already have insurance, do you want to change your approach to funding the premium in light of the tax law changes that took effect in 2013?

Chapter 9

Pay for Education

Read this chapter if anyone you love could use help with this enormous expense, now or in the future.

F or some people, providing everyone in the family with the best possible education is part of the legacy they would like to leave. Ideally, saving for this expense ought to start early. Yet it would take a skilled soothsayer to know precisely what that education will cost many years from now and what funds, including scholarships and financial aid, may be available from other sources. What's more, though you may feel generous during your peak earning years, your income may decline as time goes by, while your expenses rise with inflation. So set aside money for your retirement before you contribute to education savings accounts for other people.

In This Chapter...

- ⚜ *Custodial Accounts for Minors*
- ⚜ *Section 529 Plans*
- ⚜ *Coverdell Education Savings Accounts*
- ⚜ *Direct Payment of Tuition*
- ⚜ *Trusts*
- ⚜ *Eligibility for Financial Aid*

In this context, as in others, you need to be aware of some gift-tax basics. Currently you can give up to $14,000 each year to as many recipients as you would like without incurring gift tax. Spouses can combine this annual exclusion to jointly give $28,000 to any person tax-free. These restrictions apply whether you make outright gifts to individuals, or put the funds into trusts or education savings accounts for their benefit. Any gift that's more than the annual exclusion counts against the lifetime gift-tax exclusion – the amount that each individual can give away during life without triggering gift tax. Once you have passed the limit, which is $5.43 million ($10.86 million for married couples), gift tax of 40 percent applies.

Read on for the mechanics, pros and cons of various ways to help.

Custodial Accounts for Minors

These accounts, which function like a poor man's trust fund, are a simple, low-cost way for an adult to oversee money for a minor. Custodial accounts, typically at a bank, mutual fund company or brokerage house, are often the first savings fund that many parents and grandparents set up for young children. After that, they tend to become the repository for birthday checks and other cash gifts or small inheritances.

If you are naming a minor as the beneficiary of your IRA, some financial institutions give you the option, on its beneficiary designation form, of also naming a custodian under the Uniform Transfers to Minors Act, or UTMA. Others simply allow a parent or guardian to be appointed as custodian if the child winds up inheriting the account before reaching the age of majority. (For more about IRA inheritances, see Chapter 7.)

Though, technically, minors have title to the assets in custodial accounts, they are not allowed to exercise ownership rights, because legally they cannot enter into binding contracts. So when you put the money in an account for the person you want to benefit, there must be an adult custodian for the money. That's true even if you buy a savings bond for a minor.

But beware of two common traps associated with custodial accounts. One is that if you fund the account and also make yourself the custodian, the money plus any appreciation could be subject to estate tax down the line. That could happen if you die before the minor is old enough to take control of the funds. Then, whatever is in the account would be tallied up with everything else you own. If your estate is subject to tax, this account would be, too.

The simplest solution is to make the custodian someone who won't be making contributions to the account. This could be another person whom you trust – one parent might name the other, for example, or a grandparent could name the child's parent. Another possibility is to name a financial institution to act as custodian. Whomever you name, the custodian is a fiduciary, legally obligated to invest the funds wisely and put the child's welfare first.

The other, more common, pitfall stems from the fact that once children reach a certain age, they are legally entitled to the money you and others have been setting aside for their future. Although the statutory age of majority is 18 for most other purposes, under the UTMA, the law that most states have adopted to regulate custodial accounts, the child can generally cash out when he or she reaches age 21.

In a handful of states (California, for example), you can take action to delay such a cash-out until 25, while others allow you to provide for distributions earlier – typically at 18. So check the law in your state by searching online for "UTMA AND [your state name]." Two states – South Carolina and Vermont – still operate under the Uniform Gift to Minors Act (UGMA), which has been superseded by UTMA in most states. The main difference is that UTMA covers almost all assets, including real estate, while UGMA is limited to bank deposits, securities and insurance policies.

Did You Know ?

When putting money into a custodial account for a minor, do not name yourself as custodian. If you do name yourself and you die before the minor is old enough to take control of the funds, the money would count as part of your estate and could be taxed.

Once the child is an adult, she has control of the account, and the custodian is out of the picture. Whether your intended beneficiary spends these disposable funds on books, a car or a spring break trip to Florida, the responsibility for the money will give her some experience handling her own funds – which is, after all, an important part of growing up. Those who manage well may have cash for larger expenses like the down payment on a house, seed money for a start-up company or a subsidy for a low-paying first job. Those who deplete the fund by managing it poorly may learn, you may hope, valuable life lessons.

How much is enough for this purpose? That depends on your philosophy about money and lifestyle, as well as your assessment of what the child might need. The larger the balance in a custodial account and the closer children get to the age when they can take control of the funds, the more parents tend to wring their hands about the cash their offspring are about to get. Perhaps they're concerned that instead of using the money for tuition, the child will buy a sports car, finance a drug habit or take an extended vacation. Or maybe the amount has grown so large that the young person doesn't have the financial acumen to handle it.

It might be tempting just to take back the money or invest it all in savings bonds with the hope that the child won't find out. But that would violate the UTMA. Children are legally entitled to the money when they reach the specified age. At that point, they can claim it – or sue for it (though these cases are extremely rare) if the custodian won't give them account information, for example.

But other strategies can address such an abundance of riches. Depending on your situation, you might use one of them or a combination by dividing the custodial account into various buckets.

Spend it down. You can't use these accounts for support obligations (basically food, clothing and shelter), but it's generally safe to apply the funds to what might otherwise be unaffordable extras, such as private school, dance lessons and summer camp. You could also chip away at it during the application process – for example, by using it to pay for SAT review courses, college counseling, application fees and the cost of transportation to visit schools. Or, if your child decides to delay college and enroll in a gap-year program, you could apply the funds to that.

Another possibility, once your child starts college, is to use these funds for tuition before you tap 529 accounts (discussed below). Earnings on money in an UTMA account are subject to income tax. In contrast, a 529 offers income tax savings: You put money in one of these plans, and you don't have to pay federal or state income tax on the earnings, provided the cash is withdrawn to pay for college or graduate school tuition, fees, room and board, or books. In other words, the longer it stays in that 529 wrapper, the more tax-free compounding you get. So given a choice about which money to spend first, there are tax benefits to drawing down the UTMA account. Spending UTMA funds first can also improve the prospect of financial aid (see page 165).

Get a power of attorney. As noted in Chapter 1, this is one of the documents that every young adult should sign before going off to college or to a gap-year program. (The other is a health care proxy.) In the context of UTMA accounts, it comes in handy if you've been managing your kids' money until now and they don't yet have the skills to choose their own investments.

Still, since your child will have as much access to the account as you do, a power of attorney doesn't stop your college kid from frittering it away. But if, say, your child has reached the age of majority and tuition is due, the power of attorney will give you the legal authority to pay the bill from an UTMA account.

To avoid skirmishes with financial institutions, ask whether they have their own form that they prefer you use. Policies for handling custodial accounts may vary. Some institutions will send you a notice when your child reaches the requisite age, asking you to transfer funds held in an UTMA account into her name. Others take a more laissez-faire approach, waiting until there is some activity on the account.

Did You Know?

If you have a child or grandchild with special needs who may someday become dependent on public benefits, you should not create a custodial account or 529 college savings plan for him. To take such a step might make the child ineligible for public assistance.

Convert to a Section 529 plan. If your child isn't of college age yet, and you've overfunded savings in an UTMA account, you may want to convert it to a 529 for the extra income tax savings discussed in the next section. But the conversion must be into a special "custodial 529" and won't solve a problem with all UTMA accounts, which is that children gain legal control over the funds once they reach the age of majority. So the money could be blown on something other than college; in that case, any earnings that are withdrawn are subject to ordinary income tax and a 10 percent penalty. Another catch: Because 529 accounts can be funded only with cash, you'll have to liquidate the holdings in the UTMA, which could mean paying tax on any gains.

Invest in an asset that can't readily be converted to cash. Although this maneuver sounds clever, it's fraught with potential legal problems. Typically, it involves a limited partnership that some families use, both for investment and estate planning purposes (see Chapter 15). Here you put property – say, publicly traded stock – into a partnership, then give or sell shares of that partnership to family members. In effect, those shares are illiquid because few people outside the family would want to buy them.

By using custodial funds to buy shares of a family partnership, you make it difficult, if not impossible, for the account holder to liquidate the partnership interests when reaching majority. But you may also subject yourself to a claim that you have breached your fiduciary duty as custodian. Don't try this without good legal advice, and even then be aware of the risks.

Transfer some or all of the money to a Section 2503(c) trust. Some states allow the custodian to do this before the child reaches age 21. Note, however, that a Section 2503(c) trust (discussed more fully on page 163) must still give the child the right to withdraw at age 21 – at least for some reasonable period of time, such as 30 days.

Distribute the UTMA to the child and have the child contribute the money to a trust. If, at some point after reaching majority, the child is receptive to the idea, the custodian could distribute the assets to the child and have the child distribute them to a trust. Usually the trust is drafted so that until reaching a certain age (say, 30) the child cannot amend or revoke the trust without the consent of someone else (such as a parent).

Gentle persuasion – for instance, "a trust is a good way to protect assets from creditors" (see Chapter 17) – is sometimes enough. Alternatively, a parent or grandparent may agree to add additional funds to the trust if the child complies, so that ultimately the child will get more when the trust ends. Requiring that the trust begin to make some modest annual distributions to the child immediately may also help.

Section 529 Plans

Qualified state tuition programs, which can be used for higher education, are available in all states and the District of Columbia. You need not use the program offered by your home state, although sometimes there are benefits to doing so, such as the ability in some states to take a state income tax deduction for your contributions.

Named for the Internal Revenue Code section that permits them, these plans allow you to set up a separate account for each person whom you want to benefit. You can do this whether or not you are a relative. It's

Simple Ways to Help Out

Without any fancy estate planning, or even a lawyer's assistance, family members can help one another enormously with education expenses. Imagine a well-off couple with two adult children, both married, and four grandchildren. Here are some simple steps they can take in a single year without having to pay gift tax.

Type of gift	Amount	Total recipients	Total, this type of gift
Lump-sum deposit in 529 plan for each grandchild	$140,000 *	4	$560,000
College tuition for grandchildren (paid directly to school)	$50,000†	2	$100,000
Private school tuition for grandchildren (paid directly to school)	$30,000†	2	$60,000
Total tax-free gifts:			*$720,000*

*Counts as an annual exclusion gift spread over five years. During this time, the couple can't make any additional annual exclusion gifts to these grandchildren.
†Amounts included here are based on estimates, not legal limits.

also possible to contribute to an account that someone else has set up for the child whom you want to benefit.

A private money manager chosen by each state typically manages the funds, and you can select among different investment options. Withdrawals from a 529 account are federal-tax-exempt, provided the money is used to pay for college or graduate school. Other details of the plans, including the maximum amount you can contribute and the investment options, vary by state.

Federal law allows you to contribute to these plans up to the annual exclusion amount. The law also permits lump-sum deposits of as much as $70,000 per person at once ($140,000 for married couples), but you must file a gift-tax return electing to treat the gift as if it had been spread over five years. During this five-year period, you cannot make additional annual exclusion gifts to the person you are benefiting with the 529 plan. If you die before the five-year period is up, part of the gift, reflecting the number of years still to go, will be included in your estate.

An attractive feature of these plans (which makes them different from UTMA accounts) is that you can be the account owner and retain some control over the funds. For example, if the family member you initially planned to benefit can't use the money (perhaps because he or she received a scholarship), you can easily change the beneficiary to some-one who is a family member of the original beneficiary. However, if the new beneficiary is in a generation subsequent to the old one, there may be gift-tax consequences. Federal rules limit how frequently the account owner can change beneficiaries and investment options.

Here are some other issues to keep in mind.

Plans to benefit grandchildren. For grandparents, 529 plans are an easy way to provide for education and do some estate planning in the process (contributions are exempt from generation-skipping transfer tax because they qualify for the annual exclusion). Normally, if you want to get money out of your taxable estate, you must relinquish any claim to it. What's different with 529s is you can take back the funds – but only if you name yourself as the "owner" of the account. So if there's a chance you might need the cash, name yourself, not an adult child, as owner of an ac-count benefiting a grandchild. Keep in mind that if the funds aren't used for education, any earnings that are withdrawn are subject to ordinary income tax and a 10 percent penalty.

Naming a successor owner. This person will call the shots on invest-ments and distributions of the 529 if you pass away before the beneficiary goes to school. So be sure to name someone you trust. Young parents who establish a 529 for a child will generally do well to name the other parent as the successor owner. Should one parent die prematurely, the survivor has control of the money – and can tap it, if necessary. If the survivor doesn't touch the money, it won't be counted as part of either person's estate. Grandparents setting up a 529 will generally want to name each other, and then the child's parent, as the successor.

What if you don't name a successor? The answer depends on the terms of individual states' 529 plans. The owner could be the beneficiary of the plan, if she is older than 18, or the executor of your estate.

Investment performance. As an investment vehicle, 529 plans are too restrictive, some people find. A key disadvantage is that you must contribute cash. If you need to sell investments to obtain that cash, you may have to pay capital gains tax. Also, while you can choose among several investment alternatives when you set up the plan and you can alter the strategy once a year, you'll have far more latitude if you set up a trust that gives a trustee investment authority.

How well do 529 accounts perform? That depends on what the manager has invested in, the overall markets and the fees charged. Fees can vary dramatically from plan to plan and can be difficult to understand. Generally the fees are lower for plans you can invest in directly, without going through a broker or financial planner.

Coverdell Education Savings Accounts

These accounts, sometimes referred to as education IRAs, can pay for any level of schooling. You can set up a separate account for any family member younger than 18, even if you also fund a 529 plan for that person. A beneficiary can have more than one Coverdell account, but total yearly contributions for his or her benefit can't be more than $2,000.

Income limitations may restrict your ability to fund these accounts, however. Allowable contributions are phased out for single people whose adjusted gross income (AGI) is $95,000 to $110,000, and for married couples filing a joint return with an AGI of $190,000 to $220,000. Parents or grandparents who don't meet the income requirements can give $2,000 to each family member they want to benefit so those relatives can each set up their own Coverdell account.

Funds in the account are not taxed if they are used to pay for education expenses, including tuition, books, supplies, and room and board. Unless the beneficiary has special needs, any balance in the account must either be distributed (subject to income tax and a 10 percent penalty) when the individual reaches age 30 or rolled over into an account to benefit another family member of the original beneficiary. Gift tax may apply if the new beneficiary is in a subsequent generation to the old beneficiary.

Direct Payment of Tuition

Without using your annual exclusion or dipping into the limit on lifetime gifts, you can pay the tuition for anyone you want. Note that you must make the payments directly to the providers of those services – you can't just reimburse the person whom you want to benefit. Subject to this condition, you can pay for any level of education (from nursery school to graduate school), with no limit on how much you spend.

This often-overlooked tax break applies only to tuition – not to fees, books, supplies, room or board. When financing tuition, you can pay annually or pre-pay for multiple years, as long as the money goes directly to the educational institution for a particular student and is not refundable or transferable. The risk of pre-paying, of course, is that the payments could be forfeited if the student winds up not going to that school or completing his or her education there.

Trusts

While you are alive, the simplest way to help with education expenses – and avoid gift and generation-skipping transfer taxes – is to write a check directly to the school provider. By relying on trusts and other tools, you can leave a more lasting legacy.

Although trusts are more complicated than other methods for financing education, generally speaking they offer more flexibility. The table on page 162 summarizes some key differences between trusts and other education funding tools.

Trusts and Other Funding Tools – Key Differences

Direct Payments	529 Plans	Coverdell Accounts	Trusts
Assets that can be used/Maximum funding			
Cash/ No limit	Cash/Varies by state	Cash/$2,000 per year per beneficiary	Many types of assets/ No limit
Who can benefit			
Any person	Initial beneficiary or certain family members*	Initial beneficiary or certain family members*	Any person covered by the trust
Expenses you can pay			
Tuition	"Qualified higher education expenses," including tuition, fees, books and supplies, and, under certain circumstances, room and board†	Tuition, fees, books, supplies and other "qualified education expenses" for elementary, secondary and higher education	Expenses permitted under the trust document

*These relatives of the beneficiary are: spouse, son, daughter, stepchild, foster child, adopted child, or a descendant of any of them; brother, sister, stepbrother or stepsister, and father or mother or ancestor of either; stepfather or stepmother; son or daughter of a brother or sister; brother or sister of father or mother; son-in-law, daughter-in-law, father-in-law, mother-in-law, brother-in-law or sister-in-law; spouse of any individual listed above; first cousin. For Coverdell accounts, any new beneficiary must be under age 30 unless she has special needs.

†Covers computers only if the school requires them.

From a tax perspective, the following two hurdles must be overcome when funding a trust.

❧ Unless you plan to use part of the $5.43 million lifetime exclusion, make sure any contributions to the trust qualify for the annual exclusion.

❧ Plan for the onerous 40 percent generation-skipping transfer (GST) tax that could apply (on top of any gift tax) if the trust benefits grandchildren.

Overcoming hurdle No. 1. To be within the annual exclusion, a gift must be a present interest rather than future interest (something beneficiaries can't use right away). There are two ways that gifts to trusts can meet this requirement. By far, the most popular is to give beneficiaries Crummey powers: the right for a limited time, usually 30 or 60 days, to withdraw from the trust the yearly gift attributable to that beneficiary (see "Crummey Fundamentals," page 103). Any trust that includes this power is a Crummey trust, although it may be named for its other distinguishing features, depending on the type of trust.

To avoid these potential pitfalls, some lawyers take another tack – meeting the present interest requirement through a Section 2503(c) trust. This irrevocable trust is relatively straightforward and inexpensive to set up (maximum cost: $3,000 to $5,000), but it has some of the same drawbacks as an UTMA account. These trusts must have only one beneficiary, the trust must give the beneficiary the right to withdraw the assets at age 21, there must be no restriction on the right of the trustee to make distributions of principal and interest before that, and the trust must be includable in the beneficiary's estate if the beneficiary dies.

Although this type of trust may sound no better than a custodial account because minors can gain access to the trust assets at 21, lawyers have added an embellishment that reduces the problem: They give the child a window of opportunity – usually 30 or 60 days – to terminate the arrangement, and if the beneficiary doesn't withdraw the funds at 21, the trust continues for a preset number of years.

With this provision, the money is less accessible than it would be with an UTMA account. In other words, a child who doesn't act within the limited time frame must wait for the money. In contrast, with a custodial account, once they have reached the magic age, they can claim it any time.

What's more, as a beneficiary approaches 21, you can encourage this young person to leave the money in the trust, with the understanding that he or she will probably get something additional in your will.

Overcoming hurdle No. 2. Another tax issue comes up when making gifts to trusts that could benefit grandchildren or more remote descendants. Currently, each of us can give away $5.43 million during life or at death without paying generation-skipping transfer tax. The tax applies, on top of any gift or estate tax, once this exemption is used up. Ordinarily, when putting money into the trust, you would need to apply, or allocate, your GST exemption to whatever the gift amount was. But you can avoid that requirement if all contributions to the trust qualify for the annual exclusion and you are putting the money into a special kind of trust that generally does not give rise to GST tax.

Section 2642(c) of the Internal Revenue Code describes the requirements for this trust. It must be irrevocable, can benefit only one grandchild and the trust document must specify that if the grandchild dies before the funds have been fully distributed, the remaining funds become part of the grandchild's estate (making them potentially subject to estate tax at that point).

Did You Know?

Without incurring gift tax, you can pay for tuition at any level of education and for medical and dental expenses (including health insurance) of as many people as you want, as long as the expense is not reimbursable and you pay the providers directly.

Trusts created under this section of the code and funded with annual exclusion gifts let you save the GST exemption to use in other ways. But because these trusts can benefit only one grandchild per trust, they are not appropriate for people who want the grandchild's parents to receive benefits under the trust before the funds get distributed to the grandchild. They are also not suitable when you want to shift assets among your grandchildren. For a discussion of using the GST exemption to set up a trust for multiple grandchildren, see Chapter 14.

Eligibility for Financial Aid

If a child might qualify for financial aid (a family with parents earning as much as $200,000 could qualify if two kids are in private colleges at the same time), ownership and spending of money from various pots set aside for education can get tricky. To boost eligibility for aid, parents (and sometimes grandparents) may need to make some strategic decisions the year before the child enters college. These are issues that arise.

Whether to spend UTMA money first. Under the federal formula for calculating eligibility, based on the Free Application for Federal Student Aid (known as FAFSA), students are expected to contribute up to 20 percent of their assets, while the rate for parents is 5.64 percent. For this rubric, UTMA accounts are considered assets of the child, while 529 plans, whether owned by a parent or the child, are assessed at the lower rate. So if a child is going to a school that takes the FAFSA, it might make sense to spend the UTMA money first.

A different standard applies at about 200 schools that use the College Board's Profile form, or CSS Profile, to award their own aid (meaning price discounts). These tend to be expensive private colleges (including members of the Ivy League) but also include some public colleges, among them the University of Michigan, William & Mary and the University of North Carolina at Chapel Hill. This form counts student-owned 529 plans and UTMA accounts at the same 25 percent rate. So spending the UTMA money first won't help with financial aid.

Ownership of 529 accounts. The FAFSA doesn't ask about 529s owned by a grandparent. But once a grandparent makes the first distribution for tuition, the student must count that amount as income to her on the following year's FAFSA; a student is expected to apply 50 percent of all her income above a certain amount to annual college expenses. Therefore, a well-meaning grandparent could exhaust a 529 paying the first year's tuition and at the same time endanger a student's ability to get aid (including subsidized federal loans and work-study money) for the next year. In such a case, the 529 funds would be best spent paying senior-year tuition.

In contrast, the CSS requires the student to report all 529 savings accounts that name her as a beneficiary and that aren't owned by her parents. Such accounts could have a big impact on a grandchild's aid eligibility.

No matter which forms you fill out, you may be able to mitigate the impact on aid by transferring ownership of the account to the student's parent shortly before the student applies for college. Then, assuming the student is a dependent, the 529 would count as any other parental non-retirement account; 5.64 percent of the balance is expected to be used for college each year, but distributions from the 529 aren't income to the student or the parent.

Could the transfer of ownership be a taxable gift to the parent? Probably not, but the Internal Revenue Service hasn't ruled on the issue.

Did You Know?

You can't use custodial accounts for support obligations (basically food, clothing and shelter). However, it's generally safe to apply the funds to what might otherwise be unaffordable extras for the child whom it benefits, such as private school, dance lessons and summer camp.

The effect of other subsidies. Schools consider not only assets, but also all income from the previous year to determine what's available to pay for education. For these purposes, they would look not just at income from a 529 account; if a family member (say, an aunt or a grandparent) paid tuition for the child out of her own pocket, that also could start hurting the financial aid calculation for the following year.

Trust distributions always count as income, whether or not they are taxable to the child, and count against aid eligibility. The same rule applies to outright gifts to the student, whether with cash or by paying bills on the student's behalf: for example, a grandparent who pays the rent.

To-Do List

Mix and Match Education Funding Techniques

Which education funding tools you choose will depend on a variety of factors. Here are some questions to ask, and action to take if you answer "yes."

✤ *Do you have a lot of cash on hand – perhaps because you just sold a business or investment?*
Action: Use some of those funds to pre-pay tuition and make a five-year lump-sum contribution to a 529 plan.

✤ *Are the people you want to help already in school?*
Action: Make direct payments of tuition, and consider setting up trusts or 529 plans in case you pass away before they graduate.

✤ *If the nest egg you're creating isn't needed for education (perhaps because the beneficiary gets a scholarship), would you like the money to be available to cover post-graduation expenses?*
Action: Set up a trust that leaves open that possibility.

✤ *Is there so much money in your child's custodial account that it might reduce his or her motivation to get an education and work?*
Action: Take various steps, within the framework of the law, to spend down or divide the account.

✤ *Do you want to set up a Coverdell Education Savings account but can't because your income is too high?*
Action: Give $2,000 to family members you want to benefit so each can set up his or her own Coverdell account.

Chapter 10

Subsidize Friends Or Family

Read this chapter if you would like to offer financial help to adult children, grandchildren, parents, siblings or others.

The economic meltdown that began in 2008 continues to ripple through our lives. Prosperous baby boomers, who expected to inherit from their parents, find themselves supporting older relatives instead. In other cases, grandparents are helping adult children meet the high costs of raising their own offspring. Even as the economy appears to grow, wages lag and many young people cannot find full-time jobs sufficient to support themselves.

As noted in Chapter 9, paying for education is the most common way of subsidizing other people. For those who could benefit from a cash gift, you can give $14,000 ($28,000 for married couples) to each, and as many individuals as you want. After that, gifts of money (or other assets) count against the $5.43 million ($10.86 million for married couples) lifetime gift-tax exclusion.

In This Chapter...

- Help With Housing
- Fit the Gift to the Need
- Minimize Hassles
- Don't Gamble With Gift-Tax Returns

As far as the government is concerned, noble motives don't matter; you must follow the same rules that would apply to any other lifetime transfers. Even if you don't exceed the limit – at which point you would owe gift tax of 40 percent – your lifetime gifts reduce how much you can pass tax-free through your estate plan.

Although simply writing a check is the easiest approach, there are a variety of other strategies to help people, with or without using the annual exclusion. Some are available only to help family members; others can be used for those not related.

Help With Housing

Plenty of young families – and mature ones, as well – still struggle with housing costs. After education, this is the primary way that family members who have been more fortunate help out.

Beware, though, the pitfalls. Intrafamily deals of all kinds have psychological overtones and can ignite conflicts. Plus, you might have Uncle Sam to contend with if you don't follow the tax rules. Here are strategies to help family pay for housing without buying trouble.

Give them cash. Gift recipients could use the cash as a down payment on a mortgage, or to make extra payments and pay it off more quickly. (Again, you must adhere to the rules on annual exclusion and lifetime gifts.)

Pay off the mortgage. The value of your gift is the unpaid principal plus the accrued interest. This strategy appeals to parents who want to increase children's cash flow and give them the financial security of owning a home mortgage-free. Afraid the object of your largesse might turn around and remortgage the house? If so, give children the cash and let them decide whether to pay off the mortgage.

Lend them the money. Credit between family members requires the formalities of a bank loan, but the rate can be more favorable. You must charge a minimum rate of interest set each month by the Treasury, called the applicable federal rate. If interest rates go down while the loan is in effect, you can refinance.

Buy them a house. Here, too, you'll need to use your annual exclusion and lifetime exemption. To pack more into the tax-free amounts, you can transfer partial interests in the house over time rather than giving it all at once. (For more about this strategy, see the following chapter.)

Offer rent-free living. You can let someone live in your house, or buy a house and let them occupy it rent-free, so long as the fair market value of the rent comes within the annual exclusion. Remember, spouses can combine their annual exclusion amounts, if necessary, to come within the yearly limit.

Fit the Gift to the Need

Here are other strategies for subsidizing relatives and, in some cases, friends without having to pay gift tax.

Pay directly for medical and dental expenses. Without using your annual exclusion, you can pay the dental and medical expenses of anyone you want. These payments are exempt from both gift tax and generation-skipping transfer tax no matter how much you spend. Note that you must make the payments directly to the providers of those services, as with payments of tuition (discussed in the previous chapter). You can't simply reimburse the person whom you want to benefit.

This chance to pay for medical and dental expenses, often overlooked, can be enormously useful. For example, you can apply this tax break to pay for dental implants for a cash-strapped friend. Or if someone you know is temporarily out of work and loses health insurance coverage, you could pay the premium for that person or that person's family, or if they have a health savings account, make a contribution for their benefit. You can cover anything that the person would be allowed to deduct on a tax return as an unreimbursed expense, including therapy for special needs children, fertility treatments and orthodontia. Unless you claim a family member as a dependent, you cannot deduct these expenses.

This is a great way to help elderly parents with medically necessary home improvements, home-care attendants or nursing home bills. You can also pay part of another person's long-term-care insurance – up to $3,800 for someone 61 to 70 years old, and up to $4,750 if the person is over 70. The medical care exclusion does have some restrictions: It doesn't include cosmetic surgery and massages, for instance.

Contribute to ABLE accounts. Conceptually similar to 529 education savings plans, these tax-advantaged entities were created in 2014 when Congress added a new section, 529A, to the Internal Revenue Code. Known as the ABLE Act (the acronym stands for Achieving a Better Life Experience), this provision makes it possible to set aside up to $100,000 for disability-related expenses without jeopardizing the beneficiary's eligibility for Supplemental Security Income or Medicaid.

The law is designed to lessen the financial burden on families of paying disability-related expenses. These accounts also help remove a common disincentive for working – that accumulating more than $2,000 of their own assets (including a home or car) would disqualify a disabled person for SSI. And ABLE accounts are less expensive to set up and administer than the special needs trusts discussed in Chapter 5.

Anyone eligible for SSI can have an ABLE account, but the reverse is not necessarily true. In other words, qualifying for this program (which requires getting a "disability certification" from the Social Security Administration) does not automatically make someone eligible for SSI. Details for this provision and a number of others still need to be spelled out in forthcoming IRS regulations.

Each beneficiary, who must be blind or have a disability that began before age 26, can have only one ABLE account.

Did You Know?

John Updike lent three of his children $100,000 apiece. Through subsequent gifts, he gradually forgave those loans, but they were not totally paid off when he died, in 2009. His will provided that each child's inheritance would be reduced by the unpaid portion of the loan.

Yearly contributions from all donors qualify for the annual exclusion but can't total more than whatever the inflation-adjusted amount happens to be that year (currently it is $14,000). Within these parameters, family and friends can add funds to the account, and beneficiaries can add their own funds, too. (All contributions must be in cash and are not deductible for income tax purposes.)

There are no limits on annual withdrawals, and the money grows – and can be withdrawn – tax-free as long as it is used for disability-related expenses. The category is broad, and, according to the new law, includes: "education, housing, transportation, employment training and support, assistive technology and personal support services, health, prevention and wellness, financial management and administrative services, legal fees, expenses for oversight and monitoring, funeral and burial expenses."

Certain restrictions apply. Investment choices can't be changed more than twice a year. If the total withdrawals in a given year are more than disability expenses in that year, the excess distribution is subject to income tax plus a 10 percent penalty. There's no penalty for withdrawals after the beneficiary dies – for example, to pay bills that are still outstanding. It's also possible to change the beneficiary at any time to another member of the original beneficiary's immediate family.

Though inspired by education savings plans, several features make these state-operated accounts different. One is that a beneficiary must participate in the program of the state where the beneficiary is a resident, or what's called a "contract state" (another state running a program for a state that doesn't have its own). Since the beneficiary must be the account owner, those making contributions no longer have control over the funds. Another key distinction is that the state has a claim to some of what remains once the beneficiary dies: It is entitled to be reimbursed for Medicaid benefits received.

Employ friends and family members. Whether they provide child care, manage real estate or keep the books, the compensation you provide must be reasonable – not more than you would pay anyone else for the same work. Paying a higher salary than you would pay outsiders exposes you to a potential double whammy: Not only could you be personally liable for gift tax on the excess, but your company won't be able to deduct the full salary as a business expense. If you do hire friends and family members, you can also deduct at least part of the cost of health insurance and long-term-care insurance that they receive as a fringe benefit.

Lend and borrow money. The difference between the government-approved rate (discussed in the previous section) and what the borrowers would pay on a loan from a financial institution amounts to a tax-free gift. But if you are more generous than the government allows, the difference between the interest payments you are receiving and what you should be getting is considered a gift.

Family members can use money you lend them for any purpose.

Alternatively, you can benefit relatives by borrowing money from them and paying higher interest than they could get from money market accounts or bank CDs. There's no maximum government-set rate, but you can mimic the market by paying what a bank in your area would charge for a comparable personal loan.

Make a family member your dependent. To do that, you must pay at least 50 percent of the person's support. The law defines dependents very broadly – it can include most of your relatives and their spouses, for example.

Note, though, that you may not claim someone as a dependent if his or her annual gross income is more than $3,950. Social Security payments do not count, but required withdrawals from retirement plans, like IRAs and 401(k)s, do. Those who claim a relative as a dependent may be able to reap a huge tax benefit by adding the dependent's unreimbursed medical expenses to their own and deducting however much exceeds 10 percent of their adjusted gross income. Until the end of 2016, there's a lower threshold – 7.5 percent of AGI – if either spouse is 65 or older.

Give of yourself. If you have a talent that can relieve others of the need to pay for certain services, you may be able to give the greatest intangible gift. Whether you're a physician, architect, investment adviser, plumber, technology whiz or loving babysitter, there's no gift tax due when you lend a hand.

Minimize Hassles

Giving and receiving financial help on a continuing basis can be awkward, create resentments within a family, and leave children and grandchildren dependent on handouts in unpleasant ways – for example, to keep paying private school tuition. You can address at least some of those issues with the following steps.

Create an agency account. This reduces the paperwork if you are making direct payments for educational or medical ("ed-med") expenses. Here's how it works: you open a bank account in your own name and put in enough money to cover the expenses for an extended period of time. Then you give another person a power of attorney (as discussed in Chapter 1) to pay certain bills, such as education expenses, from the account. If, because of a physical or mental disability, you are unable to make the payments, that person now has the power to write checks in your name directly to a qualified provider.

Grandparents, in particular, may find this approach more convenient than having bills channeled to them through the child's parents. Instead, they can give one of the parents a power of attorney and relieve themselves of the paperwork. You do not need a lawyer to set up one of these accounts, but you do need to trust the person who has check-writing power not to spend the money on other things.

Create a buffer trust. The idea here is to help multiple family members without being pestered. You create a trust naming all the people you might want to benefit. Trust beneficiaries are not entitled to payouts but can request help as needed from whomever you name as trustee (it could be another family member or a professional).

Under the terms of this trust, payouts can be made only for direct ed-med payments and annual exclusion gifts, including those put into Section 529 plans. Unlike trusts used to reduce estate taxes, this one can be revoked if you decide you need the money yourself and it hasn't been spent.

Did You Know?

Without using your annual exclusion or lifetime gift-tax exemption amount, you can pay health insurance premiums for anyone you want. But you must make the payments directly to the insurance company. You can't simply reimburse the person whom you want to benefit.

Leave a safety net. When a friend or family member is relying on your largesse, make sure you provide a fallback in case something happens to you. One possibility is to leave the individual an outright inheritance. But it's much better to create an irrevocable trust that can be funded through lifetime gifts, a bequest or a combination of the two. It's possible to set up trusts to benefit multiple people and provide as much flexibility or control as you want over how the funds will be distributed. Trusts have the additional advantage of protecting assets from the beneficiaries' creditors.

You can fund the trust with the proceeds of a life insurance policy (as discussed in Chapter 8) or income-producing assets, like bonds or shares in a closely held company. Better yet, if you are able to use rapidly appreciating assets, such as stock, real estate or interests in a business start-up, both the gift and any subsequent increase in value will be out of your estate.

Using your annual exclusion, you can add $14,000 a year ($28,000 if you're married) of cash or other assets for each trust beneficiary, so the more beneficiaries, the more you can give away without paying tax. One issue you will face, assuming the trust is not expected to pay out immediately, is that to qualify for the annual exclusion, your gift must be a present interest, meaning that the recipient can use it immediately. The most common way to meet this requirement is to give each beneficiary Crummey powers – the right for a limited time, usually 30 or 60 days, to withdraw from the trust the yearly gift attributable to that beneficiary. (Crummey powers are discussed more fully in Chapter 6.)

If you are using the annual exclusion to help the trust beneficiaries with current expenses, you may need to apply some or all of your $5.43 million lifetime exclusion ($10.86 million for a married couple) to the assets you put into the trust. Depending on the type of trust you create, it may also be necessary to allocate, or apply, your $5.43 million generation-skipping transfer tax exclusion as you contribute assets to the trust (see Chapter 14).

Don't Gamble With Gift-Tax Returns

If you gave more than $14,000 in cash, property or gifts to anyone, you must report the gift on Form 709, the gift-tax return that is due on April 15 of the year after you make your gifts. Mistakes can be expensive, leading to back taxes plus interest, and perhaps penalties if you've tried to dodge Uncle Sam.

Misunderstandings abound, and many Form 709s that should be filed are not. The following answers to some frequently asked questions can help you avoid tax mishaps.

Are gifts you receive taxed? Gifts from family and friends are not considered income, so there's no income tax. That's true no matter how high the value of gifts you receive in a given year. But sometimes a gift is subject to gift tax. When it is, the person giving the gift – not the recipient – is responsible for paying the tax.

When must you file a gift-tax return? Anything above the $14,000 annual exclusion (adjusted for inflation) is considered a taxable gift, and you need to report it. Whether you will owe any tax depends on whether you have used up your $5.43 million lifetime gift-tax exclusion. One reason you must file a gift-tax return is to show the IRS how much of the exclusion amount you have used so far.

Must gifts under $14,000 ever be reported? Yes. To come within the annual exclusion, a gift must be a present interest. This becomes an issue with gifts to certain trusts whose beneficiaries don't have any rights until sometime in the future (as discussed in Chapter 6). Whenever you make a gift that isn't a present interest, it must be reported, no matter how small the amount.

Are there special rules for married couples? Yes. The most important one is that the usual limits on lifetime gifts don't apply. If your spouse is a U.S. citizen, there's an unlimited marital deduction for most gifts, even if they exceed the annual exclusion amount, and you generally are not required to file a return.

Different rules apply if your spouse is not a U.S. citizen. In that case, you must file a gift-tax return if your gifts to him or her total more than $147,000 per year (this amount is adjusted for inflation). Additional gifts to a non-citizen spouse count against your $5.43 million basic exclusion and must be reported on the gift-tax return.

Another important tax break is that married couples can combine both their annual exclusions and their lifetime tax-free amounts – it's called gift-splitting. By using the annual exclusion this way they can jointly give away up to $28,000 to each of as many people as they want each year without dipping into the $5.43 million lifetime allotment. Ordinarily couples must then file a gift-tax return and consent, on each other's returns, to gift-split.

It's also possible for spouses to share their $5.43 million basic exclusion amount during life. (Here, too, they must file a gift-tax return and consent to gift-split.) But keep in mind that this reduces the amount available to each of them to make tax-free transfers at death to someone other than each other – for example, to children. And when the first spouse dies, less unused exclusion will be left for the survivor to carry over through portability. (For more on portability, see Chapter 3.)

When married couples use the annual exclusion to gift-split, does it matter who signs the checks if the funds are coming out of a joint account? This question comes up often. The best way to handle it is for couples to each write a separate check out of the joint account. The person who writes the check is considered to be making the gift. While married couples can double up, to do that they have to file a gift-tax return to make what's called a gift-split election. By writing separate checks they can avoid the need to file a return solely for this purpose.

What if I fund a 529 college savings plan? A popular use of the annual exclusion is to put money in Section 529 college savings plans (see Chapter 9). The law also permits lump-sum deposits of as much as $70,000 per person at once ($140,000 for married couples), in which case you must file a gift-tax return electing to treat the gift as if it had been spread over five years. During this five-year period, you cannot make additional annual exclusion gifts to the beneficiary of the 529 plan. If you die before the five-year period is up, part of the gift, reflecting the number of years still to go on your five-year gift, will be included in your estate.

Is paying tuition for someone a taxable gift? As noted above and in the previous chapter, if you pay a friend or family member's tuition, dental or medical expenses (including health insurance premiums), it won't count against either the annual exclusion or your

> ## Did You Know?
>
> Married couples can combine their annual exclusions (known as gift-splitting) to give away up to $28,000 each to as many people as they like each year in three ways: Each give $14,000, give $28,000 from a joint account or give $28,000 from one of their accounts.

$5.43 million basic exclusion, and you won't have to file a gift-tax return – but only if you make those payments directly to the service provider, such as the school, doctor or insurance company.

Can a gift-tax return be filed late? Yes. To request an automatic six-month extension to file Form 709, you can file Form 8892. If you are applying for an extension for your personal income taxes, filing the necessary paperwork for that (Form 4868) automatically extends your time to file Form 709, so you don't need to request the extension separately. Either way, though, if you owe tax, you must pay it by April 15 (use the voucher on the Form 8892 for this) or you will owe interest and perhaps penalties.

If you didn't file gift-tax returns for past tax years, it's not too late to correct the situation. Generally speaking, you have until the IRS catches the problem. When you're not liable for gift tax, there's no penalty for late filing.

Should you file a return even if you're not required to? This question is not as ridiculous as it sounds. You might want to file a return if there's room for debate about what your gift is worth. Under the tax law and IRS regulations, to start the statute of limitations running on your gift-tax return, you must make "adequate disclosure" of the gift. The only way to do that is to file a gift-tax return reporting the gift.

Are gift-tax returns audited? Yes, and filing one (even just to start the statute of limitations running) means you might get audited. However, when you make a transfer that's clearly a taxable gift, the law requires you to report it. Plus, after you die, during an estate tax audit, the IRS can question – and tax – gifts you made many years earlier if you didn't file a return reporting them.

Is it ever too late to make a gift-split election? Yes. If you have already received a deficiency notice from the IRS, you can no longer make the election. Barring that, it's not uncommon to file a gift-tax return and make the election long after the gift has been made or even after someone has died.

How long should gift-tax returns be kept? Since the $5.43 million lifetime exclusion from gift tax and any gift tax you pay are cumulative, you must keep the returns indefinitely. Your heirs need them to calculate the tax, if any, on your estate. And the most likely time for the IRS to flag unreported gifts or to question the value of the gifts you made is after you die. You do everyone a favor by leaving all the documentation behind.

To-Do List

Set the Record Straight

While generosity with family members often occurs under the radar, the law is clear: If the gift exceeds a certain value and the Internal Revenue Service catches it, you could be forced to pay gift tax as well as interest, and, in some cases, penalties.

Within a family, there are also benefits to transparency. Making lifetime gifts cracks open the door to the secrets of your estate plan. Children and grandchildren may now be wondering whether that's all they're going to receive, or whether there is more money coming later.

The following steps can help you avoid conflicts in both arenas.

❧ Thoroughly document intrafamily loans, including interest rates and repayment schedules.

❧ When entering into other transactions with family members – for example, by employing them or renting to them – make sure whatever you pay or charge is at market rates.

❧ If you have made a gift that does not qualify for the annual exclusion, file a gift-tax return.

❧ When making lifetime gifts to some family members and not to others, decide whether you want to reduce their inheritance proportionately.

❧ Discuss with family members whether your estate plan will even out certain disparities that have arisen during your life. Explain your reasoning.

Chapter 11

Home Base: Factoring In Real Estate

Read this chapter if you own your primary residence or vacation home, or might move to a different state.

Our homes provide the setting for much of our lives. We've watched children grow from toddlers to young adults who tower over us. We've endured renovations, solved problems at the kitchen table, whispered in the dark. Letting go can tug at our heartstrings, whether we are contemplating a change of residence or passing along real estate to heirs. There are financial challenges as well, because a home is often one of the largest assets in an estate.

In This Chapter...

- *Giving Away Partial Interests*
- *Putting Your House in a Trust*
- *Passing Down a Vacation Home*
- *Donating a House to Charity*
- *Choosing a State of Residence*

An important question, when you are dealing with any valuable real estate, is whether your heirs want to keep the property. If not, and it's promptly sold, the cost basis will be adjusted to its value on your date of death (or in some cases an alternate date six months later). This can reduce or eliminate the need to pay capital gains tax. In contrast, if the real estate will stay in the family and its value at your death would bring your estate above $5.43 million (the exclusion amount), you might be better off using various lifetime tools to reduce the tax bite later.

Vacation homes pose special complications. If a home is in a state other than the one in which you live, unless you take certain precautions, your heirs will need to go through probate in two states, as noted in Chapter 2. And if that state has its own estate tax, that, too, poses a potential trap that you can avoid with careful planning.

Giving Away Partial Interests

This very simple way of transferring real estate during life can make the most of the annual exclusion – the $14,000 ($28,000 for married couples) that we can each give every year to as many recipients as we would like without incurring a gift tax. The strategy also packs more value into the $5.43 million lifetime exemption ($10.86 million for spouses) from gift tax that applies to gifts above the annual exclusion.

How does giving away partial interests make the gift limits go further? These interests are considered fractional shares. Since the gift recipient gets just a partial interest, the value of what's transferred can be substantially discounted, because the partial interest is not a controlling interest: The recipient can't act unilaterally and is yoked together with other interest holders.

You can make gifts of fractional shares all at once (for example, if you were giving various people an interest in the same property) or over time (most likely if there was only one recipient). Meanwhile, each part-owner must pay his or her share of property taxes, insurance and repairs.

This approach can work well in a variety of situations. Suppose you and your spouse bought an inexpensive place for your son to live in while he was in college, and he plans to stay on after graduation. Through a series of combined annual exclusion gifts worth $28,000, the two of you can gradually make him the owner of the property without having to pay gift tax.

Just remember that you need to get a professional appraisal at the time you make the first transfer, with follow-up appraisals if the value of the property has changed when you make subsequent gifts. But if you straddle two years by making your annual exclusion gifts in December and again in January, you can rely on the same appraisal for both.

If you want to benefit various people, you can avoid squabbles by making your gifts to a trust that will benefit all of them, and choose a trustee (as discussed in Chapter 6) to oversee the property management. Under this arrangement, you and your spouse together can contribute an interest worth up to $28,000 per year for each trust beneficiary. Another possibility is to put the real estate into an entity such as a family limited partnership or limited liability company, and sell or give away shares in the entity that holds the property – not in the real estate itself (see Chapter 15). You can make these transfers to individuals directly or to a trust that benefits them.

One thing you should *not* do is put your home into such an entity or give away a partial interest in the house and continue to live in it rent-free. The tax code says that if you give something away but retain the right to use it, the property is still considered part of your estate. Therefore, it could be subject to tax.

Putting Your House in a Trust

The qualified personal-residence trust, or QPRT, is a tool to consider if you are still living in a house but plan to leave it to your heirs, either for their own use or so they can sell it. The QPRT (pronounced "CUE-pert") removes part of the value of a costly home from the estate and shelters future appreciation. You just have to win a bet that you can escape the grim reaper for a specified time: the longer the period, the greater the potential tax savings.

Here's how the arrangement works: you put your primary residence or vacation home into an irrevocable trust, retaining the right to live there rent-free for a specified number of years. During that time the trust, of which you could be trustee, owns the property. When the period ends, ownership can pass to the beneficiaries, usually children, or go into another trust, often called a drop-down trust, for the rest of your life. Meanwhile, the QPRT has removed both the property and any future appreciation from the estate. Because the trust freezes the house at its fair market value when it's transferred to the QPRT, no additional tax is due after that.

The immediate attraction of the QPRT is that it discounts the value of the gift and makes the $5.43 million lifetime exemption from gift tax go further, or produces a lower tax bill if you have exceeded that limit (there's a gift tax of 40 percent). For gift-tax purposes, the value of the QPRT reflects the value of the right to acquire the personal residence (the remainder) a certain number of years from when it is set up (the trust term), discounted by the probability that the person setting up the trust (the grantor) will live that long.

Because of the discount, the QPRT can work well even if the property does not increase in value. For example, if you put a $1 million house in a QPRT and the value of the gift is $600,000, but the house later drops in value to $800,000, you will have still removed $200,000 in value from your estate.

Good Housekeeping

If you want to create a qualified personal-residence trust, you have a few housekeeping matters to address first. Because most mortgages have due-on-transfer clauses, it's best to pay off an outstanding mortgage, or, if you can't or choose not to, to get the bank's blessing for the QPRT. Otherwise, the principal portion of each payment made after the trust is in effect will count as a taxable gift, which could be an accounting nuisance and will require you to file an annual gift-tax return (see Chapter 10).

You should also have the house appraised, change the name on the property insurance policy and be sure the insurer will cover the home once it's in a trust. In states with special benefits for homeowners, such as homestead laws protecting a person's house from creditors (see Chapter 17) or tax breaks for the elderly, you may lose those benefits by putting property into a trust.

Figuring the discount involves a complex actuarial calculation based on a rate set each month by the U.S. Treasury called the Section 7520 rate (named after a section of the Internal Revenue Code). The latest Section 7520 rates are available at www.tigertables.com. The higher the rate and the longer the term, the bigger the discount and the more savings associated with the QPRT.

Let's say Sally, who is 60, has a net worth of $7 million, including a $1 million home that she wants to put into a 10-year QPRT. Assuming a Section 7520 rate of 2.4 percent, the transferred property would be valued at $673,570 for gift-tax purposes. Extend the term to 15 years and the discounted value drops to $516,400.*

The discounted value of the house in the trust will count against Sally's lifetime limit. But with a lifetime limit of $5.43 million, it's possible to transfer a home like Sally's and still have a lot of the exclusion amount left to cover other assets.

Who might want to do a QPRT? This estate planning tool could work well for a healthy homeowner who plans to retire to a different location in 10 or

---

Lawrence P. Katzenstein, Tiger Tables Actuarial Software

15 years. Another possible trust candidate is someone with a vacation re-treat that she wants to keep in the family (more about that on page 191). Note, by the way, that in the eyes of the Internal Revenue Service, a boat or a recreational vehicle counts as a personal residence and can be put into a QPRT, provided it has cooking and toilet facilities, and you've used it for more than 14 nights in a year or more than 10 percent of the time you rent it out (whichever is greater).

The QPRT is especially attractive for people with a significant portion of their wealth tied up in a personal residence. A widow with a home worth $1 million and other investments totaling $5 million might not want to give away investment assets to reduce the taxable estate: She needs to live on the income. A QPRT enables her to reap a substantial estate tax savings without disturbing her portfolio.

Did You Know?

The IRS defines a "dwelling" broadly. A mobile home, a boat or a trailer qualify, as long as it provides sleeping accommodations, a toilet and cooking facilities – and you've used it in a year for more than 14 nights or 10 percent of the time you rent it (whichever is greater).

There is one big catch, however: For a QPRT to work, you must outlive the trust term. If you don't, the property is in-cluded in your estate, at its value on your date of death, and is potentially subject to estate tax. If you used part of your exclusion amount to make the gift to the trust, that amount gets restored, so the exclusion amount that's available when you die will not be reduced by the amount of that gift (it would be if you survived the QPRT term). In the unlikely event that you exceeded your lifetime exemption and paid gift tax when setting up the trust, your estate can deduct whatever federal gift tax you paid.

One way to hedge your bets is to form multiple qualified personal-res-idence trusts with staggered terms, just as you might fill a portfolio with bonds of different maturity dates. As long as you outlast one of the trust terms, at least part of the property will be removed from the estate. The law allows you to place two residences into separate QPRTs and also to divide each property among an unlimited number of trusts. So one course might be to put your primary home in a 15-year trust and the vacation hideaway in a 10-year trust. Or you could set up four trusts on the primary home, assigning one-fourth of its value to each (or perhaps taking a partial interest discount) and setting the terms at 5, 10, 15 and 20 years.

So what happens once the trust ends? One possibility is to lease the house from the family members who will then own it. Another, which is preferable, is to have the property go to a drop-down trust and lease it from that trust.

Either way, it's important that you pay rent at fair market rates, or the IRS might decide after you die that you retained an interest in the property. Should that happen, the house would be included in your estate and taxed at its value when you die. Beware: If rents go up dramatically in the area where the house is situated, you need to be sure you can still afford the tab. Any trust that picks up where the QPRT ends should be structured as a grantor trust, meaning that the person who sets it up retains certain rights or powers. The attraction of grantor trusts is that they're not treated as separate taxable entities (see Chapter 15). That means the trust pays no tax on the rent it receives from the grantor once the QPRT term ends. And provided the rent is at fair market value, there's no gift tax, either.

In effect, you can use this trust to transfer additional money in excess of the annual exclusion gifts to family members tax-free. It's even possible to use an irrevocable life insurance trust (as discussed in Chapter 8) as the drop-down trust from a QPRT, in which case the rent money could finance the premium on a life insurance policy.

Another huge benefit of this type of trust is that if it sells the property, the transaction is treated as a sale by the grantor. Therefore, it qualifies for the same tax break that is available to homeowners if they sell their principal residence: The first $250,000 ($500,000 for married couples) of capital gain is not subject to tax if you have lived in the house for at least two of the five years before the sale.

All these features of the drop-down grantor trust should make the QPRT more palatable for people who have reservations about it. The children don't own the house at this point – the drop-down trust does – and the setup isn't really going to change your lifestyle. The trust can even require that the property be rented back to the grantor, so long as he pays rent at the fair market value. With a trustee at the helm, you don't have to worry about being evicted by your own offspring. In fact, they don't even have to know about the QPRT until after you die.

But be careful about this: A drop-down trust that passes property to children when the grantor dies should contain a specific provision to cover the contingency of a child dying during the trust term. A trust that says grandchildren will get the parent's share could subject the transfer to generation-skipping transfer tax on top of any estate tax (see Chapter 14). This rule doesn't apply if the grandchild is orphaned before the trust is created. Generation-skipping transfer tax – a whopping 40 percent – applies to gifts or bequests to grandchildren of more than $5.43 million. So a better course is not to give grandchildren orphaned during the trust term a share in this particular property but to make it up to them in the will; property can be left through your estate plan without a generation-skipping transfer tax if the grandchild's parents have died.

Did You Know?

If you change your home state, it's important to pull up roots and establish new ones. Otherwise, if your former state has an income tax or estate tax, it may chase you, or your estate, for taxes. In a worst-case scenario, you could wind up owing taxes to two states.

What if you want to sell the house before the QPRT ends? The easiest course is to roll over all the proceeds into another residence. Things get more cumbersome if you don't buy another home or if you purchase a less costly one. The trust must cover either possibility by providing the grantor an annuity from the sale proceeds each year until the trust expires. (An extensive discussion of the grantor retained annuity trust, or GRAT, appears in Chapter 15.) Alternatively, the trust could provide that the part that would have gone to the annuity trust will go to the grantor instead. (The trust can give the trustee the power to decide which of these happens.)

Among the situations in which a QPRT might not be appropriate is when the house has markedly appreciated and the heirs plan to sell it right away. In that case, they could be hit with a substantial capital gains tax. Here's why: By receiving ownership through the QPRT, the heirs aren't entitled to the adjustment in basis they would get if property passed through the estate. Instead, their cost basis in the property equals what you originally paid for the home plus the cost of subsequent improvements, with an adjustment for any gift tax paid in the transfer. Presumably, that basis is much smaller than the sale price would be.

The Sedgwick Legacy

A Federal-style house in Stockbridge, Mass., built by Theodore Sedgwick, a senator, congressman and judge, has remained in his family for more than 200 years, and recent generations have creatively funded its upkeep. Several family members bought the house from a cousin in 1940 for a nominal sum and put it in a trust to benefit all Sedgwick descendants.

Since then, bequests and lifetime gifts from family members have supplied its primary endowment, while a member of the Sedgwick family who works in the arts has occupied it. In exchange for a reasonable rent, this tenant is responsible for maintaining the house and the family graveyard nearby, hosting family weddings and funerals, and booking visits by other Sedgwicks who can spend weekends and vacations in the guest wing.

In such cases, advisers should run the numbers to see whether capital gains tax of up to 20 percent wipes out any estate tax savings achieved through the QPRT. Children who plan to use the house as a primary residence for at least two of the five years before selling it can exempt $250,000 of the profits from selling ($500,000 for married couples filing jointly).

Passing Down a Vacation Home

Whether it's a cottage on the Pacific or a château in France, the vacation home you think is a dream legacy might turn into a nightmare for your heirs. Ask whether they want to keep the property in the family as much as you do. They're not ingrates if they don't – they just have different interests, or priorities and lives of their own.

If you don't get a firm answer, the simplest approach is to leave the property to the estate and give family members a right of first refusal to buy it. You can limit that option to, say, six or nine months, and give a preference to people who want to purchase the house as a group. Even if younger generations are enthusiastic about the house, it's better not to make them joint owners. Instead, leave the property to an independent entity, such as a trust, or put it into a limited liability company and give the heirs shares in the enterprise (see Chapter 15). For tax reasons, property should not be placed in a corporation.

Whatever the vehicle, an even bigger issue than estate taxes is: How is the family going to be able to afford to keep this property intact? Some benefactors set up an endowment funded with cash, securities, business interests or the proceeds of a life insurance policy. If you can't cover the expenses forever, you might just leave enough money to take care of a year or two and permit heirs to buy out one another or sell the property to a third party after that.

The more owners and the longer that family ownership lasts, the more organization that is necessary. You may want to put the basic governing framework in place and leave your heirs to work out day-to-day details, such as choosing a caretaker, allocating time slots and resolving inevitable disparities in how much people use the house. These are some issues for you to consider.

- Who sits on the governing body, and what is the mechanism for it to make decisions?
- Which decisions rise to the level of requiring a vote by the governing body (perhaps capital expenditures of a certain amount), and which do not and could be made by whoever is in residence at the time, or discussed more informally (emergency repairs, for example, or basic maintenance)?
- What will happen if a family owner dies, gets divorced or declares bankruptcy?
- What is the procedure for selling or transferring shares? (Limiting it to your descendants rules out ownership by people who marry into the family.)
- In a buyout, how will the price be determined? (The possibilities range from having other family members pay the full share of the appraised value to imposing a discount and installment payment plan.)
- How many owners must agree before the entire property can be sold?

Donating a House to Charity

Charities are becoming more flexible about the kinds of donations they will accept, and real estate is the most popular type of gift besides cash and marketable securities. You can make these gifts during your life or through your estate plan.

Most likely the charity will sell the property and apply the proceeds to a philanthropic use. For example, the money could go into a donor-advised fund account so that you or members of your family can recommend grants. Or it could be used to fund a charitable remainder trust that will pay an income stream to you or your family and ultimately benefit charity (both these tools are discussed at length in Chapter 16). Before putting the house in the trust, you must move out, or you would violate the rules against self-dealing.

Donating real estate to charity, rather than selling the property and contributing the proceeds, offers significant financial advantages. Whether the donation is during life or through your estate plan, there is no capital gains tax on any appreciation in the property. If done through your estate plan, your estate is entitled to a charitable deduction that can reduce the tax it owes. With lifetime donations, you can deduct the fair market value of the property donated to a public charity, up to 30 percent of your adjusted gross income. (As discussed in Chapter 16, if you elect to limit your deduction to basis for all contributions made in a given tax year, you can deduct up to 50 percent.) Any deduction that can't be taken in the year of the donation (for instance, if your contribution exceeds the limit on charitable deductions) can be carried forward up to five years.

> ## Did You Know?
>
> State tax authorities are on the lookout for people who leave their home state for long-term medical or geriatric care. Even if you keep a house in the place where you have been living and hope to return, if you go into a nursing home, certain states will pursue income and estate taxes.

Most charities prefer that the property not be mortgaged, because, depending on the nature of the real estate, the term of the note and the charitable vehicle used, the gift could run afoul of various tax law restrictions. In addition, just as if it were purchasing the property, the non-profit must check for liens and be sure there are no environmental hazards that would carry cleanup obligations under federal law (see Chapter 16 for a discussion of these and other real estate issues). And since the property will generally be sold, the value must be high enough that the charity is willing to devote the effort and resources to marketing it.

Donations of real estate can take a variety of forms and must meet certain requirements. If you are considering a lifetime donation, think about these two key issues.

Do you want to continue using the property? By donating a remainder interest, you and your spouse can reserve the right to use the home for your lifetimes and have it pass to charity when you die. This technique removes the property from your taxable estate, and you get an income tax deduction for the actuarial value of charity's remainder interest, based on the ages and number of life beneficiaries (the older you are, the larger the deduction), the value of the property and the Section 7520 rate.

Most charities insist that donors who participate in these arrangements pay all maintenance costs, taxes and insurance. Home improvements, like updating a kitchen or renovating a barn, require the charity's consent, but you can get an additional charitable deduction for these enhancements based on a similar actuarial calculation. If need be, you can even sell the house during your life and split the proceeds with the charity according to its actuarial interest at the time of the sale. All these subjects should be covered in a co-ownership agreement.

Another variation on the theme that is attractive to people who can use extra cash is to donate the remainder interest in exchange for a gift annuity. (Charitable gift annuities are discussed in Chapter 16.)

Are you ready to sell the house? If so, selling the house through a charitable remainder trust can be a highly effective diversification strategy. Since the trust is a tax-exempt entity, it doesn't pay tax when it sells the asset, so you save the capital gains tax you would otherwise have to pay on a home that has appreciated. You can structure the trust to pay income to you and your spouse for the rest of your lives or for a term of up to 20 years, before the remainder goes to charity. In addition, you get a current income tax deduction based on the current value of the charity's remainder interest.

The best type of charitable remainder trust to use for this purpose is what's called a flip unitrust. Such a trust can be set up so that there's no requirement for the trust to make any payouts until it sells the property. But beware this potential trap: When you have a binding obligation to sell any non-cash asset, including real estate, before giving it to charity, the pre-arranged-sale rule forces you to pay tax on the gain. Here, too, you must move out of the house before you put it in the trust or you will violate the rules against self-dealing.

Choosing a State of Residence

Your choice of domicile – legal lingo for the place you call home – affects your finances in various ways. For people who divide their time between two or more states, saving income taxes has long been a motivation for choosing one state, rather than the other, as a place of residence. Your choice of residence can also have an impact on financial aspects of your estate plan. While that may not be enough to cause you to move, all other things being equal, you might make your domicile in a more financially friendly state.

Once you have decided where you want to live, you need to sever contacts with the old state and establish ties that bind you to the new one. Otherwise, you may not be able to take advantage of the benefits of the state you are moving to, and your former state may claim you're still a resident and chase you (or your estate) for taxes. In a worst-case scenario, you could wind up owing taxes to two states.

How do people get caught? Having what's known as source income in the former state, such as rent from a piece of property you own there, is one way. Another is by selling a business shortly after moving, say, from a state that has an income tax to one without. Tax authorities could notice that the federal tax return for the year of the departure, which includes the sale, reports much more income than the one from the former state.

Continuing to own real estate in a place with estate tax could hurt you, too. Typically, that would require a non-resident estate tax return to be filed (for a way around this, see page 197). Some states have a domicile questionnaire that must be attached, aimed at ferreting out proof that you were, in fact, a resident. Depending on the state, it may ask about everything from dates of club memberships to whether you were in a nursing home, rented a safe deposit box or were buried in the state. If you haven't kept good records, the family member or personal representative who completes the form may not have the necessary information.

It is, therefore, important to understand how state law can impact the bottom line and plan any moves carefully. These are some issues that may be affected.

Asset protection. State law has a huge influence on whether various assets are protected from creditors – a category that may include everyone from disgruntled spouses and ex-spouses to people who win lawsuits against you. Deadbeats, scam artists and people running from their debts have given asset protection a bad name. Even so, this subject has moved into the mainstream of estate planning – and rightfully so (asset protection is discussed in depth in Chapter 17). Various state-law exemptions are the first line of defense against creditors who try to reach your money and property.

> ## Did You Know?
>
> State estate taxes affect not only taxpayers who live in those states, but also those who are resident elsewhere and own property in a state that taxes out-of-state residents. By putting real estate, such as a vacation home, into a limited liability company, you may be able to avoid this potential tax trap.

State estate tax. Although most states do not have a gift tax (Connecticut is an exception), a growing number of states have imposed a separate estate tax, and the exemptions they allow may be less than the $5.43 million permitted under federal law. (Chapter 4 discussed strategies that spouses can use to plan around the differences.)

When real estate is concerned, keep in mind that state estate taxes affect not only taxpayers who live in those states, but also those who are resident elsewhere and own property in a state that taxes out-of-state residents. For example, if you live in Arizona, California, Florida or Texas, which do not have an estate tax, but own a summer home on Nantucket, you need to be aware that it can be subject to state estate tax in Massachusetts. The tax is based on the ratio of the real estate to the total estate, and with costly property, it can quickly add up.

One strategy to address this potential tax trap is to convert real property to intangible personal property by putting the real estate into a limited liability company or family limited partnership. Unlike real property, which is taxed by the state in which it is situated, intangible personal property is taxed in the state where the owner resides. So far, most states have not taken a position about whether this strategy should be permitted. But pressures to generate revenues could cause some to clamp down on this technique in the future.

Community property. As discussed in Chapter 4, the rules on property ownership and inheritance operate differently in the nine states that have community property law. The big advantage, from an estate planning perspective, is that both spouses' shares get a step-up in basis when the first spouse dies, minimizing or eliminating the capital gains tax if the property is sold soon after. The major downside is that community ownership complicates the division of property in a divorce.

It's important to think about these issues when you relocate. If you move to a community property state from a non-community property state, you and your spouse have a choice about whether to keep property acquired before the move as separate property or whether to treat it as community property. What you own when you move to the state does not automatically become community property. You specify your wishes in a contract called a community property agreement. Likewise, if you move to a non-community property state, you can enter into a similar type of agreement either to keep existing property as community or convert it to separate property.

Income tax on trusts. If you are the trustee, beneficiary or grantor of a trust, your residence can affect the taxation of the trust. Conceivably, a trust could be taxable in more than one state, and it's not always possible to get a credit for the other state's tax.

The precise rules on taxing trusts vary widely. More important than knowing which state does what is alerting advisers to any outstanding trusts before you move, so they can suggest a strategy appropriate for your situation. For example, California is one of the more difficult states regarding trusts, taxing them if their trustees or beneficiaries are residents. If the trust is revocable, the solution may be as easy as having someone who moves to California resign as trustee.

Your will. All states will honor a will that's valid in the state where it was signed, but specific terms drafted for when you were living in the old state could be problematic in the new one. For example, in Florida, you can't name someone from outside the state as executor (called a personal representative there) unless he or she is a member of your family. Some states permit people disposing of personal property to leave a memo that's binding on the executor. Others have rules that such a memo, listing particular items to go to certain people, is just advisory, and that the executor doesn't have to follow it (as noted in Chapter 2).

You won't necessarily have to redo your will if you move, but you should have a local lawyer review it, along with any other estate planning documents. Since you will be subject to a new set of state laws, you should be sure your documents are appropriate for the state you are moving to. For example, if you and your spouse move to a community property law state, you will need to have new wills drafted by a local lawyer.

Power of attorney. As discussed in Chapter 1, this important estate planning document authorizes a person whom you trust to act as your agent in a variety of financial and legal matters. State laws vary as to both what powers you can convey and the requirements for the document to be valid. Therefore, when you move, you should have any existing powers of attorney reviewed by a local lawyer. For example, in Florida, there must be two witnesses when you sign the document. If you move from a state with different requirements, the document may be ineffective for your needs. And if you become mentally incompetent before you sign a new power of attorney, it might be necessary to get a court-appointed guardian to handle certain tasks instead.

To-Do List

Beware the Ties That Bind

Changing your domicile or home state for tax purposes can be compli-cated. It's important both to establish a residence in the new state and to sever enough ties in the previous one that tax authorities will have no claim against you. Spending more than six months a year in a state is the best way to prove you live there. Evidence that you intend to remain is also helpful. These are some steps to take:

❧ Get a state driver's license and register your car

❧ Register to vote and cast your ballot

❧ Change your address for all important mail and documents, including your federal income tax return and your passport

❧ Join community groups, local clubs and, if you're religious, a house of worship

❧ File a declaration of domicile, if the state has a procedure for doing that

❧ Apply for special tax breaks, if any, that are available to residents

❧ Move your safe deposit box

❧ Make donations to local charities

❧ Establish relationships with local professionals, such as doctors, lawyers and accountants

❧ If you redo your estate plan, sign the documents in the new state and be sure they indicate that it is your residence

Chapter 12

The Family Business: a Legacy Or a Headache?

*Read this chapter if you have
your own business or a share
in a family-held enterprise.*

Whether you are an entrepreneur or own a share of a family business, thinking about what will happen next can raise emotionally charged issues. Many business owners are so consumed with day-to-day operations they don't have time to consider estate planning – and don't want to. (It's awful to contemplate a time when you won't be at the helm.) Family members who don't work in the enterprise may not share the owners' devotion to the company and could have mixed feelings about the value of sustaining it. For various reasons, most such businesses do not continue to the third generation. The death of a company founder can cause revenues to slip. The product or business model may be hopelessly out of date. If your estate is large enough to be taxed, the 40 percent levy could leave your heirs cash-strapped.

In This Chapter...

- *What Is Your Succession Plan?*
- *Do You Have a Buy-Sell Agreement?*
- *Should You Transfer Shares?*
- *How Will Your Family Pay Estate Taxes?*

Planning while you are hearty is the best way to improve the odds that your company will thrive after you are gone, but you must be realistic. Find out whether any of your children want to continue in the business. If none does, your estate plan can reflect the expectation that the company will be sold. If one or more children want to keep the company going, you can even out the inheritances of children who will not be involved; the most common way is with life insurance (see Chapter 8). To the extent that you can afford it, shift assets to younger family members while you are alive. And take steps to minimize conflicts.

What Is Your Succession Plan?

Whatever the long-term goals and the assumptions about the economic viability of the company, every family-owned business should have a succession plan. These are some issues to cover.

How much is the company worth? Answering this question is a prerequisite for various forms of succession planning, from transferring shares to children to selling the company. In the life of a business, the value can fluctuate – for example, as a result of market conditions or because a sale or initial public offering is on the horizon.

Whether the value of the business has increased or fallen, that information can help you chart a course. If things have taken a turn for the worse, advisers who work with companies in financial distress may be able to help put the business back on track or find a buyer. If your company is on the verge of increasing its worth, your estate planning should take that into account.

How long should you stay involved? Company founders often think of the business as an extension of themselves, and that makes it tough to let go. Sometimes a founder who is psychologically ready to step down can't do without the salary, or the health and retirement benefits she has been receiving. In these cases, it may be possible for the founder to continue, at least temporarily, to receive an income stream as a consultant or part-time employee, rather than giving up everything, as the business makes a transition to family management or new ownership. The company might also adopt a deferred compensation plan to provide income to the founder after she reaches a particular age, whether or not she continues working. Another possibility is to structure a transaction, either with family members or a trust, that involves an installment sale or a loan that will generate revenue for the original owner.

Who is the likely successor? This is a potential lightning rod for many families, especially when the candidates include both family members and outsiders, or when some children are involved in the company and others are not. In the most successful transitions, owners have taken steps to avoid disagreements – for example, by having children earn their spurs elsewhere before joining the family enterprise, and by equalizing inheritances.

Do You Have a Buy-Sell Agreement?

Think of this as a business prenup or postnup, depending on when owners draw it up. In a buy-sell, partners (the process is the same for corporations and limited liability companies) decide what will happen to their interest in the company if events like disability, death, divorce or personal bankruptcy occur.

By requiring a sale under certain circumstances known as trigger events and by specifying the terms beforehand, a buy-sell can prevent such evils as becoming an unwilling partner with an owner's heirs or leaving a surviving spouse illiquid because the remaining owners refuse to buy the survivor's inherited shares. The best time to arrange the details is before you begin a venture, but generally there is no harm in waiting six months or so until you're sure the business is workable. For older companies, it's better late than never. Either way, some issues must be sorted out.

What events should you include? Some events – leaving the company, starting a competing business, offering shares to an outsider – may seem obvious; others could require considerable soul-searching. If a founding partner retires, for example, the remaining owners may feel torn between a desire to reward his past work and not wanting him to get a free ride.

Who can – or must – buy the business interest when one party wants out? In what's called a cross-purchase agreement, the option or obligation belongs to the remaining owners. Alternatively, there's a redemption agreement, which designates the company as the buyer. A hybrid approach typically gives an owner the right of first refusal, with the company next in line.

When owners' interests are divided unequally – say, one is a majority shareholder – you may also want to incorporate what's known as a tag-along provision. Then, if a 90 percent owner sells to Microsoft, for example, the deal must give the 10 percent shareholder the option of selling under the same terms. Sometimes agreements include a drag-along provision, in which the 10 percent owner is required to sell if the 90 percent owner does.

How can you value the interests being sold? There are many ways to approach this. If you name a set amount, you'll need to update it annually to reflect changes in the company, the industry or the economy. A more practical solution is to describe a process for determining the value, whether through an appraisal of the company's fair market value or by using a formula.

What are the payment terms and financing? A lump-sum payout provides all the cash at once, and that cash often comes from life insurance. You'll need fewer policies if the company buys a policy for every owner rather than if each owner insures the others individually. However, company-owned policies might not be as tax-efficient as policies owned by the co-owners in a cross-purchase agreement.

The alternative to a lump-sum deal is an installment sale, with payments, plus interest, over a defined period. These arrangements are common in buyouts where the owners don't anticipate a ready source of cash, which could happen if one owner gets divorced or wants to quit the business. The legal bill to prepare a buy-sell agreement may be $2,500 to $25,000, depending on complexity. If your budget is tight, you can rely on the free buy-sell agreement that many life insurance companies offer policy buyers, but it will probably cover only an owner's death, not other trigger events, and it doesn't replace the advice of a lawyer who understands these issues.

Should You Transfer Shares?

The best time to shift business assets to family is before your company hits a home run, such as a sale or initial public offering, or the announcement of a revolutionary product. Once the enterprise soars in value, all the appreciation would be stuck in your estate. If you can afford to transfer some holdings before that happens, it is possible to shelter the increased value from estate tax.

Currently, you can make gifts of up to $14,000 in cash or other assets each year ($28,000 if you are married) to each of as many recipients as you would like without incurring gift tax. In addition to this annual exclusion, you can give away $5.43 million during your life ($10.86 million for married couples) before a gift tax of up to 40 percent applies. Various estate planning techniques, designed to minimize or steer clear of the gift tax altogether, can pack even more value into both the annual exclusion and the lifetime gift-tax exemption amount. These techniques are covered briefly later in this chapter and discussed extensively in Chapter 15.

Which transfer methods work best depends on a variety of business and personal factors. Among the most important are the maturity and current value of your business, your expectations for its future, and whether and how soon you anticipate the company might be sold or go public. You should also evaluate your cash flow needs, decide whom you want to benefit and weigh your tolerance for complexity.

At the outset, many business owners divide the company into voting and non-voting shares, recapitalizing if necessary. This serves two purposes. By retaining the voting shares, owners can maintain control over business decisions, which may be important to them as they approach a critical juncture. The strategy may also allow the value of the non-voting shares intended for transfer during life to be further discounted, because they carry no control rights.

Once you have done that, here are some possible situations to consider.

The value of the business is still relatively low. The best wealth transfer technique may be the simplest: transfer shares to family members using your annual exclusion.

You can make these gifts to individuals directly, or to an irrevocable trust that can benefit multiple people and protect the assets from creditors (see Chapter 17). You and your spouse can each put in $14,000 worth of stock each year for every trust beneficiary. Those annual exclusion gifts offer a lot of bang for your buck, especially if the company stock isn't worth very much right now. If it increases in value – for example, because of a sale or initial public offering – the trust would receive its share of the proceeds.

Your company could be a boom or a bust. A grantor retained annuity trust, or GRAT, lets you bet on the upside potential without any downside risk. Here's how it works: The person setting up the trust, known as the grantor, puts company shares into a short-term irrevocable trust and retains the right to receive an annual income stream, known as an annuity, for a preset time (for this type of asset, it is typically 5 to 15 years). If the grantor survives that period – a condition for this tool to work – any property left in the trust when the annual payments end passes to family members or to a trust for their benefit (they are the remainder beneficiaries).

The annuity should be approximately equal to the value of the assets transferred, plus an assumed interest rate that the government imposes, known as the Section 7520 rate. If the assets in the GRAT appreciate by more than that rate, all the excess passes to the grantor's heirs with little or no gift tax. On the other hand, if the appreciation never occurs, the grantor is no worse off, except for the fees paid to set up the trust, because the annuity would be paid by returning some shares to the grantor.

The GRAT is a terrific tool for shifting assets you expect will suddenly increase in value. For example, in 2008, Facebook's SEC filing shows, billionaire co-founder Dustin Moskovitz put 14.4 million shares into a GRAT; co-founder Mark Zuckerberg, 3.6 million shares; and Facebook Chief Operating Officer Sheryl Sandberg, 1.9 million shares. Based on some conservative assumptions, Forbes estimates that the tally for tax-free transfers through the GRATs was: Moskovitz, $148 million; Zuckerberg, $37 million; Sandberg, $19 million.

When the company went public, Sandberg already had children, but neither of the others did. The most likely beneficiary of Zuckerberg's and Moskovitz's GRATs is another trust – one that provides, if they don't have children, the money will go to other family or charity.

GRATs also offer enormous flexibility for parents who may be concerned that a business bonanza might make their children too rich. For example, you could provide in the trust document that if the remainder interest grows to more than a certain amount, the excess will come back to you rather than going to your children. At that point you could choose to donate the funds to charity or spend them for another purpose.

With assets that are difficult to value, as may be the case with closely held stock or real estate, a GRAT offers an additional benefit. By expressing the annuity as a percentage of the initial value of the GRAT, you permit the trust to simply pay a larger annuity if the IRS determines the property is worth more than you initially figured. This minimizes the additional gift tax the IRS might try to impose if it audits the value of the gift.

But GRATs are not ideal for transfers to grandchildren and more remote descendants. The $5.43 million exemption from generation-skipping transfer tax can't be applied until the trust term ends, by which time you hope asset values will be higher.

Your company is growing slowly but steadily. A popular alternative – or complement – to a GRAT is what's called an installment sale to an irrevocable grantor trust. With this technique, senior family members sell assets to a trust that will benefit younger relatives and, in exchange, take back an interest-bearing promissory note. Assuming a sale at fair market value and interest at the applicable federal rate – which is lower than the Section 7520 rate – there is no gift and, therefore, no gift tax.

Your hope is that the value of the business interests will increase by more than the interest rate by the time the loan term ends. If it does – for example, if a sale occurs – you will have shifted all that excess to family members without having to pay gift tax.

This strategy requires that the trust have other assets, ideally worth at least 10 percent of the trust's total assets once the property is transferred. Often the grantor supplies this seed money using all or part of the lifetime gift-tax exemption, which is $5.43 million.

Like a GRAT, this transaction involves what's called a grantor trust – so named because the grantor retains certain rights or powers (see Chapter 15). As a result, the grantor, rather than the trust or its beneficiaries, must pay income tax on the trust earnings. The benefits can be enormous. For example, if a company is sold, the trust will receive a cash infusion that triggers capital gains tax. If the grantor, rather than the trust, pays this tax, all the proceeds of the sale can remain in the trust rather than being partially depleted by taxes.

You want to support charity as well as family. When giving shares to family, you are likely to achieve maximum estate planning benefits if you transfer assets before there is any appreciation. In contrast, when giving shares to charity, you are usually better off making the donation when asset values are higher, because you maximize the potential income tax deduction. Donating company stock, assuming the charity is open to this gift, avoids capital gains tax. A non-profit, which is tax-exempt, does not have to pay tax on the proceeds of a sale or initial public offering.

With a charitable remainder trust, which can benefit you or family members as well as a charity, individuals must pay their share of the tax. But this tax is deferred and applied proportionately to each trust distribution the person receives (see Chapter 16). Note that if your company is organized as an S corporation – a company structure that avoids double tax on company earnings (first at the corporate level, and then on the individual's tax return as dividends are distributed) – putting the stock in a charitable remainder trust will cause the company to lose its S designation.

There are also drawbacks to donating closely held stock to a private foundation. The primary one for donors is that you can deduct only the basis, or initial cost, of the shares – not the fair market value. Another potential tax trap is unrelated business taxable income, or UBTI, which falls outside the tax-exempt status charities usually enjoy. Without careful planning, some donors have been unpleasantly surprised to learn that their gifts of privately held company stock to a private foundation gave rise to taxable income, defeating one purpose of making the gift in the first place.

When making charitable donations, you must also be mindful of certain restrictions imposed by law or IRS rules. If a donor has a binding obligation to sell the company before giving the stock to charity, some courts have found that the donor must pay tax on the gain. To avoid running afoul of this pre-arranged sale rule, there must still be a chance that the deal could be called off. Another caveat: Penalties might apply when a private foundation or a charitable trust enters into a transaction that involves its contributor or certain of her relatives.

Some children are involved in the company and others are not. Parents sometimes ask children who work in the business to pay for at least part of the shares they are receiving. These arrangements are most common in situations when the parent does not have other, comparable assets to give any children not working in the company.

Whether you choose just one of these strategies or use them in combination, it is best to start with the least complicated approach that will achieve your goals. Lawyers' fees for these transactions can range from less than $10,000 to many multiples of that sum, depending on the details. And any time you give away shares of a business, you should get an appraisal, which can easily cost $5,000 or more.

How Will Your Family Pay Estate Taxes?

In the past, estate taxes have presented difficulties for family business owners, particularly when the business is illiquid. Normally heirs must pay estate tax within nine months of the death of the senior family member. A substantial estate tax bill could force heirs to sell off key assets or even lose the company. Loans for this purpose may be hard to get in a tight credit market.

These issues may seem less troublesome now that we can each transfer $5.43 million tax-free, but if taxes might still be an issue, one possibility is to buy life insurance that would cover the tax bill. You should start by setting up an irrevocable life insurance trust, which can buy the policy and, when you die, hold the proceeds for whomever you have named as beneficiary. If, instead, you are the owner of the policy, it would be considered part of your estate and the proceeds could be taxed.

Next, you need to funnel money into the trust so it can pay the premiums. Your contribution does not count against the lifetime limit as long as you stay within the annual exclusion, with no limit on the number of trust beneficiaries – each counts as one recipient. (Other techniques for financing premiums were discussed in Chapter 8.)

Depending on the circumstances, your family may also be able to elect to pay the estate tax in installments. Although the rules are complex, Section 6166 of the Internal Revenue Code extends the deadline for payment of tax attributable to a closely held business that makes up more than 35 percent of an estate. Normally, heirs must pay estate tax within nine months of the death of the senior family member. An estate that makes a Section 6166 election on its tax return can stretch payments over as many as 15 years. During the first four years, it can make interest-only payments. After that, the tax and any interest due can be paid in up to 10 equal installments. Although the interest is not deductible, special rates make this an attractive option.

Unfortunately, the definition of closely held business contained in Section 6166 is very narrow: A closely held business is one with no more than 45 shareholders. But under the American Jobs Creation Act of 2004, a company with up to 100 shareholders can qualify as an S corporation. That means many S corporations can't take advantage of Section 6166.

An alternative test to qualify for Section 6166, based on ownership, is also problematic. For partnerships, the estate must own 20 percent of the company's capital to qualify. For corporations, the estate must hold 20 percent of the value of the voting stock.

Finally, the IRS can require a bond ensuring payment of the deferred estate tax or impose a tax lien. Both options could be costly. While the bond would be a direct expense, a tax lien could pose other financial harm, because lenders and customers might take it as a sign that the company is in trouble.

Although families make a Section 6166 election when the business owner dies, you need to plan ahead to make sure the option is available. If an estate is relatively illiquid, for example, make sure the value of the business represents more than 35 percent of the estate. That might mean giving away other assets through lifetime gifts – or limiting your gifts of business interests.

To-Do List

Give Your Family Business
A Stress Test

One way to determine whether your estate plan adequately accounts for your business is to run through a series of "what ifs." If something happened to you, what would be the answer to each of these questions?

❧ Would your company be able to meet payroll, fund retirement benefits and pay other operating expenses?

❧ Is there a family member or trusted employee whom you have groomed to take over?

❧ Would the company be likely to lose clients or customers?

❧ Do you have enough insurance for various purposes?

❧ If estate taxes are due, would your heirs need to sell the business at fire-sale prices in order to pay them?

❧ Could your estate get an extension of the deadline to pay these taxes?

Chapter 13

Hidden Traps
When Crossing
Borders

*Read this chapter if you or a family member
is a citizen of another country,
lives abroad or has foreign investments.*

Various links to foreign countries can affect your estate plan. The issues range from postmortem income tax woes for overseas bank accounts that you didn't disclose while you were alive to estate or inheritance tax on foreign property.

The United States is one of the few countries that impose taxes during life and at death on property anywhere in the world. These rules apply to U.S. citizens, resident aliens and domiciliaries – people who expect to live in a place indefinitely. They may be subject to income tax on money earned anywhere, and estate tax on worldwide assets totaling more than $5.43 million. In some cases, a tax credit may be available for taxes paid to foreign countries.

In This Chapter...

- ⚜ *Offshore Accounts*
- ⚜ *Estate Traps*
- ⚜ *Gifts and Inheritances Across Borders*
- ⚜ *Foreign Trusts*
- ⚜ *Expatriate Tax Rules*

A U.S. resident for income tax purposes is someone who has a green card or who meets what's called the "substantial presence" test. It's a weighted average of the time you spent in the U.S. during three consecutive years: all of the days during the current tax year; 1/3 of the days in the year before that; and 1/6 of the days two years earlier. If the total is more than 183 days, you are a resident for tax purposes.

U.S. residents who are not domiciliaries are subject to gift and estate tax only on transfers of U.S. assets (such as stocks or real estate). Foreigners who do not live in the U.S. (non-resident aliens) may be surprised to find that U.S. assets that they acquire may be subject to tax when those assets are transferred during life or at death.

Offshore Accounts

The Internal Revenue Service is on a continuing crusade against people who avoid taxes by hiding money or assets in unreported offshore accounts. Failure to report the existence of offshore accounts or pay taxes on these accounts can lead to civil and even criminal penalties. There is an increasing risk of getting caught, too, now that the Foreign Account Tax Compliance Act (FATCA), which took effect in 2014, requires foreign financial institutions to report accounts held by "U.S. persons" to the IRS. (Federal regulations define a U.S. person as a U.S. citizen or a resident alien who holds a green card.)

Heirs have inherited huge tax debts not only from relatives who were flagrant tax cheats, but also from those who didn't report certain assets, or, in advanced age, forgot to file altogether. Complex statutes of limitation make it conceivable that tax trouble will crop up a decade or more after someone dies. At that point, if the estate has no money left to pay the tax bill, the IRS can pursue heirs individually – it's called transferee liability – up to the amount of the inheritance.

You may have legitimate reasons for maintaining foreign bank and other financial accounts, but you must disclose them on a Foreign Bank Account Report, known as the FBAR, if they total more than $10,000. This requirement applies not only to owners, but also to inheritors and anyone with "signatory authority" over the account. Surprise: An adult child with power of attorney on her elderly parents' foreign accounts must file her own FBAR, even if she never took any action on the account, according to an Internal Revenue Service manual. Failure to file an FBAR is punishable with steep penalties – up to half of the account's value for each year of non-filing – and can even be criminal if a violation is willful. The FBAR is due by June 30 with no extensions allowed, and must be filed electronically with the Treasury Department's Financial Crimes Enforcement Network, known as FinCEN.

If you haven't been reporting these accounts up until now, do yourself – and your heirs – a favor by coming clean. Here are ways to do that.

The Offshore Voluntary Disclosure Program (OVDP). Under this IRS program, a taxpayer (or his estate) has to pay eight years of back income taxes, interest and penalties, plus a separate FBAR penalty, which, for most people, equals 27.5 percent of the highest balance of the account during the past eight years. Going into OVDP protects you from criminal charges, but you're ineligible for the program if you're already under audit or the government knows about your account.

For heirs, this program offers some finality. Otherwise, years later the IRS could demand more back taxes and penalties with heirs on the hook for up to the amount they inherited. Compared with that, OVDP may, in effect, be cheap insurance.

Streamlined filing compliance. While OVDP protects you from prosecution, this option does not. It requires a taxpayer (or his estate) to pay only three years of back taxes, file six years' worth of FBARs and pay an FBAR penalty equal to 5 percent of the account's highest end-of-the-year value during the last six years. (Expats can escape the 5 percent penalty altogether.) The catch? To qualify, you must certify that previous lapses resulted from "non-willful" conduct, which the IRS vaguely defines as "negligence, inadvertence, or mistake or conduct that is the result of a good faith misunderstanding of the requirements of the law."

"Quiet disclosure." This comes under the heading of what the IRS calls "delinquent FBAR submission procedures." You send the IRS amended back tax returns, including the FBAR, and a check. The idea is that you're reporting everything without calling attention to what you have done. But the risk, if the IRS discovers your delinquency, is huge, since it can assess the maximum FBAR penalty. With quiet disclosure you don't get criminal protection, either. And it's not an option if the IRS has already contacted you for an examination or asked for delinquent returns for the years in question.

Comply only going forward. Like everyone else with overseas accounts, answer "Yes" to the question on Schedule B of the Form 1040, "Did you have a financial interest in or signature authority over a financial account (such as a bank account, securities account, or brokerage account) located in a foreign county?" and file the FBAR, if required. People who comply in the future without making up for the past are gambling that an understaffed IRS won't audit their old 1040s. But beware: Although ordinarily the statute of limitations is three years, if you haven't filed an FBAR, it never starts to run. So, at least in theory, the IRS could come after you at any time.

Estate Traps

Suppose you have kept a foreign bank account that you set up during an overseas posting or are thinking of buying a retirement home in the French countryside. Since U.S. estate tax applies to your worldwide assets, both could be taxed if you leave behind total assets worth more than the $5.43 million that you can transfer during life or at death. If you give those foreign assets while you are alive to anyone other than a spouse who is a U.S. citizen, you will have to pay gift tax if the total value of your gifts exceeds the tax-free amount.

There's also the possibility of double tax on your overseas assets: inheritance tax in the country where they are situated, as well as U.S. estate tax. Only 17 countries have estate or gift-tax treaties with the U.S. that may prevent or minimize double taxation: Australia, Austria, Canada, Denmark, Finland, France, Germany, Greece, Ireland, Italy, Japan, the Netherlands, Norway, South Africa, Sweden, Switzerland and the United Kingdom.

> ## Did You Know?
>
> If you plan to spend time overseas and buy or sell real estate, transact business or open a bank account, you need a durable power of attorney that's valid in that country. This document appoints an agent to act on your behalf in case of physical or mental disability.

Forced heirship rules in some countries are another issue that may arise. These rules, which are designed to avoid disinheritance of a spouse or child, give that person a preset share of what you leave behind. Where forced heirship rules exist, they can frustrate estate planning strategies that are popular in the U.S. For example, if you have children, you may not be able to leave foreign real estate entirely to your spouse – something you would typically do in order to take advantage of the unlimited marital deduction that U.S. law affords (as discussed in Chapter 3).

If, instead, you must leave part of the property to your children and their portion is worth more than the $5.43 million federal exemption (or the state exemption if you live in a state with a separate estate tax), the foreign property could be subject to estate tax in the U.S. Were it not for the forced heirship law, you would be able to avoid that tax when the first of you dies by leaving the entire property to the surviving U.S. citizen spouse.

Likewise, an estate planning tool used to avoid inheritance tax in certain foreign countries – retaining the right to live in a house while you are alive and giving your children a remainder interest in the property after that – would be ineffective for U.S. estate tax purposes. In fact, this arrangement would cause the entire value of the property to be included in your estate. Owning real estate abroad, therefore, requires coordination between your estate planning lawyer in the U.S. and a knowledgeable adviser in the country where the property is situated. It may be possible to avoid both foreign tax and inheritance laws by putting the foreign property into a foreign corporation. That way the assets are owned by the corporate entity you create rather than by you directly. However, local taxes may be imposed on such transfers.

Did You Know?

Certain assets, including U.S. equities, real estate and tangible personal property in the U.S., are subject to U.S. gift tax, estate tax and generation-skipping transfer tax when they are transferred, even if both the owner and the gift recipients are non-resident aliens.

Another question that arises is whether you need a separate will just to cover valuable property in a foreign country, prepared in that country in accordance with its laws. This greatly complicates and adds to the cost of your estate planning and should be avoided if possible.

Some countries have entered into multinational treaties requiring certain formalities in preparing and signing a will and recognizing the validity of wills done in participating countries. The U.S. is a signatory to one such treaty, known as the Washington Convention, though the Senate has not ratified it and only 27 states have adopted it in their probate law. You might need a separate will if your assets are in a country that has not signed the treaty or in other special situations, such as when a country's succession rules are inconsistent with your estate planning goals. Trusts, for example, are rarely or never used in many countries.

Another reason to write a separate will is if you are expecting an inheritance battle; the will can include provisions, based on local law, that can minimize or avoid the kinds of problems that you anticipate.

Gifts and Inheritances Across Borders

Certain assets, including U.S. equities, real estate and tangible personal property in the U.S., will be subject to U.S. gift tax, federal estate tax (and possibly state estate tax) and generation-skipping transfer tax when they are transferred, even if both the owner and the gift recipients are non-resident aliens. Many people are not aware of this. For example, if an Indian citizen who is a resident of Mumbai dies owning a condominium in New York, his children cannot inherit that property, regardless of their nationality, until they have paid both federal and state estate tax.

Tax on transfers from foreigners. Foreigners are not eligible for the $5.43 million exclusion amount. When they transfer interests in U.S. property during life, they must pay gift tax if the value of a gift is more than the $14,000 annual exclusion. Gifts in excess of that amount are taxed, based on their aggregate value during the foreigner's lifetime, at a rate of up to 40 percent. An exception applies when the gifts are made to a spouse who is a U.S. citizen; in that case, the unlimited gift-tax marital deduction applies (as noted in Chapter 3).

Transfers through an estate plan get a credit of $14,000 (in effect, an exemption of $60,000 because of the graduated estate tax rates that apply in this context). For amounts above that, an estate tax of up to 40 percent applies. Here, too, there's an unlimited marital deduction for assets inherited by a spouse who is a U.S. citizen.

But these taxes can be easily avoided if a foreigner acquires and holds the assets through a corporation situated in a jurisdiction that does not have estate or income tax (such as Bermuda or the Cayman Islands) rather than owning them directly. That converts what would otherwise be considered U.S. assets into offshore corporate assets, which aren't subject to U.S. estate tax. Another advantage is privacy, because the shareholder of record is the corporation, not an individual.

Connecting

Ties to a foreign country can affect the tax on transfers during life and through who owns the assets, where they are situated and who is receiving them.

Whom does the tax cover?	What assets does the tax cover?
U.S. citizens/domiciliaries	Worldwide
Foreigners (non-resident aliens or resident aliens who are not domiciliaries)	U.S. equities, real estate and tangible personal property
Expatriates who gave up U.S. citizenship after June 17, 2008	Worldwide

*Unlimited marital gift-tax deduction or estate tax deduction applies to transfers to a spouse who is a U.S. citizen.

the Dots

your estate plan. The tax that applies in a given situation may depend on

When does the tax apply?	How much is exempt?	Tax rate (once exemptions exceeded)
• Lifetime gifts	• $14,000 annual exclusion • $147,000 annual exclusion gift to non-citizen spouse • $5.43 million lifetime exemption*	Up to 40%
• Bequests	• $5.43 million*	Up to 40%
• Lifetime gifts	• $14,000 annual exclusion*	Up to 40%
• Bequests	• $14,000 credit*	Up to 40%
• Lifetime gifts to U.S. persons	• $14,000 annual exclusion*	Highest rate in effect
• Bequests to U.S. persons	• $14,000	Highest rate in effect

Often shares in the corporation are owned, in turn, not by individuals but by an offshore trust that is also situated in a tax-friendly jurisdiction. The trust can shield the assets from creditors and provide for distributions under its terms, both during life and afterward. This can avoid tax on the assets by either the U.S. or the foreigner's home country. It also can avoid forced heirship in countries that have such rules.

Different rules apply when the transfers do not involve U.S. property. These assets are generally not subject to gift or estate tax. So, for example, a U.S. person could receive a gift or inheritance of any amount from her Canadian father and not have to pay any U.S. tax (though there may be foreign tax implications).

Did You Know?

Planning is more complex if your spouse is not a U.S. citizen. You can't rely on the unlimited gift-tax and estate tax marital deduction and neither of you can benefit from portability. Annual gifts to your spouse of more than $147,000 count against the $5.43 million lifetime limit.

However, money coming into the U.S. is tightly regulated, and it may be necessary to report the gift or inheritance even if there is no tax on it. Consider the U.S. child with a Canadian father: If the amount she receives in a given year from him and any other non-resident aliens and foreign estates totals more than $100,000, she must report them to the Internal Revenue Service on Form 3520.

Why? The IRS is on the lookout for income masquerading as gifts and wants to decide for itself, based on the information you supply, whether what you received is taxable income rather than a non-taxable gift. Assuming the transfer is indeed a gift, no tax will be due, but you must still file the form – there is a penalty of up to 35 percent of the amount of the gift if you are required to file the return and don't. The reporting requirement does not include direct payments of tuition or medical expenses, which are discussed in Chapters 9 and 10.

A much smaller threshold – $15,601 in 2015, indexed for inflation – applies to gifts received from foreign partnerships, foreign trusts or foreign corporations. The rule covers funds you receive directly, as well as money doled out on your behalf, such as the payment of credit card bills.

Thinking ahead, if you are a U.S. citizen or green card holder and expect a significant gift or inheritance of non-U.S. assets from a resident of a foreign country, you should set up a trust to receive it. That prevents the gift or inheritance from later being taxed as part of your own estate.

Transfers to a non-citizen spouse. If your spouse is not a U.S. citizen, you will not be able to rely on the unlimited gift-tax and estate tax marital deduction, and neither of you can benefit from portability (discussed in Chapter 3). Annual gifts to your spouse of more than $147,000 (indexed for inflation) count against the $5.43 million lifetime exemption.

Assume Lucy, an American, marries Ricky, a Cuban who has a green card, and they live in Miami. If Lucy dies first and leaves Ricky more than $5.43 million, anything above that limit is immediately subject to tax of 40 percent unless it goes into a special kind of trust, called a qualified domestic trust, or QDOT. If this trust distributes principal, it must withhold estate tax – at the rate that was in effect when Lucy died. (When Ricky receives distributions of income, they are subject to income tax but not estate tax.) The QDOT was discussed extensively in Chapter 3.

In contrast, if Ricky gives or leaves property to Lucy, these transfers are entitled to the unlimited marital gift-tax or estate tax deduction. Therefore, a QDOT to benefit Lucy is not necessary.

Complications arise when you own property jointly with rights of survivorship or in tenancy by the entirety, two forms of title discussed in Chapters 3, 4 and 17. Typically, when spouses own property this way, only half its value is included in the estate of the first to die, but a different rule applies when one of them is not a U.S. citizen.

For real estate, the tax treatment in this situation depends on when the couple acquired the property. If it was after July 14, 1988, the whole property is included in the estate of the first to die unless the survivor can show how much he contributed to the purchase price. In that case, what is counted as part of the estate would be reduced to reflect the portion that he paid. For real estate bought before 1988, state law determines how each spouse's interest is calculated.

Likewise, if the property is sold or the couple ends the joint ownership arrangement by putting title in just one of their names, any proceeds or share in excess of what the recipient contributed is considered a gift. The non-citizen spouse can make this transfer to the citizen spouse without paying gift tax (just like Ricky's gifts to Lucy). But if annual gifts from the citizen spouse to the non-citizen spouse exceed $147,000 (indexed for inflation), it counts against the $5.43 million lifetime gift-tax exemption.

Similar issues arise with joint bank accounts or brokerage accounts that give each spouse the right to make withdrawals freely. If either spouse takes out more than the portion he or she put in, it's considered a gift. And when one spouse dies, his contribution and share of the appreciation is considered part of his estate. These rules make it very difficult for spouses to hold valuable property as joint owners when one is a citizen and the other is not.

Foreign Trusts

From a tax perspective, U.S. citizens and resident aliens who hold a green card are better off being beneficiaries of domestic trusts than foreign ones, but under federal rules, a trust could easily be characterized as a foreign one instead. To make matters worse, U.S. beneficiaries can get nailed with taxes on foreign trust earnings, and the law on who falls into this category is very broad.

Unless the trust is a grantor trust – one in which the person creating the trust retains certain rights or powers – it typically pays the income tax on its earnings but takes a deduction for net income (income minus expenses) distributed to beneficiaries. With non-grantor foreign trusts, however, the trust pays tax only on income that comes from a U.S. source, such as dividends from corporations, rents from real estate or capital gains from the sale of real estate. In contrast, U.S. beneficiaries of these trusts are taxed on all distributions of income, including income from capital gains, whether it comes from a U.S. source or a foreign one. And any time a U.S. person transfers property to a foreign trust, there's a presumption under federal law (very hard to overcome) that it has a U.S. beneficiary.

Likewise, the scale tips toward foreign trusts more often than some people realize. Under the Internal Revenue Code, a trust is treated as a domestic trust only if it meets both these criteria: a U.S. court can exercise primary supervision over the administration of the trust (the "court test") and one or more U.S. persons have the power to control all substantial decisions of the trust (the "control test"). Under the regulations, "substantial decisions" include whether and when to distribute income or principal; the amount of any distribution; whether to remove, add or replace a trustee; and the power to make investment decisions. A trust can have a foreign investment adviser without being considered a foreign trust if the adviser can be dismissed by the U.S. trustee.

If a trust flunks either test, it is considered a foreign trust. The fact that the trust says the laws of a particular state apply to it or that it was created under a will that was probated in a U.S. state doesn't change the result.

How might you inadvertently turn a domestic trust into a foreign one? Having a foreigner serve as a trustee with the power to make substantial decisions is one way, for example, when non-resident aliens set up trusts to provide for U.S. beneficiaries. Their inclination might be to name a family member from the home country as trustee. That could make the trust a foreign trust.

The IRS is on the lookout for foreign trusts. On the annual federal income tax return, you must indicate whether you have received distributions from foreign trusts during the past year or whether you set up or transferred any funds into one of these trusts. If so, you must report that on Form 3520, filed with the return. The penalty for not filing is 35 percent of the distribution. Other penalties apply if the trust distributes accumulated income from previous years.

Expatriate Tax Rules

Tax law discourages people from expatriating just to avoid taxes. Two provisions of the tax code, added in 2008 through the Heroes Earnings Assistance and Relief Tax Act of 2008 (the so-called HEART legislation), could have a significant impact on expatriates or U.S. persons who receive gifts or inheritances from them.

Who's covered? These provisions apply to someone who expatriates on or after June 17, 2008, by giving up his citizenship or, in the case of long-term residents (those who have spent at least 8 of the 15 years before expatriating living in the U.S.), by giving up his green card, if in either case they fit at least one of these descriptions:

⚜ Their average annual income tax for the previous five years was more than a specified amount ($160,000 for 2015), adjusted for inflation

⚜ Their net worth is $2 million or more (including interests in trusts)

⚜ They fail to certify, under penalty of perjury, that they have complied with the tax law during the previous five years

There are exceptions for certain minors and for those who have been dual citizens since birth who remain a citizen of another country at the time of expatriation and have not been U.S. residents for more than 10 of the last 15 years before expatriating.

What's the tax pain? When you expatriate, the law imposes an exit tax on your worldwide property (not just your U.S. assets), including property in a trust if you are the grantor. Whether or not you sell that property when you expatriate, it is treated as if you had on the day before you expatriated, and there is capital gains tax due on appreciation of more than a certain amount ($690,000 for 2015), adjusted for inflation. If you want to defer that tax until the asset is actually sold or you die, you must make a deal with the IRS – for example, by posting a bond.

Certain interests in deferred compensation plans and trusts that you did not set up are not subject to the exit tax. Instead, there is a 30 percent withholding tax on payments from these plans or trusts as you receive them.

Perhaps more importantly, once you expatriate, there's a steep tax when you benefit U.S. citizens or residents through lifetime gifts, distributions from trusts that you have set up or bequests under your estate plan. (Note that, in this context, the income and net worth thresholds are applied as of the date of a gift or immediately before death, not at the time of expatriation.) Anything they receive that exceeds the $14,000 annual exclusion amount (indexed for inflation) is subject to gift tax or estate tax at the highest rate in effect at the time. Recipients, whether they are individuals or U.S. trusts, are liable for the tax unless you have filed a gift-tax return or your estate has filed an estate tax return. Payments that would qualify for the unlimited marital deduction are not subject to this requirement (again, special rules apply if your spouse is not a U.S. citizen).

There is no $5.43 million gift-tax or estate tax exclusion in this context. If you are planning to expatriate, you should consider using at least part of that exclusion to make gifts to friends or family before you do. Otherwise, the tax-free amount will be lost when you expatriate.

To-Do List

Get the Right Advisers on Your Team

International estate planning is a highly specialized field. Although most competent trust and estate lawyers could handle the basic issues involving a U.S. citizen who is married to someone who isn't, for anything more complex, it pays to consult a sub-specialist (for general advice on finding a lawyer, see Chapter 18). You may also need whomever you choose to coordinate with advisers in the country where you live, own assets or have family. You should seek an international estate planning expert if you are:

❧ A U.S. citizen or green card holder and expect a significant gift or inheritance from someone who is a resident of a foreign country

❧ A U.S. citizen or green card holder and the beneficiary of a foreign trust

❧ A U.S. citizen or green card holder and the grantor of a trust that names a foreigner as trustee

❧ A U.S. citizen or green card holder and own or are about to buy property, such as real estate or business interests, in a foreign country

❧ Planning to live abroad – for example, to work or retire – but still consider the U.S. your home country

❧ Thinking of giving up your U.S. citizenship or green card

❧ An expatriate and plan to make a significant gift or bequest to a U.S. person

❧ A citizen and resident of another country and own or are about to buy U.S. equities, real estate or tangible personal property

❧ A citizen and resident of another country and want to benefit a family member who is coming to the U.S. to work or study or who is a U.S. citizen or green card holder

Chapter 14

What You Can Do For Grandchildren

*Read this chapter if you would like
to provide a financial cushion for your
descendants in the years ahead.*

There are many ways to make gifts to grandchildren. The possibilities range from cash gifts to various ways of financing tuition and medical expenses to complex trusts that can offer grandchildren and subsequent generations a financial cushion for the rest of their lives. These techniques give you a chance to give away money gradually, as grandchildren's needs change and as you feel comfortable parting with the funds. Wealthy people can also take advantage of some devices to move significant sums downstream tax-free.

As you know from earlier chapters, when you make lifetime gifts, you need to be concerned about gift tax. When you transfer assets at death, estate tax may be an issue. Any time you give assets directly to grandchildren, or set up or add assets to trusts that benefit this generation or future ones, you need to plan for the 40 percent generation-skipping transfer, or GST, tax. This tax applies on top of the other two taxes.

In This Chapter...

- ♣ *Gifts That Don't Count*
- ♣ *A Trust for One Skip Person*
- ♣ *When – and How – to Apply The GST Exemption*
- ♣ *Pitfalls in Existing Plans*

GST tax is relevant whenever you make transfers, during life or at death, to what are called skip persons. Within a family, this means anyone other than your spouse who is two or more generations younger than you. Outside of the family, it covers anyone who is more than 37.5 years younger than you. A skip may be direct, meaning that the assets immediately go down at least two generations (for example, a grandmother gives her diamond ring to her granddaughter), or indirect, so that an earlier generation gets a share first – as would happen with a trust that provides payouts first to children and then to grandchildren.

GST tax can be imposed at one of two junctures. Perhaps the easiest to identify is when transfers are made to a skip person. These transfers can take various forms. They can involve a direct skip – such as when you make an outright gift to an individual or put money into a trust that exclusively benefits skip persons. Or there may be a taxable distribution: for example, when a trust that benefits both skip persons and older family members makes a payout to a skip person. Generally, with a direct skip, you or your estate pay any GST tax; with a taxable distribution, the recipient pays it.

The other type of event that could generate GST tax is what's known as a taxable termination. This is when the interests of all non-skip persons in a trust have ended, and skip persons are the remaining beneficiaries. For example, in a trust set up to pay income to your child for life and then give principal to the grandchildren, there could be a taxable termination when your child dies, because only grandchildren are eligible for trust payments. When there's a taxable termination, the GST tax is paid by the trustee using funds in the trust.

Generation-skipping transfer tax does not generally apply to you if a grandchild's parent (your own child) dies before you make a gift or create a trust. Under this exception to the usual rule, the child's share is treated as if it drops directly to the grandchild rather than skipping a generation.

There are several ways to avoid or minimize GST tax, which was given its current form in 1986. Certain types of gifts don't

The Back of the Envelope

Let's say you have a $7 million estate and leave everything to your grandchildren. Together, estate tax of $628,000 and generation-skipping transfer (GST) tax of $269,143 reduce the inheritance to $6,102,857.

What's the calculation? You can do the multistep process on the back of an envelope.

Step 1: Apply the $5,430,000 estate tax exclusion to the $7 million estate. On the remaining $1,570,000, there's a 40 percent estate tax = $628,000.

Step 2: Subtract the $628,000 estate tax from the $7 million estate before you compute the generation-skipping transfer tax. The result is $6,372,000.

Step 3: Allocate, or apply, the $5,430,000 generation-skipping transfer tax exemption to $6,372,000. The amount that isn't covered, $942,000, is your base for GST tax.

Step 4: With a little algebra, subtract the tax from the tax base before you calculate the 40 percent tax (so you don't pay GST tax on the tax).
x (GST tax) = 40 percent ($942,000 minus x)
GST tax = $269,143
Total tax = $269,143 + $628,000 = $897,143

Source: Lawrence P. Katzenstein, Tiger Tables Actuarial Software

count as generation-skipping transfers at all, so no GST tax is associated with them. There is also a special type of trust that you can fund without paying GST tax, so long as you make your contributions using the gift-tax annual exclusion, discussed on page 234. (Under these conditions, money distributed from the trust is not subject to the tax, either.) And for anything that doesn't fit within these categories, each of us has a $5.43 million GST tax exemption that we can use before the tax even kicks in. Here, too, married couples can combine their exemption amounts but only for lifetime gifts. Widows and widowers cannot carry over an unused portion of the GST exemption, the way they can with the amount that's free of estate tax. (This process, known as portability, was discussed in Chapter 3.)

But let's say this kind of wealth transfer strategy is out of the question for you (it certainly is for most people) – maybe you don't expect to give your grandchildren more than a tiny fraction of the GST exemption amount. In that case, you might get the impression that you don't even need to think about this subject. That would be a mistake – just the kind of mistake that causes people to have to pay the GST tax unexpectedly. A common blunder is setting up a trust that could benefit members of an older generation and grandchildren while not allocating, or applying, at least part of your exemption to the trust at that time. What could happen? If the value of the trust assets increases dramatically, you might not have enough exemption left to cover that amount along with any other gifts you have made. This would cause a GST tax as grandchildren receive distributions or there's a taxable termination.

GST planning can help you avoid such mishaps and take advantage of the many opportunities to benefit grandchildren without having to pay the tax.

Gifts That Don't Count

C ertain types of gifts commonly made to grandchildren are exempt from
GST tax. They include the following.

Cash gifts that come within the annual exclusion. You are allowed to
give $14,000 in cash or other assets each year to as many individuals as
you want without having to worry about gift or GST tax. Married couples
can combine this annual exclusion to jointly give $28,000 to any number of
people tax-free – a practice known as gift-splitting. There are three ways to
gift-split: each give $14,000 from an individual account; give $28,000 from a
joint account; or give $28,000 from one of your accounts (the rules on filing
gift-tax returns are discussed in Chapter 15).

Any gift to a grandchild that's more than the annual exclusion counts
against both the GST exemption and the lifetime gift-tax exemption – the
amount that each individual can give away during life without having to
pay gift tax. Once you have passed the limit, which is $5.43 million
($10.86 million for married couples), gift tax of 40 percent applies.

If the grandchildren are minors, their portion of a cash gift would often go
into a custodial account that designates an adult to oversee the money until
the child is able to withdraw the assets under state law (usually at age 18
or 21). You should not name yourself as the custodian, because the money
plus any appreciation could be considered part of your estate. You can name
the child's parent, who can use the fund to pay for what might otherwise be
unaffordable extras, such as dance lessons, summer camp and after-school
programs. If you are concerned that the assets may fall into a child's hands
too soon, the gift can be made in a specially designed trust. (How to deal with
custodial accounts that have grown too large was discussed in Chapter 9.)

Contributions to college savings plans. Another way to apply the
grandchildren's portion of the annual exclusion is to put money in Section 529 education savings plans (discussed extensively in Chapter 9).
You can set up a separate account for each family member whom you
wish to benefit. Money in a 529 account is federal-tax-exempt, provided it
is withdrawn to pay for college, graduate, vocational or other accredited
school and for related expenses.

The law permits lump-sum deposits into Section 529 plans of as much as $70,000 per person at once ($140,000 for married couples), but you must file a gift-tax return electing to treat the gift as if it had been spread over five years. If you die before the end of five years, the portion of the gift reflecting the number of years remaining will be included in your estate. During this five-year period, you cannot make additional annual exclusion gifts to the person you are benefiting with the 529 plan.

Direct payments for medical, dental and tuition expenses. Without using your annual exclusion or $5.43 million lifetime exemption from gift tax, you can pay for tuition and unreimbursed dental and medical expenses of anyone you want. These payments are exempt from both gift tax and GST tax no matter how much you spend. But you must make the payments directly to the accredited providers of those services (as discussed in Chapter 10).

You can make tuition payments at any stage, from preschool to graduate school, as long as you write the check directly to the institution. Tuition may be paid annually or pre-paid for multiple years. The risk of pre-paying is that the payments must be non-refundable, according to the Internal Revenue Service, and could be forfeited if the child winds up not going to that school or not completing his or her education there.

A Trust for One Skip Person

By far the most popular way of making gifts to grandchildren is to put assets in a trust, because a trust generally provides the greatest flexibility and control over how the funds will be distributed. Unfortunately, this is also the most difficult terrain to negotiate.

The first strategic decision is whether you can accomplish your goals with a special kind of trust that will not cause generation-skipping transfer tax, so you can save the GST exemption for other gifts. Section 2642(c) of the Internal Revenue Code describes the requirements for a trust that generally does not give rise to GST tax.

The trust must be irrevocable and can benefit only one skip person – for example, a grandchild. If the grandchild dies before the funds have been fully distributed, the trust must say that the remaining funds become part of the grandchild's estate (making them tax vested – potentially subject to estate tax at that point).

Most estate planners meet this last requirement by giving the grandchild what's called a general power of appointment: the right to name the next person to receive the trust property. Unless the grandchild is married and wants to be sure the interest will go to his spouse, that power doesn't usually get exercised. Anticipating that the power probably won't be exercised, the trust usually has a general provision directing how the assets should be distributed if the beneficiary dies before the funds are completely paid out. Typically, the assets will go to other grandchildren.

But setting up the perfect Section 2642(c) trust is not enough. As noted above, adding more money to the trust than is covered by the gift-tax annual exclusion is a direct skip, requiring you to pay GST tax for the transfer to the trust (though not for distributions from the trust to the skip person) if you don't have enough GST exemption to cover it. But you can avoid the need to pay the GST tax or use your GST exemption if the gift itself is exempt from GST tax. Gifts that use the gift-tax annual exclusion accomplish this goal. When you fund a Section 2642(c) trust using these gifts, the gift to the trust does not use your GST exemption or give rise to a GST tax.

As discussed in Chapter 10, to come within the annual exclusion, a gift must be a present interest rather than a future interest. There are two ways for gifts to trusts to meet this requirement. By far the most popular is to give beneficiaries Crummey powers: the right for a limited time, usually 30 or 60 days, to withdraw from the trust the yearly gift attributable to that beneficiary. Each year, the trustees notify the beneficiaries (or the parents, if the beneficiaries are minors), in what is called a Crummey notice, that they have the right to withdraw their portion of the annual gift to the trust. Any trust that includes this power is called a Crummey trust, although the trust may be named for its other distinguishing features (for example, "a Section 2642(c) trust with Crummey powers").

You can also meet the present interest requirement through a Section 2503(c) trust, discussed in Chapter 9. Like a Section 2642(c) trust, these trusts must have only one beneficiary and must be subject to estate tax when he dies. The main difference between the two is that the beneficiary of a Section 2503(c) trust must have the right at age 21 to withdraw all the assets (although there are ways to persuade the child to leave the assets in the trust), and there must be no restriction on the right of the trustee to make distributions of principal and interest before that.

A common way of leveraging the annual exclusion amount in trusts to benefit grandchildren is to fund the trust with the proceeds of a life insurance policy. In this case, the 2642(c) trust would also be an irrevocable life insurance trust, or ILIT, described in Chapter 8. The trust buys life insurance on behalf of an older family member and holds the proceeds, when that person dies, for the beneficiaries. The named insured can be the grandparent or even the child's parent. The annual exclusion gift is only the money you put into the trust to finance the premium, not the full policy proceeds.

When there are multiple grandchildren, a trust for each of their benefits can buy a separate policy on the same person's life – say it's Grandpa's. Alternatively, a number of trusts can, in effect, function as partners, sharing the premiums and proceeds from a single policy.

However you choose to fund Section 2642(c) trusts, they are not appropriate for every situation. For example, because these trusts can benefit only grandchildren, you can't use them when you want the child's parents to receive benefits under the trust before the funds get distributed to grandchildren. Nor are they appropriate when you want the flexibility of being able to shift assets among your grandchildren, as the need arises – for example, to help pay for education or a first home. To accomplish these goals and many other purposes that trusts can serve (discussed in Chapter 6), you will need to consider the more complicated structure of a non-exempt trust – a trust that would trigger tax if you did not allocate your exemption to it, or if you had already used up the exemption.

When – and How –
To Apply the GST Exemption

The GST exemption can be applied to an outright transfer or to a non-exempt trust. This might be a trust that has older family members (like your spouse or children) as the primary beneficiaries but that could benefit grandchildren afterward. Or it might be a dynasty trust, which can go on in perpetuity in the states, including Alaska, Delaware, South Dakota and Wisconsin, that permit them. You do not need to be a resident of one of these states to choose that state as the situs, or location, of a trust. This

A Variety of Choices for Tax-

Certain gifts can be used in combination, *if* you don't exceed the annual

	When does grandchild have direct access to the funds?	Does gift qualify for the annual exclusion?
Outright gift	Immediately	Yes
Gift to custodial account for a minor	Age 18, 19 or 21, depending on the state	Yes
Direct payment of medical or tuition expenses	Never; payments must go directly to the provider or the institution	Gift doesn't count against annual exclusion or $5.43 million lifetime gift-tax exemption
Gift to Section 529 plan	Never; withdrawals must go directly to college, vocational or graduate school	Yes
Gift to 2642(c) trust	Controlled by terms of the trust	Only if trust is also a Section 2503(c) trust or includes Crummey powers

Free Gifts to Grandchildren

exclusion of $14,000 ($28,000 for married couples).

Can gift exceed the annual exclusion amount?	Is gift exempt from GST tax?
Yes, but counts against $5.43 million gift-tax exemption	Yes, up to annual exclusion amount and above that by allocation of GST exemption to the gift
Yes, but counts against $5.43 million lifetime gift-tax exemption	Yes, up to annual exclusion amount and above that by allocation of GST exemption to the gift
Yes, without counting against $5.43 million lifetime gift-tax exemption	Yes
Yes, up to $70,000 per recipient ($140,000 for spouses) but must elect on gift-tax return to treat it as spread evenly over five years	Yes, up to annual exclusion amount (including lump-sum spread over five years)
Yes, but counts against $5.43 million lifetime gift-tax exemption	Yes, up to the annual exclusion amount, and above that by allocation of the GST exemption to the gift

is done in the trust document, which should choose the same state's law to govern the trust. However, in most cases, you need some connection with the state, such as having a trustee there, in order to be sure that its law will apply. Like certain other trusts discussed in this book, dynasty trusts can be structured so that while the property is in the trust it should not be subject to estate tax, either.

Although tax law provides for automatic allocation for lifetime transfers to trusts that fit its definition of GST trusts, it's not always clear whether a particular trust fits. To be on the safe side and have a record of what you wanted to do, you should make the allocation when first transferring funds to a trust you want to be a GST-exempt trust. After that, you can elect to have it treated as a GST trust and have the exemption automatically allocated to all future transfers to that trust.

Conversely, if for some reason you don't want a trust to be treated as a GST trust even though it may fall within the law's definition, you can make a one-time election not to treat it as one. The place to make the allocation – or opt out of it – is on Form 709, the federal gift-tax return that is due on April 15 of the year after you make your gifts.

What if you already funded a trust and forgot to make the allocation? If the assets haven't appreciated in value (or have declined), you might be fine making a late allocation. Otherwise, you would typically need to get a ruling from the IRS – a costly procedure – granting you an extension of time to make your allocation. If you succeed, your allocation would be considered timely and could reflect the value of the assets when you put them into the trust.

A classic GST pitfall that the law only partially addresses involves the problems that surround the premature death of a trust beneficiary. Say you set up a trust to pay income to your son until age 35, at which time the son gets the principal. You wouldn't normally allocate the GST exemption to such a trust because you would expect the son to survive to 35, and you might want to use your GST exemption elsewhere. But if the son dies before then and has children, the trust assets would go to your grandchildren, creating a taxable termination.

Because such a trust doesn't fit the definition of a GST trust, there wouldn't have been automatic allocation to it. But if you still have GST exemption left, you can elect to allocate it retroactively to the trust. You would do this on a gift-tax return filed on time for the year in which the child died.

Another issue you need to consider when setting up GST trusts is the inclusion ratio – generally the portion of assets in a given trust that are GST-exempt. Over time, exempt and non-exempt assets can get mixed in the same trust. This can happen when gifts to the trust exceed your GST exemption, for instance. The result is a blended inclusion ratio. In lay terms, the effect is the same as if any distribution to a skip person was partially exempt and partially subject to GST tax.

Estate planners try to design trusts covered by the GST exemption to have what's called a zero inclusion ratio, meaning that it's completely GST-exempt. That way, there isn't any tax on either a taxable distribution or a taxable termination. Other trusts would have an inclusion ratio of one, meaning that they would be entirely subject to GST tax. However, there would be no GST tax when those trusts make distributions for tuition and health care expenses directly to the providers of those services, even to benefit skip persons. These trusts can be extremely useful for that purpose.

Ideally, you would use non-exempt trusts to benefit only non-skip persons, but there is a remedy when trusts have become blended: In many cases you can now split the trust into totally exempt and non-exempt trusts going forward. You don't need to go to court to do this, assuming the terms of the trust or state law allows such a severance. This rule is helpful in planning for new trusts and trying to correct problems in old ones.

Pitfalls in Existing Plans

With even the slightest oversight, generous gifts to grandchildren could be reduced by the onerous GST tax. These other common GST traps may be lurking within your current estate plan.

IRA skips. Leaving individual retirement accounts to grandchildren is a great income tax strategy (discussed in Chapter 7). The main advantage is that the young person can stretch payouts out over his or her life expectancy and thereby defer income tax on the withdrawals.

Just remember that IRAs left to grandchildren may be subject to GST tax in addition to estate tax and income tax. (Beneficiaries are entitled to an income tax deduction for the portion of the estate tax and, in some cases, for GST tax attributable to an inherited IRA.) As with any other asset, an IRA left to the owner's child could be hit with GST tax if the child disclaims, or turns down, the inheritance, passing it to a grandchild.

If you don't have more effective ways to use your GST exemption, you might choose to generation-skip an IRA. This might appeal to people who are not extremely wealthy but happen to have sizable IRAs, whose children don't need the money and who are not in a position to make large lifetime gifts.

Formula clauses. If you have not reviewed your estate planning documents lately, you should consider whether there is more money destined for GST trusts than you would like. This could happen if your will includes formula clauses to fund these trusts. Terms like "that portion," "that fraction" or "that amount" (without saying what it is) are signs of lawyers trying to take maximum advantage of the exemption, which kept changing. Instead of naming a specific sum that will go into a trust, many old wills refer to an amount up to the exemption or express the sum as a percentage of whatever the limit happens to be when the person dies.

This used to be good standard practice, but remember that the GST exemption, which went up gradually starting in 2001, is currently $5.43 million. Wills written long ago might not reflect your intentions anymore: Too much may now be going to benefit grandchildren and too little to older family members. If so, you will want to change your plan.

Future gifts. When adding funds to trusts in the future, keep another potential trap in mind: Just because a particular transfer to a trust uses the gift-tax annual exclusion does not mean it is always exempt from GST tax. Unless the trust is a 2642(c) trust, GST exemption needs to be allocated when you add assets to a trust that benefits skip persons. Otherwise, even if there is no GST tax when you make the gift, there could be tax later.

To-Do List

Set Your Priorities

When setting up trusts for grandchildren, discuss these questions with your advisers.

❧ What purposes can the trust funds be used for?

❧ How long should the trust last?

❧ If you have multiple grandchildren, should you have a separate trust for each one?

❧ When should the grandchildren have direct access to the money?

❧ Do you want the trust to benefit children as well as grandchildren?

❧ Who should be the trustee?

❧ What assets are available to fund the trust?

❧ Should you supplement these assets by having the trust buy a life insurance policy on your life?

❧ Should an independent trustee have the power to amend some or all of the trust provisions to anticipate changing family circumstances?

❧ Do you want to pay income taxes on trust assets while you are alive?

Chapter 15

Make Lifetime Gifts Go Further

*Read this chapter if you have
the resources to transfer large
sums of money while you are alive.*

Most chapters of this book include at least some information that will resonate with almost everyone. This chapter focuses on tools that are generally useful only to people whose heirs will be saddled with estate taxes. Now that the federal applicable exclusion amount has been raised to $5.43 million per person, far fewer folks are in this category. In addition to the super-rich, they include less affluent elderly or infirm single people whose net worth is more than $5.43 million, and widows and widowers who lost a spouse before it was possible for married people to carry over each other's unused tax-free amount.

In This Chapter...

- *The Annual Exclusion and Lifetime Exclusion Compared*
- *Trusts That Offer Income Tax Benefits*
- *GRATs Explained*
- *Using Family Entities to Discount Values*
- *Selling Assets Instead of Giving Them Away*

Methods of reducing or eliminating estate tax involve pruning your net worth through irrevocable transfers that leave less for the government to tax. If the assets increase in value after you have passed them along, the appreciation is received by your heirs free of gift and estate tax. The trade-off is that your heirs could get stuck with substantial capital gains tax (see Chapter 3).

This chapter looks at techniques designed to pack as much value as possible into both the $5.43 million per person lifetime exclusion and the annual exclusion, which allows you each year to give up to $14,000 each to as many people as you choose. Which tools you use depends on: how much you expect the assets to appreciate, your cash flow needs and your tolerance for complexity.

The Annual Exclusion and Lifetime Exclusion Compared

A threshold question for anyone thinking about giving away assets during life is: Can I afford it? First, you should be sure you are leaving yourself enough – and, to be on the safe side, assume that you will live to an advanced age. "How much will I need?" has always been a difficult question with a very personal answer, influenced by both economics and psychology. The financial crisis that began in 2008 continues to have a ripple effect, leaving many people feeling financially shaken.

If, upon reflection, you still want to prune your estate, consider the difference between the annual exclusion and the lifetime exclusion. Here's what you need to know.

Annual exclusion. This is the amount, in cash or other assets, that you can give every year to each of as many individuals as you want, without incurring gift tax. The annual exclusion is currently $14,000 for individuals ($28,000 for married couples). Periodically adjusted for inflation in $1,000 increments, it hasn't been raised since 2013. This is a "use it or lose it" tax break. In other words, if you do not make gifts in a given year, you cannot carry over the exclusion and give more to each person the following year. Other chapters covered the many uses of the annual exclusion – for example, to provide cash to needy family or friends, fund trusts or contribute to Section 529 plans.

To wealthy people who want to cut estate taxes dramatically, gifts of $14,000 per recipient every year may seem like peanuts, but over time the tax savings can add up. Let's say Sally, whose husband died long ago, has a total of 10 children and grandchildren and makes annual exclusion gifts to each of them for 20 years. If the recipients invested that money and earned 5 percent annually, at the end of 20 years her tax-free annual gifts totaling $2.8 million ($140,000 per year times 20 years) will have created $4,860,695 for the recipients.*

Without these gifts, if Sally died at the end of 20 years, the family would be left with much less. Assume that the estate tax rate when she dies is 40 percent and that her exclusion (whatever it is at the time) is fully applied

*Calculation by Lawrence P. Katzenstein

to other assets. Under that scenario, her heirs would need to pay roughly $1,944,278 in estate taxes on the assets if she had not given them to her family. Not counting the generation-skipping transfer tax that may also diminish sums going to grandchildren (see Chapter 14), the inheritance would be reduced to $2,916,417.

Although cash is the most common type of gift – to help a child who wants to buy a car, pay off a loan or start a business, for example – you can transfer assets, too. For gift-tax purposes, you count the value of the asset at the time of the transfer. Any appreciation after that is not subject to estate or gift tax. You may want to give appreciated stock, if the recipient can sell it at a lower capital gains rate than you would pay. But don't transfer stock with a built-in loss – the recipient's basis will be the current market value and the income tax deduction for the loss will be eliminated. Instead, sell the stock, book the loss yourself and give the cash.

Did You Know?

When making gifts of tangible personal property, you should hand over the items as soon as possible. You can't write a child's name on a painting and keep it on your wall, for example. If you do and you die, it will be considered part of your estate.

The most tax-efficient use of the annual exclusion is to make gifts of appreciating assets, such as stock that has declined in value but is expected to recover, real estate or interests in a business start-up that has growth potential (but, again, this should not be property with a built-in loss). The gift is valued at the time of the transfer. If the asset later increases in value, that appreciation benefits your family member and will not be subject to estate or gift tax (though of course the gift recipient would need to pay income tax on the sale of appreciated assets). If you make a gift of anything other than cash or marketable securities, you need to get a professional appraisal at the time you make the transfer, especially if it is a hard-to-value asset, like a share in the family business.

One condition for the annual exclusion is that the gift must be a present interest, meaning something the recipient can use right away rather than a future one. This is an issue when using the annual exclusion to fund trusts, because they are usually not expected to pay out immediately. One way to meet the present interest requirement is to give each beneficiary a Crummey power – the right for a limited time, usually 30 or 60 days, to withdraw from the trust the yearly gift attributable to that beneficiary (as discussed more fully in Chapter 6).

Annual exclusion gifts must be complete (received and, in the case of a check, either deposited or cashed) by Dec. 31 of the year in which you make them. When starting an annual giving program, some people make gifts in December and again in January, effectively doubling what they can give away in a short stretch of time. Going forward, it's best to make gifts early in the year rather than waiting for the December holiday season. That gets one more year of appreciation out of your estate. And if you die during the year ahead, the property will have already been transferred.

Lifetime exclusion. One reason that annual exclusion gifts are so appealing is that they pass outside of the transfer tax system. Therefore, they don't count against what the tax law calls the "basic exclusion" but which most people refer to as the "lifetime exemption" (or exclusion) or the "estate tax exemption." Which term you use depends on the context. The main thing to understand is that once you've gone over the annual exclusion, there is currently a $5.43 million limit on the total amount you can give away – either during life or through your estate plan. You are allowed to transfer assets at either stage or a combination of the two. If you exceed the limit, you (or your heirs) will owe tax of 40 percent.

On the estate tax return, your $5.43 million estate tax exclusion is reduced by the amount of lifetime gifts. If you exceeded the limit, heirs can take a credit for the gift tax you paid. Even if you don't exceed the limit while you are alive, your lifetime gifts will reduce how much you can pass tax-free through your estate plan.

Most people can accomplish their estate planning goals without ever using the lifetime exclusion amount. With portability (discussed in Chapter 3), spouses can avoid estate tax until their combined assets total more than $10.86 million. They might not want to shed assets until their net worth is significantly more than that, especially given the unlimited marital deduction that permits them to postpone estate tax until the second of them dies. Unmarried couples, however, do not have the benefit of the marital deduction and might be inclined to use their exclusion amount

A Mayor's Missed Opportunity

Edward I. Koch, the former mayor of New York, was worth about $10.5 million when he died, in 2013, according to papers filed in New York City Surrogate's Court. But between federal and state estate taxes, Uncle Sam and the State of New York together got almost one-fourth of what he left behind.

Deathbed gifts could have significantly lowered the estate tax bill. By using the annual exclusion to give $14,000 while he was ailing to each of the nine people benefited in his will, Koch could have reduced his estate by $126,000. Additional gifts of up to $5.25 million using the federal lifetime exclusion then in effect would have completely wiped out what he could pass at death tax-free. But since New York doesn't have a gift tax, the gifts would have reduced the size of his taxable estate without affecting what was then a $1 million New York estate tax exemption.

So instead of paying New York estate tax of up to 16 percent on $9.5 million ($10.5 million minus a $1 million exemption), his estate would have paid that tax on $4.25 million ($9.5 million minus $5.25 million transferred during life). The savings on the state estate tax would have been $726,000.

Paying less state estate tax reduces the federal deduction for state estate tax, though, so Koch's heirs would have had to pay an additional $290,400 in federal estate tax. Therefore, the net tax savings from this strategy would have been $435,600 ($726,000 minus $290,400).

Calculations by Gideon Rothschild

sooner (see Chapter 4). So might surviving spouses who became a widow or widower before 2011 and hold much more in the marital share than will be covered by their own $5.43 million exclusion.

Although there is no urgency to make lifetime gifts, the sooner you use the exclusion amount, the more future income and potential appreciation you shift out of your estate. The lower the value of the assets (for example, because markets are depressed or because you are transferring shares of a start-up enterprise), the less exclusion amount your gift will consume. A variety of techniques discussed later in this chapter can get even more bang from each buck.

Be aware, though, that the cost basis for assets transferred during life is different from that of inherited assets. Those that are inherited get a basis adjustment to the fair market value on the date of the owner's death. The advantage of this fresh start is that it limits the capital gains tax inheritors must pay if they sell the property. In contrast, if you transfer assets during life and they go up in value, as you would hope, there will be more gain to tax than if those same assets were inherited. If asset values decline, on the other hand, you will have wasted part of your gift-tax exclusion by applying more than you would have if you had waited to make your gift.

Note: If you gave more than $14,000 in cash, property or gifts to anyone in a given year, you must report the gift on Form 709 – the federal gift-tax return. The rules and protocols are discussed in Chapter 10 and in the "To-Do List" on page 263.

Trusts That Offer Income Tax Benefits

Sometimes an income tax strategy offers enormous estate planning benefits. Converting a traditional IRA to a Roth (discussed in Chapter 7) is a great example of that. Setting up a grantor trust is another, and a hugely effective way to transfer wealth to the next generation without incurring gift tax.

A grantor trust is not a single variety of trust but a set of characteristics that can be incorporated into various types of popular trusts. The term refers to the fact that the person who creates the trust, known as the grantor, retains certain rights or powers. As a result, the trust is not treated as a separate entity for income tax purposes, and the grantor, rather than the trust or its beneficiaries, must pay tax on trust earnings.

A 2004 Revenue Ruling made clear that paying the tax is not considered a gift to the trust beneficiaries. Yet this tax, on income that the grantor probably never receives, shrinks his estate. At the same time, assets can appreciate inside the trust without being depleted by ordinary income taxes or capital gains taxes.

For example, let's say a couple set up a trust to benefit their five grandchildren and fund it with annual exclusion gifts of $140,000 per year

($28,000 times five grandchildren). Consider the benefit of grantor trust status if this trust successfully invests a single year's contributions – perhaps by purchasing stock in a new business that one of the grandchildren has started. Let's say that five years later the company goes public and the stock originally bought for $140,000 is worth $2 million. If the trust sells this stock, the grandparents, rather than the trust, would pay the capital gains tax on the $1.86 million in appreciation. The top rate for long-term capital gains is now 20 percent, plus there would be a 3.8 percent Medicare surcharge on this investment income, making the effective tax rate 23.8 percent. By paying the $442,680 tax (23.8 percent of $1.86 million), the grandparents effectively make an additional tax-free gift to the trust.

Another attractive feature of these irrevocable trusts is that assets placed in the trust are removed from the senior family member's estate. From an estate and gift-tax perspective, the transfer is treated as a completed gift. The value of the assets is frozen at the time of the transfer, so that future appreciation is not subject to estate or gift tax. These trusts can be useful for a broad range of people, from young entrepreneurs with mushrooming assets to elderly couples with securities portfolios.

Creating a grantor trust. A variety of powers, contained in the trust document, will have the effect of conferring it with grantor trust status. Examples include the right of the grantor or the grantor's spouse to receive loans from the trust without collateral, and the option to reacquire certain trust assets and substitute others of equivalent value. Whether such powers are actually exercised – and often they are not – putting them into the instrument makes it a grantor trust.

Types of trusts that can be grantor trusts. Grantor trust powers can be included in trusts established for many different purposes, which are discussed elsewhere in this book. For instance, they work well in trusts designed to receive gifts under the annual exclusion. They are also extremely helpful in an irrevocable life insurance trust, or ILIT (as discussed in Chapter 8). The more quickly funds accumulate inside the trust, the sooner it will be able to pay the premiums without further gifts from the grantor. When an ILIT is a grantor trust, both the grantor and the trustee will have more flexibility to adapt the insurance and other trust assets to changing circumstances. For example, the IRS has ruled several times that insurance policies can be transferred between two grantor trusts without triggering taxable gain.

The Power of a Grantor Trust

Tax-free compounding within a grantor trust can translate into significant sums. Let's say a trust is funded with $1 million of assets, invested for growth to produce a total return of 5 percent per year before tax, or 5 percent per year after tax.

Compare what the value of the assets would be in 20 years if the grantor pays this tax, so the assets can grow tax-free, with the value if the trust pays the tax.

Year	Grantor pays the tax (Assets grow tax-free)	Trust pays the tax
5	$1,276,282	$1,159,274
10	$1,628,895	$1,343,916
15	$2,078,928	$1,557,967
20	$2,653,298	$1,806,111

Source: Lawrence P. Katzenstein

Making your spouse the beneficiary of a grantor trust. There may be times when you will want to make your spouse a beneficiary of the grantor trust. This strategy has several advantages.

One is that you can reduce the size of a trust that has grown too large. Perhaps your own financial circumstances have changed, and you need extra funds to maintain your lifestyle. Or maybe you are afraid of spoiling your descendants. In such cases, you can funnel some money out of the trust by making distributions to your spouse. Depending on the situation, your spouse can either keep those funds or donate them to charity, which would generate a charitable income tax deduction (see Chapter 16).

Naming a spouse as beneficiary also offers a means to finance the trust income taxes, which can become a major concern. If, for any reason, the income tax burden becomes unmanageable, the trustee can make distributions to your spouse, who can then use the funds to pay the tax for which you would be liable on a joint return. One downside is that in funding the trust, you will not be able to exercise the option, available only to married couples, of combining your lifetime exclusion amounts and annual exclusions. Instead, you will be limited to your own exemption of $5.43 million and one $14,000 annual exclusion. Typically, grantor trust status ends when you die, at which time the trust becomes responsible for paying its own income taxes.

Escape hatches. With all estate planning techniques, you must be able to part with the property you are transferring, but grantor trusts create a new financial obligation: to pay the tax bills if the trust assets hugely appreciate. For example, if the trust owns a large position in low-basis stock that is about to soar suddenly in value – say, because the company is being sold – the tax liability could be more than you are prepared to pay.

As noted above, naming your spouse as a beneficiary provides a vehicle for channeling money to you as a couple that can be used to pay the taxes.

Another option if the tax bill becomes unaffordable is to terminate, or turn off, grantor trust status. How you toggle off the grantor trust treatment will depend on the provisions that made the instrument a grantor trust in the first place. For example, you could renounce the power to reacquire certain trust assets and substitute others of equivalent value. Some lawyers rely on grantors to relinquish any relevant powers. Others set things up so that an independent party, known as a trust protector (as noted in Chapter 6), can modify all the appropriate provisions. While it is possible to draft a trust so that someone can also restart grantor-trust powers, it is not a good idea to structure things this way, because it starts to look as though the grantor is retaining enough control over the trust that it might be subject to inclusion in his estate.

GRATs Explained

A grantor retained annuity trust, or GRAT, is a special type of grantor trust. You put appreciating assets into an irrevocable trust and retain the right to receive an annual payment for a specified trust term. This annuity is based on a rate set each month by the U.S. Treasury called the

Section 7520 rate (named after a section of the Internal Revenue Code). The latest Section 7520 rates are published monthly by the IRS and available at http://1.usa.gov/1DTGEAS.

If the value of the trust assets increases by more than this rate, your GRAT will be economically successful. In that case, the excess appreciation will go to family members (the remainder beneficiaries) or to trusts for their benefit when the GRAT term ends. But if the appreciation never occurs, you are no worse off; the trust would simply satisfy its payout obligations by returning its assets to you. At that point it's possible to "re-GRAT" the assets – to create another GRAT – in the hope that they will do better in the future. It is currently possible to set up a GRAT that results in no taxable gift – or at least a nominal one. That way, there's little or no lifetime gift-tax exclusion wasted if the asset does not perform as you hoped.

Within this basic structure, many variations are possible, and you can engineer both the GRAT term and the annuity for maximum financial benefit. Since you must live until the end of the trust term for a GRAT to

Did You Know?

The financial crisis that began in 2008 created opportunities. Low asset values and the decline in interest rates used in some wealth-transfer tools drastically cut the tax cost of lifetime transfers. Heirs would benefit from any appreciation with no additional tax due.

work, many people choose short-term GRATs – 366 days is the minimum. (If you die before the GRAT term ends, all or a portion of the trust will be included in your estate.)

A short-term GRAT is also the better approach if you're dealing with a volatile asset, anticipate it will appreciate significantly and want to capture that gain before the value dips. You can even hedge the mortality and investment risks by forming a series of short-term GRATs created over a certain time span – say 10 GRATS, each with a two-year term.

With longer-term investments – for example, shares in a family business passing to children through a GRAT – those who are hearty and optimistic might opt for longer trust terms. This locks in the Section 7520 rate, which would be desirable if interest rates are low when you set up the GRAT.

GRAT Results

Sally is 50 and puts $1 million worth of property into a two-year GRAT. If the Section 7520 rate is 2.4 percent and the GRAT is designed so there is no taxable gift, Sally would receive a yearly annuity of $518,081.*

If the assets increase at the rate shown below, the GRAT will have the following results:

Rate of annual trust earnings	Gift-tax-free transfer to children when GRAT ends
7%	$72,472
10%	$122,030
15%	$208,626

This example assumes that the payments are equal, although many GRATs are designed so the second payment is 20 percent more than the first one.

Source: Lawrence P. Katzenstein, Tiger Tables Actuarial Software

Whether you go short term or long term, you can use the annuity stream to fund additional trusts, creating a series of cascading GRATs.

Likewise, you can structure the payout to reflect your expectations about investment performance. Often, GRAT annuities are designed to be lower in the first year and increase by a preset percentage of up to 20 percent annually in successive ones, as the trust asset appreciates. But if the GRAT asset is very volatile – as it would be for a call-spread option, a put-spread option or a currency trade, for example – or if you expect a big capital gain in Year 1, you can provide for a higher initial payment to reflect that.

With assets that are difficult to value, such as closely held stock, a GRAT offers an additional benefit. By expressing the annuity as a percent-age of the initial value of the GRAT, you permit the trust to simply pay a larger annuity (with no gift-tax consequences) if the IRS determines the property is worth more than you initially calculated. This avoids the assessment of additional gift taxes.

Note that GRATs are not appropriate for transfers to grandchildren and more remote descendants. The $5.43 million exemption from generation-skipping transfer tax can't be applied until the trust term ends, by which time you hope asset values will be higher. (The generation-skipping transfer tax was discussed in Chapter 14.)

Once you have created a GRAT, you or your financial advisers need to monitor the performance of the assets you put into it. Although you can't add assets to a GRAT, it is possible to reacquire trust assets and substitute others of equivalent value. There are three situations when you might want to do that. One is when asset values have declined, making the GRAT unsuccessful. Another is when assets have increased in value but you think that they may go down before the GRAT term ends. The third is where the value of the assets has increased to the point where you do not want the beneficiaries to receive any further increases, for personal or financial reasons.

In each of these cases, there might be a benefit to getting volatile assets out of the GRAT and putting them into a new one at the lower rate, essentially giving you a fresh start. You can do this by exchanging the property either for cash or for another asset of equal value. Alternatively, you can buy the assets from the GRAT using a promissory note.

Since a GRAT is a grantor trust, it is possible to do all of these transactions with the trust and not have to pay income tax.

Using Family Entities to Discount Values

Some people use closely held enterprises, such as family limited partnerships, or FLPs, and limited liability companies, or LLCs, to maximize investment opportunities and for asset protection (see Chapter 17). They can also be used to discount the value of assets before transferring them to family members or to trusts for their benefit.

Here is how these family-controlled entities work: A senior family member puts assets, such as marketable securities, real estate or shares of an operating business, into the entity, which is most often an FLP but may be an LLC (some lawyers are more familiar with that structure). Then the individual sells or gives away shares in the entity that holds the assets – not the assets themselves. Since the interests can't readily be sold outside the family, their value is discounted for both lack of marketability and lack of control (often a total discount of 20 to 30 percent).

By reducing the value of partnership units or membership shares for gift-tax purposes, discounts enable you to minimize the tax cost of transferring assets. That can make your gift fit within the annual exclusion or lifetime exclusion amount or, for gifts that exceed these amounts, reduce how much gift tax you will have to pay.

Note, though, that using family-controlled entities for estate planning purposes is an invitation to an estate tax audit, in which the IRS disputes the amount of the discount you took when selling or transferring the shares. Good records are essential to settling the audits favorably. For starters, you need to get a professional appraisal at the time you set up the entity and make the first transfers, with follow-up appraisals if the value of the entity has changed when you make subsequent transfers. Those appraisals, which should be attached to the gift-tax return due on April 15 of the year after you make the gift, can cost $10,000 or more.

Avoiding or defending a tax audit goes far beyond that. The IRS has brought numerous cases challenging these arrangements, winning some and losing others. Although the decisions are sometimes hard to reconcile, certain facts have tipped the scale in the government's favor (with a strong case, taxpayers have been able to settle with the IRS for 25 to 30 percent of the disputed amount). Family-controlled entities seem especially vulnerable to attack when:

- ⚜ The senior family member who sets up the entity and primarily funds it retains control over critical decisions or the right to income or use of partnership property
- ⚜ One partner withdraws funds from the partnership without making corresponding distributions to the other partners
- ⚜ The entities are formed by people who are terminally ill or extremely old

Not surprisingly, taxpayers also tend to lose these cases when they transfer most of their assets into the entity, use it to pay personal expenses, commingle personal assets with partnership ones or put a home into the entity and continue to live in it rent-free. In fact, the biggest problem with these entities is not the legal documents but the way people run them after they leave the lawyer's office. The IRS has been successful in demonstrating that people did not respect the formalities of the FLP as a business. So far, the best defense against an IRS challenge has been to show that there was a non-tax reason for using a partnership. Here are some examples.

❧ *Protecting property from creditors.* As a rule, creditors of a limited partner cannot take partnership assets or force a liquidation, although they can reach distributions the entity makes to the partner.

❧ *Streamlining or facilitating wealth transfer.* Instead of struggling to divide certain assets like real estate or stock portfolios, which may be difficult to apportion, it's possible to transfer the assets to an entity and give various people shares in the enterprise.

❧ *Avoiding probate on real estate you own in other states.* By putting the land or building into a family partnership, you convert real property, which must be probated in the state where it is situated (as discussed in Chapter 2), to intangible personal property that is probated in the state where the owner lived.

❧ *Reducing investment management costs by consolidating the assets of various family members in one portfolio.* Many financial institutions offer reduced fee schedules for large accounts.

In an IRS audit, it's not enough to allege that you are using the partnership for these purposes. You also need to show how they apply to your particular family circumstances. That is, you cannot just say that you want to avoid creditor claims. You have to show that you actually have a reasonable fear of creditor claims and that the entity would help avoid them.

Another issue to think about is your tolerance for the sort of administrative details that will help the arrangement withstand an audit. Basically, you must operate the entity like a business. That means making distributions only in proportion to each person's partnership interest. You should also hold regular partnership meetings, keep minutes of those meetings and make sure they reflect some of the non-tax purposes the entity is serving.

Finally, you need to consider these entities in the context of your own family dynamics. Since family members will be tied together in the enterprise, it's preferable that they get along well.

Selling Assets Instead of Giving Them Away

Although you can make gifts of any assets, including partnership interests, using the annual exclusion and lifetime exclusion amounts, you can avoid gift tax altogether by selling the assets to the people whom you want to benefit instead of giving them away. Here, too, both the property sold and any future appreciation are removed from your estate, though the amount paid for the asset is included in your estate. Since you will need to set a fair sale price, it is preferable to use assets that are not difficult to value.

If you, like many people, worry that lifetime transfers will leave you short of money, you may feel more comfortable with a technique like a sale that creates an income stream. (A GRAT has the same virtue.) The drawback is that cash received as interest and principal payments on the note bring assets back into your estate, even as you strive to trim what will ultimately be taxed. These sales can be financed in several ways.

Fixed-payment installment note. Typically, the sale is done in exchange for a promissory note with interest. You must charge interest at the applicable federal rate, set each month by the Treasury. Otherwise, the "missing interest" could be treated as a taxable gift. In some cases, the IRS can also attribute interest income to you and tax you on the amount you should have earned.

While you can sell the assets directly to family members, there is a distinct advantage to using a grantor trust in these installment sales. Here's why: Since the trust is not treated as a separate entity for income tax purposes, the grantor, rather than the trust or its beneficiaries, is treated as the owner of the trust assets. Therefore, there is no capital gains tax on the sale to the trust and no tax on interest payments you receive. And by paying the taxes on income generated by the trust, you, in effect, make an additional tax-free gift to the trust beneficiaries.

This tool requires that the trust have other assets – as a rule of thumb, at least 10 percent of the value of the assets being transferred through the installment sale. Often the grantor supplies this seed money using the lifetime gift-tax exclusion. Now that the exclusion amount has been raised to $5.43 million, it is possible to put more seed money into the trust without having to pay gift tax.

The installment sale to an irrevocable grantor trust is a popular alternative to a GRAT because it addresses the two key drawbacks of the GRAT: the risk of dying during the trust term and the inability to use the generation-skipping transfer tax exemption until the GRAT ends. However, installment sales have their own set of potential drawbacks. One is that only scattered court cases – but no federal law – support them.

Other risks relate to the vicissitudes of the market. If asset values plummet, the note could easily be worth more than the trust property.

> ## Did You Know❓
>
> You should make gifts to individuals or to trusts early in the year rather than waiting for the December holiday season. That removes one more year of appreciation from your estate. And should you die during the year ahead, the property will have already been transferred.

In that case, the trust might need to use some of its initial funding to make interest payments. The grantor, who would be getting back assets he put into the trust, will have wasted any lifetime gift-tax exclusion or gift tax used to fund the trust.

On the other hand, if the trust assets wildly appreciate, a grantor who has not set aside enough money to pay the tax bills could be wiped out. Although this problem can be avoided if you and your advisers anticipate it, the situation can be more difficult to address after the fact.

Private annuity. This tool, typically used for people who are elderly or in poor health, involves a sale of assets in exchange for an unsecured promise to pay an annuity for the rest of the seller's life. The payout is based on the seller's life expectancy under the government's actuarial tables. If the seller lives for less time, the buyer gets a bargain. Federal regulations prohibit people from using these tables if there's more than a 50 percent probability that they're going to die within a year.

The greatest drawback to this transaction, typically done between parents and children (or a trust for their benefit), is that it involves an unhealthy emotional dynamic: a bet against Dad or Mom. The sooner the parent dies, the better off the buyer is financially; the longer the parent lives, the more children have paid for the property. Understandably, many people find the idea distasteful.

These arrangements also have various financial complexities. The buyer's basis, which at the time of the sale equals the value of the annuity, must be recomputed if the seller doesn't live until his life expectancy. The reason: The buyer has, in effect, paid less for the property.

To further complicate matters, under IRS rules, the party paying the annuity must have assets sufficient to make the payments not just for the seller's actual life expectancy but until he reaches age 110. This exhaustion rule, as it's called, is only a problem for trusts and other entities. If the trust or entity doesn't have adequate funding, it won't be permitted to value the annuity based on the seller's life expectancy but only until the money would run out.

Self-canceling installment note. An alternative to the private annuity is selling assets to family members or to a trust for their benefit in exchange for a self-canceling installment note, or SCIN. This financing technique works just like any other installment note, except that the debt is forgiven if the seller dies during the note term. The advantage of a SCIN is that family members can potentially wind up with the property without paying the full sales price. (With an ordinary note, if the seller dies while the note is outstanding, the balance is payable to the estate.)

Buyers pay a price for this potential windfall: In order for the transaction to be legitimate, the SCIN must incorporate a premium for the cancellation feature. This premium is based on current interest rates and the seller's age. It can be added either to the principal or the interest portion of the note.

Another financial drawback of the SCIN is that when someone dies with one of these notes in place, all unrealized gain is taxable to the estate as income in the year of death. The estate may not have enough income tax deductions to offset it. In contrast, with a note that doesn't have the self-canceling feature, the children would continue making payments to the estate, and the gain would be deferred over the remaining years of the note. Therefore, in deciding whether to use a SCIN, it's necessary to compare the premium associated with this device and the income tax the estate would have to pay with the estate tax savings of having the note canceled.

To-Do List

Avoid Audit Risks

Under tax law and Internal Revenue Service regulations, to start the statute of limitations running on Form 709 – the federal gift-tax return – you must make "adequate disclosure" of the gift on that return. You need to file the form even if you don't owe tax. (For answers to some common gift-tax questions see pages 177-180.)

Since the $5.43 million lifetime exclusion from gift tax and any gift tax you pay are cumulative, you must keep the returns indefinitely. The most likely time for the IRS to flag unreported gifts or to question the value of the gifts you made is after you die. The following steps can help you avoid some common audit flags.

❧ Report annual exclusion gifts on the gift-tax return any time there's room for debate about what the interest is worth.

❧ When lending money to family members, charge interest at the applicable federal rate and document the transaction.

❧ If you apply annual exclusion gifts to forgive all or a part of an intra-family loan, keep a record of the gift and the loan balance.

❧ Send annual Crummey notices each year letting trust beneficiaries know about their right to withdraw their portion of your annual exclusion gift to their trust. Keep copies with your important papers.

❧ Make GRAT annuity payments on time.

❧ When you give an asset away, do not retain the right to use it.

❧ Document your decision to transfer tangible property with a letter to the recipient. If you pass away before actually transferring the item, the property will be out of your estate.

❧ Get an appraisal when there is any question about the value of a gift, and each time you transfer shares in a family entity. Attach this documentation to your gift-tax return.

Chapter 16

Your Charitable Legacy

*Read this chapter if there are causes
you care deeply about and would like
to benefit now or later.*

Philanthropy is ingrained in our culture, and most of the money comes from individuals rather than from corporations or foundations. Whether you give to charity during your life or through your estate plan, philanthropy can create a meaningful legacy. For many people the choices they make reflect the schools they attended, cultural pursuits that gave them pleasure, ties to their community or diseases that have afflicted family members.

Gifts made during life, if you can afford them, give you a chance to see your money put to good use. They can also be much more tax-efficient. With lifetime gifts, you can take an income tax deduction for the year in which you

In This Chapter...

- ⚜ *Benefiting Family (or Yourself) As Well as Charity*
- ⚜ *Creating a Continuing Fund Rather Than a One-Shot Gift*
- ⚜ *Choosing the Best Assets to Donate*

make the gift. Such gifts also have the effect of reducing the size of the estate you will leave behind, though that is an issue only for people whose estates will exceed the exemption from federal estate tax (currently $5.43 million for individuals and $10.86 million for couples).

Some people are reluctant to make large lifetime donations because they depend on income from their investments or want to make a priority of taking care of family first. But there's a middle ground: split-interest gifts made during life (or through an estate plan) that provide an income stream for you or a person you designate, as well as a payout to charity.

Minimally, every estate plan should include what's sometimes called a bomb clause, saying what will happen if you and your closest heirs are wiped out simultaneously, as in an accident. If so, you might prefer to benefit charity rather than some distant relative. Those who go further carve out a portion of their estate or a specific dollar amount for charity (see Chapter 2).

The simplest way to make a bequest is to designate one or more charities in your will or living trust, or on the beneficiary designation form of your retirement account (see Chapter 7). This may be any charity to which you could make a gift and then take a corresponding charitable deduction from your taxable income.

Perhaps you aren't prepared to make significant charitable bequests through your estate because you're not sure if your heirs will need the money or can't decide which charities you would like to benefit. In that case, there are a couple of steps you can take now to maximize flexibility.

One is to pave the way for your heirs to shift assets to charity by disclaiming within nine months of your death. This means turning down an inheritance and having it go to whomever is next in line – typically a person (see Chapter 2). If you want at least part of the disclaimed assets to go to charity, your estate planning documents must name the specific charity, or charities, or a charitable trust that will receive whatever is disclaimed; the choice is not up to the people who would otherwise inherit the assets.

Another way to postpone tough choices is to make your charitable beneficiary a private foundation or a donor-advised fund. By naming family members to recommend future grants, you can use either of these entities to support your charitable legacy or encourage your heirs to develop charitable interests of their own.

Benefiting Family (or Yourself) as Well as Charity

Even very wealthy donors who previously might have made an outright gift to charity have become more cautious after the financial crisis of 2008, whose effects are still being felt. "Will I have enough to retire comfortably?" and "Could a charitable bequest shortchange my family?" are reasonable questions that might dissuade people from philanthropy and make charity a second-choice beneficiary.

If you share these concerns but still want to include charity in your estate plan, there is another option: gifts that provide funds for you or your family and also benefit charity. These are the possibilities.

Charitable gift annuity. This is a contract in which the donor contributes assets – typically cash or marketable securities – and the charity agrees to pay a fixed amount of money annually to that person and perhaps the surviving spouse. The size of an annuity payment is based on the contribution and the age at which it begins. Most charities use suggested maximum rates from the American Council on Gift Annuities (available at www.acga-web.org). Gift annuities factor in an assumption that when the donor dies, the charity will get about 50 percent of the initial value of the amount transferred. Therefore, the rates are lower than those of annuities from commercial insurance carriers.

A gift annuity is backed by the assets of the charity, even if it must dip into other funds to make the payment. But these contracts are not a certainty. If the endowment dries up or the organization shuts, the payments will stop. In a bankruptcy case, the annuity holder becomes an unsecured creditor.

At the time of your donation, you can take an income tax deduction. It is based on actuarial tables that take into account the rate the charity is offering, the age of and number of annuitants (one or two) and federal interest rates at the time you enter into the arrangement. A portion of each annuity payment is considered return of principal and not taxed. The rest is taxed as ordinary income if you contributed cash. If you contributed appreciated property held for more than a year, part will also be taxed as a long-term capital gain.

Charitable trusts. Two major types of trusts can be set up during life or through an estate plan and used to benefit both individuals and charity: the charitable remainder trust and the charitable lead trust. Both of these trusts

The Legendary Lead Trust That Never Materialized

When Jacqueline Kennedy Onassis died, in 1994, the nation got an up-close look at a sophisticated estate planning tool that has since become part of the Jackie O legend. In her will, the former First Lady described a trust that would pay an annuity to charity for 24 years. After that, whatever was left would go to her grandchildren or their descendants. Onassis called this charitable lead trust the C&J Foundation, using the initials of the first names of her two children, Caroline Kennedy Schlossberg and John F. Kennedy, Jr.

In theory, the trust was an effective way to combine philanthropy with smart tax planning. It could be structured to avoid estate tax on money going into the trust, as well as generation-skipping transfer tax on funds eventually paid out to grandchildren. Anything that exceeded the required payout to charity would go to the family tax-free.

When the will first became public, the provision for this trust received widespread publicity, as various commentators speculated that the Onassis estate was worth $100 million or more. Under that scenario, by some estimates, as much as $192 million would be distributed to charity through the trust and the grandchildren might receive $98 million when it ended in 2018.

Funding for the trust was to come from the residuary estate – what remained after family, friends, lawyers and taxes had received their share. In the will, Onassis gave her children the option of disclaiming, or turning down, a portion of their inheritance. In that case, certain items would go to the Kennedy Library, and the rest would go into the residuary estate and be available to fund the charitable lead trust.

As things worked out, though, the trust was never created. That's because the children did not disclaim, except for property going to the Kennedy Library. When the dust settled, the family's lawyers said the residuary estate was valued at $18 million but owed $23 million in estate taxes, which would need to come out of the children's inheritances.

Still, this trust-that-never-was lives on in estate planning lore.

Doing the Math

Oone powerful incentive to use charitable remainder trusts is the present income tax deduction available to the donor or the estate when this irrevocable trust is funded.

The deduction equals the value of the charity's remainder interest – the right to receive the trust assets at some point in the future. To calculate it requires the use of the Section 7520 rate, set each month by the IRS.

With an annuity trust, the higher this discount rate, the bigger the deduction (for a unitrust, the interest rate doesn't affect the deduction). You're allowed to use the most favorable rate during a three-month period of the month when you set up the trust and the two previous months. Other factors that will influence the value of the remainder are the term of the trust (for those that last only a preset number of years) and the number and age of the beneficiaries.

To illustrate, let's say Jack, who is 70, sets up a $1 million charitable remainder annuity trust that will pay him 5 percent, or $50,000, each year for the rest of his life. Using a 2.4 percent discount rate, the present value of the annuity is $578,515, so the value of the remainder interest is $421,485 (the two must total the initial trust value of $1 million). When setting up the trust, Jack would get a deduction for $421,485. If, instead, the discount rate was 5 percent, the annuity would be worth $474,565, and the remainder would be worth $525,435, so Jack would get a higher deduction.*

Two requirements for charitable remainder annuity trusts can be difficult to satisfy when interest rates are low. One is that the present value of charity's interest must be at least 10 percent of the initial trust funding. The other is that there must be no more than a 5 percent probability, based on IRS actuarial tables, that the trust funds will run out before the charity's remainder interest vests. If these rules prevent you from creating an annuity trust, you might want to consider a unitrust instead. Although the same 10 percent requirement applies, it is not as sensitive to interest rate fluctuations.

Assumes payments will be made at the end of each quarter.

Source: Lawrence P. Katzenstein, Tiger Tables Actuarial Software

are split-interest arrangements, meaning that charitable and non-charitable beneficiaries each get a share of the assets but at different times. In a charitable remainder trust, individual beneficiaries receive income for whatever period of time you specify – their lifetimes or a term of up to 20 years. When this interest ends, the charity receives what is left, known as the remainder interest. The charitable lead trust is the same idea in reverse. The charity receives its payout up front for the period you select. When this payout ends, the non-charitable beneficiaries, usually family members, get what is left.

Each of these vehicles, which are irrevocable, carries significant tax advantages. With a charitable remainder trust, you or your estate receives an income tax deduction upon transfer of assets into the entity (see "Doing the Math," page 270). A charitable lead trust, on the other hand, can produce gift-tax and estate tax savings, and, in some cases, income tax savings. If the trust earnings are sufficient, the money gets added to the principal. Down the line, this appreciation not only goes to family members – but most important – goes to them tax-free.

The charitable lead trust is for people who can afford to give the income to charity and whose families can do without the principal for a long time. Depending on how investments perform, it's possible that the charitable lead trust will be depleted by the end of the term, in which case the family would get nothing. Because these features don't appeal to many people, the charitable remainder trust is the more popular of the two.

The payout can be structured as either an annuity or a unitrust interest. In a charitable remainder annuity trust, the non-charitable beneficiary receives a fixed dollar amount at least annually – the minimum is 5 percent of the initial trust value. With a charitable remainder unitrust, the income interest is expressed as a percentage of the fair market value of the trust revalued each year (again, the minimum is 5 percent). While the amount of the annuity interest stays constant, the payout in a unitrust will change from year to year.

A popular variation is the net income with make-up charitable remainder unitrust, which expresses the payout as the lesser of net income or a fixed percentage of the trust assets valued annually. There's also the appropriately named flip charitable remainder unitrust, used for trusts funded with assets that produce little or no income, such as real estate or closely held stock. With this trust, there's no payout requirement until the assets are sold. At that point it is converted into a standard unitrust, with payments according to the predetermined rate.

Charitable remainder trusts can be established during life or at death, and the benefit need not be limited to a single charity. A key attraction of lifetime charitable remainder trusts funded with highly appreciated property is that no capital gains tax need be paid when the assets are put into the trust. Nor is there any tax due as the assets appreciate or are sold inside this vehicle, since the charitable remainder trust is tax-exempt. As individual beneficiaries receive yearly payouts, they pay tax according to a four-tier system. Under this method, to the extent the trust has ordinary income from the current year or accumulated income from a previous year, it is distributed first and taxed at ordinary income rates. Next comes capital gain, then other income and, finally, trust principal.

It's possible for the remainder interest to go to multiple charities or to a donor-advised fund (see "Creating a Continuing Fund Rather Than a One-Shot Gift," below). You can retain the right to change the remainder beneficiary to a different charity or postpone the choice of charity altogether and leave it up to the trustee.

If there is a special needs child in your family, you might want to make a special needs trust the income beneficiary of a charitable remainder trust (see Chapter 5). In this case, the remainder beneficiary might be a charity concerned with the child's particular disability.

Creating a Continuing Fund
Rather Than a One-Shot Gift

For people who want to benefit multiple charities over a period of time, the typical choice is between a donor-advised fund and a private foundation, both of which can be set up either during life or as part of an estate plan.

Private foundation. Starting a private foundation involves forming a separate legal entity and applying for tax-exempt status from the Internal Revenue Service. Complex tax code provisions regulate these entities, covering everything from the types of investments and grants a private foundation can make to transactions with officers, directors, trustees and substantial contributors (most are off-limits). To justify the expense of establishing and running a private foundation, many advisers recommend an initial endowment of $5 million to $10 million. Those who start with less may find that the hassles outweigh the benefits.

People who set up private foundations often assume that there will be extensive family involvement. Yet a variety of factors conspire against that. Sometimes adult children simply aren't interested. Even when they are, if they are scattered geographically, it can be difficult to build consensus for grant proposals and other relevant matters without assistance. Siblings who don't get along may be unwilling to work together toward a charitable goal. Sometimes no succession plan is in place, or asset values have declined to the point where the expense of running the operation is disproportionate to the endowment. A common solution is to dissolve the foundation and distribute its assets to a public charity.

Another possibility for avoiding family friction is to design a foundation with a limited life span rather than thinking of it as something that will last forever. This approach might include a sunset provision providing that the entity will terminate when a specific event occurs, such as when the last of the founders dies. For example, the Bill & Melinda Gates Foundation is scheduled to close within 50 years after its current trustees have died. This avoids the threat that grants will stray from the donor's intent with succeeding generations.

Donor-advised fund. These funds have become a popular alternative to a private foundation because they offer many of the same virtues without the expense and paperwork. Contributors make irrevocable contributions to a non-profit organization that administers the fund in conjunction with funds set up by other donors. You can make these contributions while you are alive, through your estate plan or a combination of the two. At any time in the future, you or your heirs (or any other people you designate) can recommend which non-profit organizations should receive grants from the account.

Organizations sponsoring donor-advised funds include religious entities, universities and community foundations. Some large financial institutions have started donor-advised funds that are public charities. To set up a donor-advised fund account during life, you make a donation to the charity offering the program and claim a federal income tax deduction for your irrevocable contribution. It is also possible to fund a donor-advised account through your estate plan, by making it a beneficiary of a charitable trust, a revocable trust (see Chapters 1 and 2) or simply naming it under your will.

Depending on how you want the funds disbursed after you are gone, you can appoint friends or family members as advisers to recommend

Weighing the Possibilities for a

The advantages and disadvantages of using a

	Assets contributed	Deduction limits*	Donor's role in investment
Private Foundation	• Cash	30% of adjusted gross income (AGI)	Able to exercise investment management, within certain rules
	• Marketable securities	20% of AGI Deductible at fair market value (FMV)	
	• Shares of closely held stock • Real estate • Tangible personal property	20% of AGI Limited to cost basis	
Donor-Advised Fund	• Cash	50% of AGI	Fewer investment choices
	• Marketable securities • Shares of closely held stock • Real estate	30% of AGI Deductible at FMV	

*Any deduction that cannot be taken in the year of the donation – for instance, if the donor's contribution exceeds the limit on charitable deductions – can be carried forward up to five years. Tax deductions mentioned here refer specifically to federal taxes. At the state level, rules and regulations regarding tax deductions for charitable giving vary.

future grants, or have the money go into the charity's central fund, in which case the organization would decide how it was spent.

Which works best? For people with sufficient funds for either a private foundation or a donor-advised fund, the deal-maker or -breaker is often how much control they want over both investment management and

Continuing Fund for Charitable Gifts

private foundation or a donor-advised fund.

Donor's role in grant-making	Required distributions	Role of donor's family	Privacy
Complete control	At least 5% of value of non-charitable assets each year	Donor can: • appoint relatives to board • give them responsibility over day-to-day activities • pay them salary, within limitations	None: yearly tax filing, Form 990-PF, is a public record of assets, contributors and grants
Can recommend grants to any IRS-qualified public charity	None, unless fund rules require it (proposals to change this are circulating)	Donor can appoint successors to recommend grants	Donor can request anonymity

grant-making. With a private foundation, donors have total investment oversight, and they can manage the assets themselves while adhering to specific rules, or they can hire an investment manager. With donor-advised funds, donors can recommend that grants be made to IRS-qualified public charities, but legally you have given up the money and your grant recommendations are not binding. Fund trustees have the ultimate say over whether recommendations are followed.

Still, there are certain kinds of grants you can't make with a donor-advised fund. Donors generally can't recommend grants to individuals or create scholarships. Many donor-advised funds won't allow you to support charities organized under the laws of other countries. On the other hand, a private foundation can do all these things. So it's only with a private foundation that you retain ultimate control over grant-making.

Choosing the Best Assets to Donate

To satisfy charitable bequests, the trustee of your living trust or your executor, the person you designate to carry out your wishes under a will, is likely to liquidate your estate and donate the cash. If you plan to make lifetime gifts – for example, by funding a charitable trust, gift annuity, private foundation or donor-advised fund – you have strategic choices about the best assets to donate.

For gifts to a public charity, donors are entitled to an income tax deduction for up to 50 percent of adjusted gross income (AGI) for cash contributions and up to 30 percent for donations of other appreciated assets held more than 12 months. Any deduction that cannot be taken in the year of the donation can be carried forward up to five years.

There are significant benefits to giving away appreciated property. With marketable securities, for example, your deduction, which is subject to the AGI limitations, is based on the full market value of the securities. Since you are not selling the property – merely donating it – you do not have to pay capital gains taxes. Therefore, by donating these assets, rather than selling them and donating the after-tax proceeds, you can, in effect, make the dollars earmarked for charity go much further. And if you still want your portfolio to include that stock because you think it will increase further in value, you can simply buy additional shares at the higher price. In the process, you acquire a new, higher cost basis than you had on the donated shares, which could be beneficial if the assets go up further and you decide to sell them.

Raising the Ceiling on Charitable Deductions

Generally deductions for gifts to a public charity are limited to 50 percent of adjusted gross income (AGI) for cash and to 30 percent for assets held longer than a year, with the possibility of applying a five-year carryover in both cases. But you can elect to deduct up to 50 percent of AGI for certain gifts that would ordinarily qualify for only a 30 percent deduction.

The election is available for gifts to a public charity of appreciated property held longer than one year and applies to securities, real estate and tangible personal property related to the charity's exempt purpose. The trade-off is that instead of being able to deduct the full fair market value of the property, you are limited to cost basis. But if the property being donated hasn't appreciated much, there is less benefit to valuing the donation at fair market value.

Who should consider making this election? Someone who, for one reason or another, is not likely to be able to deduct the full fair market value of a 30 percent gift even using the five-year carryover. That could be true if the value of the donated property is very high, or the person is elderly or in poor health and might die before the end of the carryover period. This election is also used when preparing the final income tax return for someone who has died (the carryover will be lost after that).

You can make the election on a year-by-year basis, so in each case you will want to run the numbers before making a decision. Remember, too, that if you choose to make this election for a particular gift, you must also make the election for all other long-term property donated during the same tax year. While the election doesn't change any deduction that you took in earlier years, it does reduce any carryover from those years, because the initial donation is treated as a gift valued at cost basis rather than at fair market value.

On the other hand, if an asset has declined in value, you are better off selling it, using the loss to offset investment gains and donating the proceeds. In other cases, people living on income from investments may not want to donate those securities at all.

Innovative donors have looked for other assets to give. Open-minded charities have become increasingly receptive to gifts of certain kinds of assets that are not cash or marketable securities.

One potential tax trap to consider: When a donor has a binding obligation to sell any non-cash asset, including real estate, before giving it to charity, the pre-arranged-sale rule forces the donor to pay tax on the gain.

For all gifts other than cash and marketable securities, it is necessary to get a qualified appraisal before taking a deduction for more than $5,000 – more than $10,000 for gifts of stock in a closely held company. Under federal regulations, the appraisal cannot be made more than 60 days before the donation and must be complete by the time the income tax return is due. And don't expect appraisers to grossly overvalue things on your behalf. Those who do risk stiff penalties. If total non-cash donations in a given year (including publicly traded stock) total more than $500, you must file Form 8283 – Noncash Charitable Contributions – with your tax return.

Within these parameters, here are some non-cash assets you could donate.

Real estate. Although real estate remains the most popular type of non-cash gift, these donations carry certain complications. Most charities prefer that the property not be mortgaged, because, depending on the nature of the real estate, the term of the note and the charitable vehicle used, the gift can run afoul of various tax law restrictions. In addition, just as if it were purchasing the property, the non-profit must check for liens and be sure there are no environmental hazards that would carry cleanup obligations under federal law. And since the property will generally be sold, the value must be high enough that the charity is willing to devote the effort and resources to marketing it.

Assuming the charity would like to receive the real estate, there are a variety of ways to contribute it in addition to an outright donation. If you are holding appreciated property that you are prepared to sell – perhaps you invested in land that has since been developed – donating the property to a charitable remainder trust offers a way to avoid capital gains tax and diversify.

If you want to continue using the property, such as your home, you can donate a remainder interest in the personal residence. With this arrangement, you and your spouse can reserve the right to use the property for your own lifetimes and have it pass to charity when you die. Meanwhile, you get an income tax deduction for the actuarial value of charity's remainder interest, based on the ages of the life beneficiaries (the older you are, the larger the deduction), the value of the property and what is known as the Section 7520 rate (named after the section of the IRS Code that applies).

Another possibility, typically used when the charity plans to keep the property, is to enter into a bargain sale: sell the asset to charity for less than the fair market value and take a charitable income tax deduction for the difference.

Tangible personal property. In addition to real estate, charities are receptive to a wide range of other donations, including collectibles and art. In one sense, gifts of art and collectibles are especially beneficial. While the capital gains rate is up to 20 percent for sales of appreciated stocks, bonds and real estate (plus the 3.8 percent Medicare surtax on investment income), the rate for tangible personal property is 28 percent. By donating valuable assets like art, you can avoid paying this tax and can take a charitable income tax deduction. Note that an artist who donates his own work can take a deduction only for his basis (for example, paint and canvas), not the fair market value. The same rule extends to someone who received a piece of art as a gift from the artist during life.

Keep in mind a limitation that applies to these types of gifts: In order for your donation to qualify for a full fair market value deduction, the charity must use the asset in a manner related to its exempt purpose. If the item donated does not satisfy this related use rule, your income tax deduction is limited to your basis in the asset or its fair market value, whichever is less. For example, a donor who gives violins to a symphony orchestra can deduct the fair market value (assuming the orchestra will use them rather than sell them), but giving the same instruments to an animal rights group would limit the deduction to cost basis.

There's a harsh mechanism for enforcing this rule when deductions of more than $5,000 are involved. If the charity sells the asset within three years, part of the deduction is recaptured. If the sale was in the year of your donation, your deduction will be reduced to cost basis. For sales in subsequent years, you must include as income the difference, if any, between your cost basis and the deduction you took. Various penalties apply, including a $10,000 fine for someone who identifies property as having a related use knowing that it is not intended for it.

Bitcoin. Charities, including the United Way and the Wikimedia Foundation, which runs Wikipedia, are starting to accept donations of virtual currencies. So far, the IRS has not outlined the rules on charitable deduc-

Timing Is Everything

If you want favorable tax treatment for your charitable donations, they must be complete in the eyes of the Internal Revenue Service by Dec. 31 of the year for which you want to take a deduction. Here are the rules to keep in mind.

Form of gift	Complete to charity
By check	On the postmark date if sent by U.S. mail (provided the check is honored)
	On the arrival date if sent by private courier (provided the check is honored)
By credit card	Date charge is posted, even if you have not ' yet paid your credit card bill
Stock *If you hold certificate*	On the postmark date if you have sent an endorsed certificate by U.S. mail
	On the arrival date if you have sent an endorsed certificate by private courier
If held by the broker	When you have relinquished control over the asset and the broker has transferred control to the charity

tions for these donations. But the guidance it issued in March 2014 provided some clues. Notice 2014-21, its only pronouncement so far on virtual currency, indicated that, notwithstanding popular nomenclature, for tax purposes it is treated as property (rather than cash).

Presumably, then, the various tax principles that apply to donations of assets such as stocks, bonds and real estate also apply to donations of virtual currency. Therefore, when you donate Bitcoin to a public charity, you generally ought to be able to take a tax deduction for the fair market value of your Bitcoin donation, up to 30 percent of your AGI, if you held it for more than 12 months. If you held it for less than that period, your deduction would be limited to your cost or the fair market value, whichever is less, deductible up to 50 percent of your AGI.

A different rubric would most likely apply if you were tech savvy enough to mine the currency yourself rather than purchasing it from someone else. That would make it "ordinary income" property in the eyes of the IRS rather than an investment that is governed by the tax rules on capital gains. Under that scenario, you could deduct only your cost basis (the fair market value when you mined it), up to 50 percent of AGI, no matter how long you held the property.

The rules on appraisals apply to Bitcoin as they do to other property that isn't publicly traded. With Bitcoin, you need the appraisal if your total gifts of this virtual currency (not just your gifts to one charity) are valued at over $5,000 in a calendar year.

Stock in a closely held company. During the booming 1990s, Internet entrepreneurs donated pre-initial public offering stock to charity, anticipating that their businesses would go public. Ten years later the whole idea seemed quaint, and charities had become much less enthusiastic about these donations. But it's conceivable that they may fly again.

The main impediment for donors is to find a charity willing to accept the gift and to get the shares appraised before you donate them. These appraisals can be expensive – they could easily cost $25,000. The appraiser would have to look at the company's financial statements as well as those of comparable businesses.

IRA assets. Charities, unlike individual beneficiaries, do not need to pay income tax on withdrawals from these accounts. Since money in a retirement account usually passes outside of a person's will or living trust, it's necessary to spell out your wishes to leave it to a specific charity on the beneficiary designation form that you give to the IRA custodian (see Chapter 7). The options include making the charity a 100 percent beneficiary of the IRA or indicating that the charity is a beneficiary of a certain percentage of the IRA, and that the rest should go to individual beneficiaries.

Since 2006, it has also been possible for people 70½ and older to make lifetime gifts of as much as $100,000 per year directly from their traditional

IRAs to charity. The donation can count against the minimum required distribution (MRD) the IRA owner would otherwise be required to take. In that case, the donor doesn't get a charitable deduction, but there's no tax on the distribution, either.

IRA funds donated this way cannot be used for contributions to donor-advised funds, supporting organizations or private non-operating foundations. Subject to those constraints, the money can go to any organization to which you can make a gift that would qualify as a charitable deduction on your tax return.

Appealing as this so-called IRA charitable rollover is from a tax perspective, it has been an on-again, off-again rule that Congress keeps extending (sometimes retroactively) to cover one or two tax years at a time. But here's a strategy you can use while waiting for the next extender: Make the donation, up to $100,000, directly from your IRA to charity. If the charitable rollover is extended, you can count it as your MRD and there will be no tax on the funds you have donated. If not, you'll pay tax on the distribution but, if you itemize, can take a charitable income tax deduction for your donation (subject to AGI and carryover rules).

Life insurance. Life insurance offers a way to benefit charity without reducing your family's inheritance. As noted in Chapter 8, sometimes donors use life insurance to back up a large pledge – for instance, one that would be recognized in the naming of a building, an endowment or a school within a university. That way, if the donor dies before the pledge is fulfilled, the life insurance proceeds can be used to carry out the donor's intentions. Although state insurable interest laws generally prohibit investors from owning insurance on the lives of strangers, most states make an exception for charities so they can insure key donors and continue their endowments.

As with most other charitable donations, this entitles you to an income tax deduction. How you calculate that deduction will depend on whether the policy is new or older, and whether it is paid up, meaning no further premiums remain to be paid. For tax reasons, if a policy still requires premium payments, it's best to donate funds to the charity and let it pay the premiums.

To-Do List

Back to Basics

Providing for charity in your estate plan doesn't necessarily mean giving like Andrew Carnegie. But it does require you to think ahead and update your plan periodically. Whether you want to allocate a lot or a little to charity, here are some basic steps to take.

❧ Identify any charities that you would like to benefit, either through a specific bequest or as alternate beneficiaries if family members disclaim the funds or none of them survives you.

❧ Check that your estate planning documents, including your will, trusts and IRA beneficiary designation forms, include charity as either a primary or an alternate beneficiary.

❧ Ask your children or grandchildren if they would like you to create a fund that they can use for their own charitable giving and whether they are prepared to devote the considerable time needed to administer it.

❧ If your net worth recently increased or decreased and you have included a specific bequest to charity in an earlier version of your estate plan, make sure the balance between how much would go to family and to charity still reflects your wishes.

❧ If your estate plan includes a substantial gift to charity, notify the nonprofit of your intentions and discuss any preferences you have about how the money will be used.

❧ If you are concerned that a charitable bequest will shortchange your family, give heirs the option, through your will or beneficiary designation form (for IRA assets), to disclaim, or turn down, the inheritance and have it go to the charity you have named on the relevant document.

Chapter 17

Create Roadblocks To Creditors

*Read this chapter if you
worry about being sued.*

Preserving resources for yourself or future generations goes beyond sound investment and money management. You also need to guard against losing assets to creditors, a category that may include everyone from disgruntled spouses and ex-spouses to people who win lawsuits against you.

The best defense is to erect a variety of roadblocks that make it difficult, if not impossible, for creditors to reach your money and property. These asset protection strategies can range from relying on state-law exemptions to creating multiple barriers through the use of trusts and family limited partnerships or limited liability companies. The strategies vary by state.

In This Chapter...

- *Specific State-Law Exemptions And Traps*
- *Special Protection for Retirement Accounts*
- *Trusts to Benefit Other Family Members*
- *Limited Partnerships and Limited Liability Companies*
- *An Irrevocable Trust to Benefit Yourself*
- *Trusts in Certain Foreign Jurisdictions*

Among the many people who might benefit from asset protection are those whose work could generate lawsuits: doctors, lawyers, accountants, construction contractors and real estate developers; executors and trustees; and directors of public companies. Keep in mind that in tough economic times, people find reasons to sue. It's prudent to ensure you are not an easy target.

A well-constructed asset protection plan may guard against risks not covered in your malpractice, errors-and-omissions, property and casualty, and other insurance policies.

Asset protection is not limitless, however. State and federal laws against fraudulent conveyance prohibit transfers with the intent to hinder, delay or defraud creditors. Unfortunately, no hard-and-fast rules spell out what these terms mean, and they are applied on a case-by-case basis. So if a court finds there has been a fraudulent conveyance, it can declare the transfer void and order the assets be made available to creditors, even if it means returning them from a foreign country.

Asset protection does not inoculate people who commit crimes. But it may insulate those who did business with a crook and can demonstrate they did not know of the crime – provided they took asset protection measures long before the crime came to light. Financial fraud has been much in the spotlight recently, with Bernard L. Madoff acknowledging that he engaged in the largest fraud in Wall Street history – a decades-long Ponzi scheme that appears to have cost investors tens of billions of dollars. He pleaded guilty in 2009 to fraud, money laundering, perjury and theft, and is now serving a 150-year prison sentence.

An ideal time to address the issue of asset protection is in the course of creating or revising an estate plan. It is possible that some of your assets are already beyond the reach of creditors, and others could be, with minor adjustments.

When thinking about asset protection, consider your net worth, as well as the potential liability that surrounds your profession. Take account not only of assets you already own, but also wealth you might inherit or generate – for example, if an existing or start-up venture is sold or goes public. Depending on your situation, it may be possible to rely on a variety of strategies, either separately or in combination with one another.

Specific State-Law Exemptions and Traps

The simplest and sometimes the best way to protect your assets is to take advantage of any state-law exemptions that apply. These vary. Some states, for example, offer creditor protection for annuities, life insurance (either for the cash value, the death benefit or both) and individual retirement accounts. Others do not. You must be a resident of the state to take advantage of its exemptions.

People living in Florida, a debtor-friendly state, can take advantage of its unlimited exemption for the equity in a personal residence, subject to certain restrictions that apply if you file for bankruptcy. Other states with such generous homestead laws, as they are called, include Iowa, Kansas, Oklahoma, South Dakota and Texas. Elsewhere, the homestead exemption may be limited to a certain dollar amount. Depending on state rules, it might make sense to pay off your mortgage, if you are able to, because doing that could make both that sum and your existing equity in the property secure from creditors.

> ## Did You Know?
>
> Even in states that protect a home from creditors, limitations apply for bankruptcy filers. You must have lived in the state for more than two years. And you can't exempt more than $125,000 unless you acquired the home three years and four months before the filing.

Another asset protection strategy that varies by state is the option for spouses to hold property in tenancy by the entirety. When assets are owned this way, only the couple's joint creditors have access to them; creditors of just one spouse cannot collect on a lien unless there is a divorce or until one spouse dies. Even then, the creditor can reach the property only if it is the debtor who survives.

Twenty-six states permit tenancy by the entirety, some of them only for real estate – not for stocks, bank accounts and other assets. Roughly a handful of states allow it for all such investments. In these states, a married couple that held its brokerage account in tenancy by the entirety could ensure that only the couple's joint creditors would have access to the brokerage account, so it could not be used to satisfy a judgment against one of them alone.

But beware another form of joint ownership, and the most common one, at that – joint tenants with rights of survivorship. This form of joint ownership (it appears on some joint bank or brokerage statements abbreviated "JTWROS") is available to both people who are married and those who are not.

The advantage of joint tenancy is its convenience. Both owners have access to the assets during life, and when one dies, the survivor immediately becomes the sole owner of the whole property, regardless of what the will says, or even if there is no will. These features make this type of ownership universally appealing – to aging parents and their adult children, siblings, spouses and domestic partners.

The drawback, from an asset protection perspective, is that joint tenancy exposes each owner to the other's potential liabilities. For example, if you are a joint tenant on your mother's brokerage account and someone wins a lawsuit against you, half the assets in your joint account could be wiped out.

Perhaps a better choice for people who are not married or who can't own assets as tenants by the entirety is a type of ownership called tenancy in common. With this form of title, you own just part of the property, known as an undivided interest. Typically, your share would equal whatever you contributed, though if someone gave you the asset – say an interest in land – as a gift or bequest, it would equal whatever percentage of ownership you received. Legally, you cannot do anything with the property unless your co-owner consents. When one owner dies, just that person's share gets included in his or her estate. As a rule, creditors have access only to the portion owned by the person who owes them money rather than to the whole thing.

Special Protection for Retirement Accounts

Even in states where the law is unfavorable to debtors, federal law provides an important exemption for retirement plans covered by the Employee Retirement Income Security Act (ERISA), making such plans one of the most solid asset protection tools. Remember, though, that ERISA plans are subject to federal (but not state) tax liens.

IRAs, however, are not covered by ERISA. If the account holder has filed for bankruptcy, federal bankruptcy law protects up to $1 million, unless the account is an IRA that has been rolled over from a company plan. In that case, the entire account balance is protected in bankruptcy. In other situations, state laws determine whether IRAs (including Roth IRAs) are shielded from creditors' claims. Most states exempt 100 percent of the assets while they are in the account. But state laws vary widely on whether withdrawals are covered, protections extend to inheritors as well as the initial owner and former spouses can reach the funds. The Supreme Court made clear in a 2014 decision that inherited IRAs (as opposed to those you set up and fund yourself) are not protected in bankruptcy.

If you recently retired or changed jobs, you have the option of rolling over assets from a qualified plan, such as a 401(k), into an individual retirement account. From an estate planning perspective, this strategy has various benefits

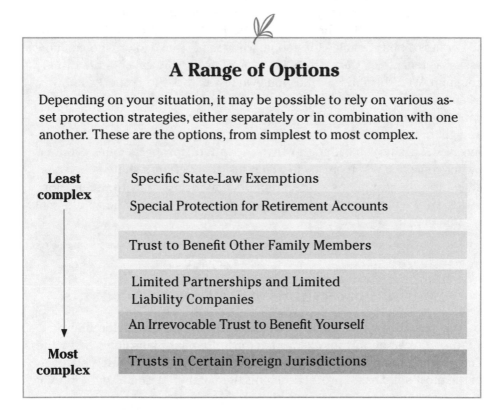

A Range of Options

Depending on your situation, it may be possible to rely on various asset protection strategies, either separately or in combination with one another. These are the options, from simplest to most complex.

Least complex

Specific State-Law Exemptions

Special Protection for Retirement Accounts

Trust to Benefit Other Family Members

Limited Partnerships and Limited Liability Companies

An Irrevocable Trust to Benefit Yourself

Most complex

Trusts in Certain Foreign Jurisdictions

(see Chapter 7). However, if you have a large retirement account and live in a state where IRAs are not protected from creditors, you may prefer to leave the assets in the company plan if your former employer allows it. You should consult a lawyer familiar with the rules of the state where you live.

Trusts to Benefit Other Family Members

Many people are concerned about keeping family money in the family, especially as children grow, get married and embark on lives of their own. Trusts are an efficient way to do that (see Chapter 6). They are also an excellent means of sheltering assets from creditors. For many people this is the main reason to set up trusts and to leave assets permanently in this legal wrapper.

Even if you do not think of trusts as a long-term arrangement, you might want to rely on one until children or grandchildren reach a certain age, are able to handle the funds or are in stable marriages. You can choose arbitrary ages at which the trust should make payouts of income or principal, or leave the choice up to the trustees. Another option is a hybrid approach, in which the trust specifies payouts at specific ages but the trustee can postpone distributions if the beneficiary is a spendthrift or has creditor problems.

> ### Did You Know?
>
> If you plan to leave IRA assets to family, they may not be protected from your beneficiaries' creditors, depending on where they live. But you can shield the assets by leaving the IRA to a trust. To do that, you must name the trust on the IRA beneficiary designation form.

The more flexibility you build into the trust, the better it can provide protection from creditors. For example, you can give trustees the power to move the situs, or location, of the trust in response to new state laws that achieve better creditor protection. In some states, trustees can decant the trust – pay out funds from one trust to another, which could help them continue creditor protection.

What you should *not* do is make your beneficiaries the co-trustees of their own trusts, with the power to make distributions to themselves. While it is generally fine for them to participate in investment decisions, giving them discretion over payouts could interfere with the creditor protection that the trust affords.

Limited Partnerships
And Limited Liability Companies

Some people are already using family limited partnerships (FLPs) and limited liability companies (LLCs) for estate planning purposes or to maximize investment opportunities (see Chapter 15). They can achieve the additional benefit of asset protection.

Here is how they work: A senior family member puts assets into the entity, which is most often an FLP but may be an LLC in states where the LLC law is the more favorable for valuation purposes. Then the individual gives or sells shares in the entity that holds the assets to family members or to a trust for the family members' benefit.

From an asset protection perspective, the chief attraction of FLPs and LLCs is that in many states creditors cannot take all the assets in the entity or force a liquidation, no matter how much they are owed. In these states, the only thing they can get is what is known as a charging order – a court order giving them the right to the debtor's distributions up to the amount of the debt plus interest.

For even better asset protection, it may be possible to use an FLP or LLC in conjunction with a trust – for example, by selling or transferring an interest in the entity to a trust that benefits other family members. This popular estate planning strategy also helps with asset protection by creating two layers of insulation.

Using a family limited partnership does subject you to a different kind of risk, however: scrutiny by the Internal Revenue Service. The IRS does not like the fact that wealthy families use these entities as a tool to discount the value of assets transferred to younger generations, and there have been many audits – and tax court cases – challenging them. Even if your main concern is asset protection, you will need to be mindful of the tax traps discussed in Chapter 15.

An Irrevocable Trust to Benefit Yourself

Known as a domestic asset protection trust, or self-settled spendthrift trust, this type of trust is a relatively new option available in certain states – but not permitted in most states.

Domestic asset protection trusts are designed to give you access to the income and principal of the trust while protecting the assets from the claims of future creditors. These trusts typically include a spendthrift clause that prevents beneficiaries from assigning their interests and creditors from reaching the trust assets.

In most states, the general rule is that whatever trust assets the grantor (the person who set up the trust) can reach are also available to creditors. Fourteen states – Alaska, Delaware, Hawaii, Mississippi, Missouri, Nevada, New Hampshire, Ohio, Rhode Island, South Dakota, Tennessee, Utah, Virginia and Wyoming – have changed their laws to permit self-settled trusts to be outside the reach of creditors. These states require that the trust be irrevocable and be administered in the state, that there be at least one local trustee and that at least some trust assets be held in the state. Whether or not you live in one of these states, it is possible to set up an asset protection trust there by designating the state as the situs for the trust.

> ## *Did You Know?*
>
> Among the people who would benefit from asset protection are those most likely to be sued: doctors, lawyers, contractors, real estate developers, executors and trustees. An asset protection plan may guard against risks not covered by insurance.

So what happens if someone gets a judgment against you in a state that does not permit asset protection trusts, like Texas, and you have set up a trust in a state that allows them – for example, Alaska? The full faith and credit clause of the Constitution says a judgment in one state must be honored in another. But, so far, there is little, if any, track record of how courts will apply the clause to these trusts.

Nor can all assets just as easily be put in self-settled trusts. Marketable securities are the best candidates, because the certificates can be readily transferred to an account in the state where the trust has its situs. Real estate, on the other hand, can be problematic, because it is generally subject to the jurisdiction of the state where it is situated (for a way around this, see Chapter 10). Operating businesses are troublesome for the same reason.

If you are interested in a domestic asset protection trust, discuss it with your financial advisers. They can help you determine whether this strategy makes sense and the best way to create this type of trust.

Trusts in Certain Foreign Jurisdictions

Offshore trusts can provide significant tactical advantages, because theoretically they are beyond the reach of the United States courts. Therefore, a creditor faces the inconvenience of having to litigate in the country where the trust is formed. Generally a U.S. judgment would not be enforceable in this location.

Popular locations for offshore trusts include the Bahamas, Belize, the Cook Islands, Liechtenstein and Nevis. Their fraudulent conveyance rules may be more lenient than U.S. laws, affording asset protection even when a trust is set up shortly before a lawsuit is filed.

Offshore trusts have several drawbacks, however. The U.S. courts have not looked favorably on them, and in one notorious case, a couple who used a Cook Islands trust to stash the cash from their fraudulent investment scheme were jailed for contempt because they refused to bring the assets back. The trusts can be expensive and complicated to create and maintain. In addition, some individuals may be more comfortable keeping their assets on U.S. soil. Keep in mind, also, that even if assets are offshore, they are still subject to U.S. income tax.

Whether you are considering a domestic asset protection trust or an offshore trust, it is best not to fund it with everything you own. You will also want to make sure the value of the assets used to fund the trust is large enough to justify the associated costs. And be sure any lawyer you retain to help you set up and monitor the trust has done dozens of them before (see Chapter 18). You don't want to turn into a test case.

To-Do List

Follow the Asset Protection Continuum

The best approach to asset protection is to start with the least complicated strategy necessary to achieve your goals. It is possible that some of your assets are already beyond the reach of creditors. Others could be, with minor adjustments. Here are some issues to explore with your financial advisers.

❧ *Does your state have a homestead exemption?*
If so, find out whether paying off a mortgage would make both that sum plus your existing equity in the property secure from creditors.

❧ *Does your state allow spouses to hold property as tenants by the entirety? (Most cover only real estate, but some permit it for other assets.)*
If so, and you are married, determine whether, for asset protection reasons, any property should be transferred from one spouse to the other or out of joint ownership into the name of one spouse individually in order to protect the assets from creditors. Note that special tax rules apply to transfers to non-citizen spouses (see Chapter 3).

❧ *Did you recently retire or change jobs, or do you expect to soon?*
If so, consider the pros and cons of rolling over assets from a qualified plan, such as a 401(k), into an individual retirement account.

❧ *Does your family have any trusts?*
If not, discuss the possibility of creating trusts for this purpose. If so, ask advisers whether they need to be adapted, or whether you should create additional trusts to address your family's need for creditor protection.

❧ *Does your estate plan include the use of a family entity, such as a limited liability company or family limited partnership?*
If not, determine whether there are reasons to set one up, including the possibility of protecting your assets (see Chapter 15).

Chapter 18

Keep Your Plan Current

*Read this chapter even if you think
you can leave well enough alone.*

I t always feels painful to spend money on estate planning, because you don't live to reap the benefits, even if you know your heirs will. But by now you should be convinced of how important it is to move forward. Estate planning starts with a fundamental goal: Once you have provided for your own needs, take care of those you love. That's true whether you have a lot of money or a little.

Your estate plan does not have to be complex, especially now that the amount that is exempt from taxes has reached $5.43 million ($10.86 million for married couples) and will be adjusted for infla-

In This Chapter...

- ⚜ *When to Update Your Plan*
- ⚜ *How to Start a Family Conversation*
- ⚜ *What Value a Lawyer Can Add*
- ⚜ *How to Find Good Legal Advice*
- ⚜ *The Seasons of Estate Planning*

tion. If you haven't revised your estate plan in 5 or 10 years, the current tax-free amount may be much higher than it was when you last met with your lawyer. With very little effort you may now be able to structure your plan so that taxes will not be an issue.

You can accomplish a great deal just by having the basic documents prepared and applying simple strategies to take full advantage of the estate tax exemption. That, plus avoiding some key estate planning mistakes covered throughout this book, might be all you need to do right now.

As your finances and personal concerns change, you may have to update or completely revise earlier arrangements. A guiding principle mentioned again and again in this book is that when various means to an end are available, you should generally choose the simplest tool that achieves your goals.

When to Update Your Plan

Vast sums of money have been lost through missed estate planning opportunities and family battles over documents that had not been updated. Estate plans should be reviewed at least every five years, more often if there is a change in the law, your finances or personal circumstances. These important developments, most of which are covered more extensively in other chapters, may require action on your part.

Changes in the law. The year 2010 was a watershed because the amount of an estate that is exempt from federal estate tax and from generation-skipping transfer tax in each case took a big jump, to $5 million, from $3.5 million in 2009. This system was made permanent, with inflation adjustments in the American Taxpayer Relief Act of 2012, and the tax-free amount is now $5.43 million. That, coupled with the financial crisis that lowered many people's net worth, makes a review urgent.

Near term, check to see if your will includes formula clauses, which are recognizable because they include phrases like "that portion," "that fraction" or "that amount" (without saying what it is). These are signs of lawyers trying to take maximum advantage of the exemption, which kept changing.

Instead of naming a specific sum that will go into a trust, such as a bypass or credit-shelter trust (see Chapter 3) or a generation-skipping trust (Chapter 14), many wills refer to an amount up to the exemption or express the sum as a percentage of whatever the limit happens to be when the person dies. This is good standard practice, but with the exemption at $5.43 million, make certain the will reflects your intent. For example, it's possible that under your current arrangement, the designated fraction, or percentage, means less money would go to your spouse than you would like (Chapter 4) or that too much would go to your grandchildren.

State estate tax is another issue to consider if you live in or own real estate in a state that has such a levy (14 states and the District of Columbia). Often the state exemption is smaller than the federal one, and this poses a dilemma for spouses. Two of these states, Maryland and New Jersey, also have an inheritance tax, and another five have inheritance tax instead of estate tax. Unlike estate tax rates, those for inheritance tax are typically based on the family relationship between the inheritor and the person who died.

The 2013 Supreme Court decision in *United States v. Windsor* will change estate planning for same-sex married couples. They can now take advantage of the unlimited marital deduction, portability, gift-splitting and IRA inheritance strategies. So it may be possible for them to simplify their documents. State estate or inheritances taxes, in states that have them, remain a separate concern, in states where same-sex marriage is not legal. The U.S. Supreme Court may resolve the problem in a case that was pending as this book went to press. (For a more detailed discussion, see Chapter 4.)

To stay current about laws that may affect your estate plan, visit the Web site for this book, www.estateplanningsmarts.com. You can also register at the site to receive occasional e-mail notifications of recent articles, book updates, products and services, and follow the author on Twitter at http://twitter.com/djworking.

Impending good fortune. Whether you have made a promising investment or own a business and are expecting a huge success (such as a sale or initial public offering, or the introduction of a revolutionary product), think about shifting some of the upside potential to family. Once the appreciation occurs, making transfers will consume more of your $5.43 million lifetime gift-tax exemption or require you to pay gift tax on a larger amount. If you can afford to transfer some holdings before they increase in value, that appreciation will be sheltered from both gift tax and estate tax. Various methods for making these transfers while minimizing or eliminating gift tax were discussed in Chapter 15.

Economic decline. The financial maelstrom that began in 2008, and has continued to have an effect, created extraordinary estate planning opportunities. A combination of low asset values and the decline in interest rates used in structuring various wealth transfer tools drastically reduced the tax cost of making lifetime transfers, whether through gifts or intrafamily transactions.

Unfortunately, the same economic forces also made people extremely anxious about their own financial security and less inclined to reduce their net worth through lifetime transfers – even of beaten-down assets. Still, the potential to turn lemons into lemonade is something to remember. Strategies such as the grantor retained annuity trust, or GRAT, and installment sales to family members or to trusts for their benefit (covered in Chapter 15) create an income stream for the person making the transfer. This may be an attractive feature if you worry that reducing your net worth in order to save estate taxes later will leave you short of money.

Change in committed relationships. Providing for your spouse or partner is covered extensively in Chapter 4. Keep in mind that if you get divorced or split up, you should not procrastinate about changing your plan. This applies not only to your will or living trust, but also to assets that pass outside of probate (Chapter 2), such as retirement assets, life insurance and savings bonds, as well as jointly titled bank accounts, brokerage accounts and real estate.

In some states, the law provides recourse if you forget to change the paperwork – say, for your life insurance or IRA – when you get married. But even where this fallback exists, your spouse may wind up with less than he would have received if you had changed the forms to make him the beneficiary.

Divorce poses special complications, especially with respect to jointly held accounts and retirement assets. The non-employee spouse generally has a right to half the retirement assets acquired during marriage. But determining what's marital property and what's separate property can be tricky.

Witness the battle over ownership of the Los Angeles Dodgers, which became an issue in 2010 during the divorce proceedings of Jamie and Frank McCourt. He said she had signed a postnuptial agreement six years earlier, ceding any ownership rights in the team (reportedly a strategy to protect this valuable asset from creditors' claims). She argued in court papers that she didn't realize she was signing away her rights. There was speculation that she wanted to continue as co-owner in order to secure an interest in the team for the couple's four sons.

A court ruled that their agreement was invalid. Of the six copies the couple had signed, three listed the team as Frank's separate property (California is a community property state) and three did not (seemingly a lawyer's error). This made their intent unclear, the court found. The battle went into extra innings before they ultimately settled.

Another issue to consider is the inheritance rights spouses may have once they are separated but not yet divorced. That became a gossip item after Elizabeth Edwards, wife of the philandering former Senator John Edwards, died in 2010. Elizabeth's will, signed about a week before she died, did not mention John, from whom she was separated. At the time of her death, the couple was waiting out the one-year period before they could get a divorce. And during that time, under the law of North Carolina, their home state, John had the right to inherit one-third of what she left behind, regardless of what her will or living trust said.

This conflict, which could have been averted by a postnuptial agreement, might trip up other couples. However, it has not posed a practical

Now or Later?

The increase in the estate tax and generation-skipping transfer tax exemption to $5.43 million ($10.86 million per couple) should compel some people to radically change their estate plans. Others can leave well enough alone. This self-test will help you determine which category you're in. It's not a substitute for consulting your lawyer but will give you some idea of how soon to make that appointment.

1. How old are you?
a. <40	4	points
b. 40-50	6	points
c. 51-60	8	points
d. 61-75	10	points
e. >75	20	points

2. Describe your health.
a. Good or excellent	0	points
b. Fair	5	points
c. Poor	10	points
d. Terminally ill	50	points

3. Are you married?
a. No	0	points
b. Yes	10	points

4. What is your estate worth, including insurance and retirement plans?
a. <$5.43 million	0	points
b. $5.43 million-$10.86 million	10	points
c. >$10.86 million	8	points

5. When did a lawyer last review your estate plan?
a. Less than five years ago	6	points
b. More than five years ago	8	points
c. I have not done an estate plan	40	points

Source: Gideon Rothschild

6. Have there been any major changes in your finances or personal circumstances?

a. No	0	points
b. Unsure if changes are considered major	6	points
c. Yes	10	points

7. Are you expecting a big increase in your net worth?

a. No	0	points
b. I don't know	3	points
c. Yes	5	points

8. How important is it for you to minimize estate taxes?

a. Unimportant	0	points
b. Somewhat important	5	points
c. Very important	10	points

9. How important is it for you to protect inheritances from creditors?

a. Unimportant	0	points
b. Somewhat important	5	points
c. Very important	10	points

10. Does your will provide for a credit-shelter (bypass) trust or a generation-skipping trust?

a. No	0	points
b. Unsure	5	points
c. Yes	10	points

11. Do you live in a state that has an estate or inheritance tax?*

a. Yes	10	points
b. No	0	points

Score:

<20	You may not be significantly affected by the $5.43 million exemption.
21-50	You should consider a review within the next few years.
>51	See your estate planning lawyer at once.

These states are: Connecticut, Delaware, Hawaii, Illinois, Iowa, Kentucky, Maine, Maryland, Massachusetts, Minnesota, Nebraska, New Jersey, New York, Oregon, Pennsylvania, Rhode Island, Tennessee, Vermont and Washington, as well as the District of Columbia.

problem in the Edwards case: He was substantially more wealthy than she and had not taken steps that would reduce his children's share of their mother's estate – an estimated $1.5 million covered by the will plus unspecified additional assets poured into Elizabeth's living trust. Since the trust is a private document, it is not clear whether it benefited John.

Still, as this case suggests, whether you are getting hitched or un-hitched, there are situations when estate planning should certainly be a subject of negotiation and a business-like agreement. Macabre as it may sound, inheritances often are covered in prenuptial agreements, especially when there are children from a previous marriage.

Now that spouses can share each other's $5.43 million exclusion amount – either through lifetime gifts or bequests – some couples may also choose to cover how these amounts will be applied, in prenups or postnups. This will be especially true in remarriages, when one of the couple is wealthy, and the other enters the marriage with an unneeded $5.43 million exclusion – call it a tax dowry. They might agree on an arrangement to combine the two exclusion amounts for lifetime gifts (a process called gift-splitting) so that the wealthier spouse can give more to her children tax-free.

Becoming a parent. Whether you're married, single or cohabiting, and no matter how much you're worth, if you're a parent or about to become one, get serious about planning. Most importantly, be sure you name a guardian for your children and provide for them financially in case something happens to you (Chapter 5). If you start a family with your current spouse and have children with a previous one, make sure you update your plan as soon as the new child arrives. Blended families pose special challenges. To head off future problems, some couples provide in the divorce decree for the purchase of life insurance to benefit their child.

Becoming a grandparent. In the flush of a grandchild's birth, whether it's your first or you are lucky enough to have many, "revise estate plan" might not be the first item on your to-do list. But when the excitement subsides, there are a few items you should check. Make sure that your will and any trusts that are part of your plan cover this new family member if his or her parents die before you (assuming, of course, that's your intent). The same goes for assets that pass through beneficiary designations; in this regard, pay special attention to retirement accounts. If there are other ways you would like to help these children and their parents, you'll find information elsewhere in this book on

Postmortem of Gandolfini's Estate Plan

James Gandolfini was best known for his portrayal of Tony Soprano, a ruthless mob boss who struggles with depression. In real life his situation was also complicated. He married twice and had a child from each union. His son, Michael, from his marriage to Marcy Wudarski, was 14 when Gandolfini died suddenly, in 2013, at age 51. At the time of his death he was married to Deborah Lin. The couple's daughter, Liliana, was born two months before he signed his will; her birth likely motivated him to redo his estate plan.

Gandolfini provided amply for both children, but they may not wind up with equal shares. Under the will, Michael will receive all his father's clothing and jewelry. He is also the beneficiary of a $7 million life insurance policy owned by a trust – an arrangement required as part of the divorce settlement with Wudarski.

The will gives Liliana 20 percent of the residuary estate – what is left after estate expenses, taxes and specific sums have been paid to others named in the will. She gets control over these funds at age 21, which is sooner than many people think advisable (better to wait at least until she's finished college).

There was also a house in Italy that Gandolfini wanted his children to share and keep in the family, according to his will. It is to be held in trust until they have both reached age 25, at which time they will own it outright, in equal shares.

After the will became public, tax pros had a field day commenting on what they consider to be faulty planning that will cause Gandolfini's heirs to pay more estate tax than necessary. Much of this analysis is speculative, since the actor probably also had significant assets that do not pass through probate. Had he relied on a living trust, which unlike a will is not a public document, his plan would have remained much more private.

allocating funds for college (Chapter 9), subsidizing young families (Chapter 10) and setting up special grandchildren's trusts (Chapter 14).

Losing a spouse. This life-altering event can leave you feeling emotionally adrift for a very long time. In the short term, it also will saddle you with finan-

Updike's Oversight

In most respects John Updike, the author, was vigilant about updating his estate plan. With handwritten changes, he kept track of outstanding loans that were to reduce his children's inheritances. And in 1991, in notations on the will he had signed six years earlier, Updike crossed out a section in which he bequeathed $35,000 to his mother, Linda G. Updike. Above it, he inserted wording that left the "remaining" Pennsylvania real estate that he had inherited from her to his four children in equal shares. (Linda Updike died in 1989.)

Updike reiterated these changes in a 2006 codicil (amendment) to his will, with some elaboration. The children were also to get the money obtained from the sale of 36 acres of their grandmother's real estate and invested for their benefit. The funds, the codicil indicates, were in a Fidelity account managed by his wife, Martha R. Updike (who was not the children's mother). Records of these investments were kept in a tall gray filing cabinet in Updike's office in a file labeled "MOM-MOM MONEY."

In the same codicil, Updike left each of his children one of his possessions: a two-volume edition of Samuel Johnson's dictionary to his daughter Elizabeth; a gateleg table to his son David; a framed and inscribed drawing by Saul Steinberg to his son Michael; and a framed James Thurber drawing to his daughter Miranda.

Another item, a 17th-century veneered bench left to his former wife, Mary Pennington Weatherall, proved problematic. In a 2012 affidavit filed in Massachusetts Probate and Family Court, Updike's widow indicated that before he died, in 2009, Updike "gave the bench to one of his sons." Apparently he never revised his will to reflect that fact, and it became an issue in administering his estate.

cial paperwork at a time when you may be at your most vulnerable. The 2012 tax law has added to this burden in ways that affect your own estate planning.

Keep in mind a couple of deadlines. A surviving spouse can add any unused estate tax exclusion of the just-deceased spouse to her own $5.43 million exclusion; this is called portability (see Chapter 3). So a widow can pass on as much as $10.86 million, untaxed, through either lifetime gifts or her will. But portability is not automatic. To get it, the executor of the estate of the first spouse to die must file an estate tax return within nine months (a six-month extension is allowed). Surviving spouses should see to it that the form is filed even if they have nowhere near $5.43 million of their own, because who knows what the future holds?

Nine months is also the deadline if you plan to disclaim (turn down) any portion of what you inherited so that it can go directly to other family members or into a trust for their benefit. The 2012 tax law makes it more likely that spouses will leave everything to each other outright. Others may want to give the survivor the right to disclaim at least some money and have it go into a bypass trust (see Chapter 4). This allows the survivor to make an informed decision based on her own financial resources and federal and state estate laws at that time. If you want to use this postmortem tax planning strategy, you need to keep an eye on the calendar.

Meanwhile, make sure you have a durable power of attorney, appointing a family member, friend or adviser whom you trust as an agent to act on your behalf in financial and legal matters if you become unable to because of illness or disability (Chapter 1). Also revisit your health care proxy, a separate document that authorizes an agent to make medical decisions on your behalf. Many spouses give each other these powers. When a spouse passes away, you need to be sure that you have designated someone else to take care of you and your finances.

Another thing to do as soon as possible is name beneficiaries for any retirement assets you inherited from your spouse. If you die without doing that, your heirs will lose valuable income tax benefits associated with these accounts. Other options for spouses who inherit these accounts don't have the same urgency (Chapter 7).

Once things have settled down, you should revise your will and living trust. Unless you remarry, you will have the last word about which assets ultimately go to family, charity or the tax man. If you have amassed more wealth than is covered by the exclusion amount (including what you carry over from your spouse), you may want to take steps to minimize estate tax. Start by converting traditional IRAs to Roth accounts – one of the simplest, most tax-efficient estate planning tools available and one that costs nothing in legal fees and can sharply reduce income taxes (Chapter 7). Then consider various ways to transfer assets to family members during your lifetime (Chapter 15). If you're thinking of moving to another state or dividing your time between various places, factor in how that would affect your estate plan (Chapter 11).

Bad health. With any luck you will never need the information under this heading, but keep in mind that it's here, and come back to it if you do.

The diagnosis of a degenerative disease or terminal illness throws families into crisis. Between doctors' visits, prolonged hospital stays and seemingly endless waits for what often turn out to be unfavorable test results, each new day can challenge our coping mechanisms. These are all things we can't control.

During the rare calm moments in the eye of the storm, some people take comfort in getting their estate plans in order. This is the time to have your lawyer review any documents and bring them up to date. If estate taxes are a concern, you can use the annual exclusion that allows you to give up to $14,000 ($28,000 for married couples) each year to as many recipients as you would like without incurring gift tax.

Often a power of attorney (see Chapter 1) authorizes your agent to make these gifts if you can no longer write the checks. Since transfers under the annual exclusion are not considered taxable gifts, they are not subject to the general rule, contained in the Internal Revenue Code, that if you do not survive more than three years after making a gift, any gift tax you paid on the transfer will be counted as part of your estate.

Annual exclusion gifts are the most common form of planning when a death is imminent. Checks need to be cashed before the death occurs, or the assets are considered part of the estate. To alleviate this problem, wise donors make deathbed gifts using certified or cashier's checks.

Another relatively simple estate planning device is available if someone who is ill survives for more than a year. It involves transferring an asset (such as a house) that has appreciated in value from a healthier person to an individual (typically a spouse) who is expected to die first. Assuming the person receiving the asset is a U.S. citizen, spouses are entitled to an unlimited gift-tax exemption when they make such transfers.

Why would you want to do this? When the healthy person inherits the assets, he is entitled to a basis adjustment to their value on the date of death. If the house has appreciated, the basis step-up could reduce or eliminate the capital gains tax your heirs have to pay if the property is sold.

There are two other more complicated techniques that lawyers sometimes recommend for people who are in poor health. One is the private annuity. It involves a sale of assets in exchange for an unsecured promise to pay an annuity for the rest of the seller's life. Another is selling assets to family members or to a trust for their benefit in exchange for a self-canceling installment note. These wealth transfer techniques are discussed in greater detail in Chapter 15.

How to Start a Family Conversation

For many people, estate planning is both a private matter and a morbid topic – not something they want to discuss. It's essential for spouses to have these conversations. Increasingly, they're taking place between parents and their adult children, too.

Families that speak freely about estate planning can sometimes address awkward situations that might arise, like the choice of the executor – who is in charge of distributing assets after someone dies – or succession plans for a family business or the leaving of assets in trust. While clearing the air takes a lot of courage, it can help avoid surprises, lead to better financial planning and promote family harmony.

How families handle delicate issues depends both on the particular circumstances and the personalities involved. Sometimes it is best to have a series of talks rather than covering everything at once. Depending on whom you are talking with, here are some conversation starters.

With your spouse or partner. Couples have their own special ways of communicating, and you know better than anyone which approach will play best with your mate. You can emphasize your own mortality ("I'd like to talk about ways to provide for you and the family in case something happens to me"), make it a subject of mutual concern ("We're not getting any younger – I think it's time we did our wills") or focus on the children ("Now that we are parents, we really shouldn't procrastinate any longer about doing our wills").

Sometimes it's easier to start with current events or an anecdote about other people. Perhaps it's a movie you saw, a book you read, a news report about someone your age who recently died or a sudden death in your community. If a friend or family member has talked to you about her or his own plan (say you're the godmother of a friend's new baby), it can help take the sting off confronting the awful thought that one of you is likely to go first. Those who encounter pushback from a spouse or partner have a card to play that's probably not appropriate for other people who are broaching the topic: "We owe this much to each other" or "Please do this for my sake."

With adult children. While parents have no obligation to change an estate plan after hearing a child's preferences, disclosing what they plan can help refine their approach. For example, maybe you are thinking of leaving one child a larger inheritance than the others because he has more children. By sharing these details with this child, you might learn that he would prefer to receive the same amount as his siblings rather than face their wrath.

Above all, explaining the principles that have influenced your decision could make them easier for children to accept. For instance, don't assume it's obvious that you left the summer home to one child because he used it most; a parent's death or even illness can rekindle sibling rivalries from decades earlier.

Of course, parents who share their thinking risk hostility from adult children who do not like what they hear. To reduce the possibility of a hostile audience, parents may talk to each child separately instead of addressing them as a group. Afterward, ask each child, "What do you think?" You may be surprised to find that adult children have great ideas and interesting opinions.

With your parents. A trickier situation involves adult children who notice signs of a parent's mental decline. Once parents become incompetent, they lack the legal capacity to make binding commitments, so it is important to sign estate planning documents before that happens. But bringing up the matter may threaten a parent's independence and desire for control.

One possibility is for the child to say: "I just did my own estate plan. Don't you think you should update yours?" Another is to convey a story about a friend's parent who did not take the necessary measures (for example, by not signing a durable power of attorney) and how much hardship was caused for those children.

Sometimes there is a fine line between being well-meaning and protecting your own inheritance. For that reason, lawyers typically insist that they have an opportunity to meet with the parent separately, even if a child provides transportation to the office.

Their goal is to guard against the two most common grounds for contesting a will or trust. One is undue influence, which refers to efforts to coerce someone to sign estate planning documents that favor one heir over others. Another is the argument that the client lacked capacity when signing the document.

Sure, it is easy to get frustrated with parents who do not put their affairs in order. But keep in mind that having the conversation requires them to confront their mortality. For both parents and children, that can be a gigantic step.

What Value a Lawyer Can Add

Lawyers aren't cheap, so it's reasonable to ask why you need one rather than relying on books or software and Web sites that help you create your own documents at a fraction of the cost. We can expect more people to ponder that issue now that the exclusion from federal estate tax is $5.43 million a person ($10.86 million per couple). Especially if you don't need sophisticated tax advice, you may be tempted to save some money and forgo professional help. The risk of doing that and relying on do-it-yourself estate products is that your documents might not accomplish your wishes, mistakes will delay the administration of your estate and sorting things out after you die will saddle your heirs with hefty bills.

A will is the document people most often try to do themselves, and the one most fraught with land mines – some of which only an experienced lawyer can spot. One problem that often arises with do-it-yourself products is inadvertently cutting a family member out of your estate plan. For example, some software will automatically disinherit a special needs child if you answer yes-or-no questions a particular way. (If you have such a child, always get professional help.)

Certainly not every will written without a lawyer leads to a horror story, and some written by lawyers go awry, too. But owning a home, being married or having children complicates estate planning and increases the risk of foul-ups. Even now that we can each pass $5.43 million free of federal estate tax, some married couples will face decisions about whether to use trusts for non-tax purposes.

If you have a lawyer prepare your will and perhaps a life insurance trust (see Chapter 8), she may throw in the other, simpler documents for free, or for a nominal additional cost, and useful help to go with them. For example, with a durable power of attorney, a lawyer can help you determine what rules apply in your state and whether, if you own real estate in more than one state, you will need a power of attorney in both. Other issues you might cover in a consultation: Whom can you trust? What powers should be included (for example, the power to make gifts or create a trust)? When should the document take effect?

Likewise, with a health care proxy, the rules vary from state to state – whether you can appoint more than one person and whether you can name a successor, for example. If you're not sure about whom to choose, you may want to discuss that with someone experienced in these matters.

How to Find Good Legal Advice

Y ou might be doing an estate plan for the first time or giving your existing plan a tune-up or a total overhaul. Either way, it's best to choose someone who not only has the necessary skills but with whom you feel comfortable. To find the best lawyer for the job and pay only for what's essential, consider these issues.

Do you need a new lawyer? If you have never done any estate planning, the answer is probably yes. This is not a job for the real estate lawyer who did your house closing, for example.

If you are updating an existing plan, the professional who created it might be able to make the changes after a brief conversation with you by phone or in person. But if your situation has changed and you need sophisticated advice about generation-skipping transfer tax (see Chapter 14), special needs trusts (Chapter 5) or protecting assets from potential future creditors (Chapter 17), make certain you are getting the expert guidance you need – and be prepared to pay for it. Don't be afraid to ask, "How many of these kinds of matters have you handled?" If the answer isn't dozens, consider finding someone else.

How do you choose the right lawyer? Start with referrals from people you know who are in similar situations or from professionals whose judgment you trust, like accountants, financial advisers or other lawyers. State and local bar associations can direct you to lawyers in your area but can't vouch for their skills. Names can also be found on martindale.com, the nationwide lawyers' directory that you can search by location and area of practice, and on www.actec.org, the Web site of The American College of Trust and Estate Counsel, a group of trust and estate lawyers.

Depending on where you live, you may have a choice between large national firms with many practice groups or estate planning boutiques – small firms that specialize in trust and estate work. The latter tend to be less expensive because their overhead is lower.

Contractions in the legal workforce can be your gain, as well-trained young or midcareer lawyers cast off by big firms hang out their shingles. These lawyers keep overhead low by sharing space with bigger firms or renting no-frills space near the government offices where public records must be filed. For certain matters, city dwellers can reap additional savings by seeking out small-town lawyers, whose rates are far below those of their urban or suburban counterparts.

Going to the lawyer who has done an estate plan for other family members (for example, your parents) poses confidentiality problems. That lawyer can't reveal any aspect of the others' plan to you without the consent of the individual or couple. If this poses a conflict of interest so that the professional can't handle the matter, the same issue typically applies to other lawyers at the firm. But she can probably recommend a colleague elsewhere.

Whomever you are considering, meet before you decide to work together (most professionals charge for this initial consultation only if you go forward). Pay attention to chemistry. Is the lawyer listening, or does she seem to have her own agenda? You want someone who can empathize with your concerns and put herself in your shoes. Also consider whether you would feel comfortable revealing highly personal information that bears upon your estate plan. This might include not only your finances, but also the state of your marriage, relationships with other family members and whatever concerns keep you awake at night.

Hourly rate or flat fee? While most lawyers charge an hourly rate, some offer flat fees for a package of basic estate planning documents, like a will, living trust, power of attorney, living will and health care proxy. Each billing arrangement has pros and cons. With a flat fee you know in advance what you will have to spend and you avoid surprises. But it's also possible that your lawyer is using a standard form without taking much time to adapt it to your situation. Ask the lawyer how much customization you can expect in a flat-fee arrangement.

You strengthen your hand when negotiating fees by doing a little homework to cut down on the time your matter consumes. Start by reading the chapters of this book that apply to your situation (the Table of Contents can help you identify them). Before contacting a lawyer, give some thought to the items on the To-Do list at the end of each chapter, such as those on pages 43, 97 and 137.

Another way to control costs – and an alternative you could propose if you don't think a flat-fee arrangement will meet your needs – is to ask your lawyer to bill by the hour but give you an estimate of the total cost and a warning (with an explanation) if it looks as though you will incur additional charges. Either way, lawyers commonly charge for such expenses as photocopies, long-distance calls and faxes, sometimes marking them up (so clarify this in advance). You should also have a clear idea of what kind of service to expect. It's perfectly legitimate to ask questions like: "What would be the next step?" or "How long will this process take?" and "How quickly do you typically respond to telephone and e-mail messages?"

All the terms should be summarized in a contract, called an engagement letter, that your lawyer prepares. It ought to cover the scope of the work, the fee, the prices for disbursements and how disputes will be resolved. This agreement should be easy to understand. Don't hesitate to ask questions if anything isn't clear.

Should you and your spouse have separate lawyers? This adds to the cost, because two people will need to get up to speed on your situation and draft documents rather than having one lawyer produce his-and-hers versions of the same wills and trusts. But under most state laws, when couples are jointly represented, everything you tell the lawyer, even privately, is not confidential from your spouse.

Separate representation may be desirable in second marriages when children from a previous marriage are part of the landscape. It's even more important for people in troubled marriages or when one spouse has skeletons in the closet – like a secret companion or an out-of-marriage child. Having your own lawyer may also be appropriate when one spouse is an heir to a family business and the tradition has been to exclude in-laws from ownership and management.

The Seasons of Estate Planning

As you move through life, expect your estate planning needs and priorities to evolve, though events that require you to update your estate plan may or may not coincide with specific life stages. Such stages tend to be driven not only by chronological age, but also by your finances, maturity and relationships – especially those with a spouse or partner, and children or grandchildren. Consider these situations.

You are single. Be sure you have all the basic estate planning documents to provide for your own care, if you can no longer handle your affairs,

(Chapter 1) and to leave your assets to the people (Chapter 2) or charities (Chapter 16) that you wish to benefit. You may not need life insurance, but if your employer or union provides a policy, make sure you have properly completed the beneficiary designation form (Chapter 8). Beneficiary designation forms for your retirement accounts should also be filled out and coordinated with the rest of your estate plan (Chapter 7).

You have a spouse or partner. In addition to the documents that single people need, you should consider the best way to take advantage of the $5.43 million estate tax exclusion (Chapter 3). Most likely, your primary goal in planning is to leave your spouse or partner well provided for financially (Chapter 4).

Married couples have more built-in protections than unmarried ones. This often lulls them into postponing planning until they have kids. That's a mistake, as the seven-year legal battle between Terri Schiavo's husband and her parents illustrates. Schiavo slipped into a coma at age 27. A court named her husband her guardian, but since she hadn't signed a living will, her parents were able to delay for years his decision to remove her feeding tube. She died in 2005, after the tube was removed.

Less dramatically, your state's law governing what happens to your assets if you die without a will may differ from what you would want done. In most states parents share the estate with a surviving, childless spouse; in some, siblings and more distant relatives have a claim on separately titled assets, too.

You have young children. People's financial situations at this stage vary hugely. Those who had business successes at a young age or had children after their careers were well established might be in a position to take advantage of some sophisticated planning techniques described in Chapter 15 to create a financial cushion for their children in the years ahead. Others have so many current expenses that they can't think much beyond that. Even if you fall in the second category, this is the ideal time to start saving for the enormous education expenses that await you (Chapter 9). And if you never thought you needed life insurance, you might want to reconsider (Chapter 8).

You have children who are young adults. Life has gotten simpler in some ways and more complicated in others. (Are you surprised to find you still lie awake at night worrying about your children?) If you accumulated $10.86 million or more during your peak earning years, you may be in a position to transfer some money now to save estate taxes later. This could be as simple as giving children a hand as they buy a first home or start a business (Chapter 10), or might involve complex transactions designed to shift large sums while minimizing gift tax (Chapter 15). The more money at stake, the more attractive you may find estate planning devices like long-term trusts that will protect assets from potential future creditors and others who prey on the wealthy (see Chapters 6 and 17).

Another issue to consider: In most states parents don't have the authority to make health care decisions or manage money for their kids once they turn 18, even if they still have those kids on their health insurance plans and claim them as dependents on their tax returns. That means if a young adult is in an accident and becomes disabled – even temporarily – a parent might need court approval to act on his or her behalf. So it should be a rite of passage for every 18-year-old to sign a health care proxy, living will and power of attorney.

You have grandchildren or great-grandchildren. They give you so much joy, and if you've done well financially, you may feel especially generous toward them. Just beware the onerous 40 percent generation-skipping transfer tax (Chapter 14) that could diminish your gifts.

Keep in mind that you're at the time in life when estate planning might become more complicated and more costly. Perhaps you're thinking about the legacy you would like to leave – for example, by providing everyone in your family with the best possible education (Chapter 9), developing a succession plan for the family business (Chapter 12), keeping a vacation home in the family (Chapter 11) or making meaningful gifts to charity (Chapter 16).

To-Do List

Keep Advisers Current

We talk to our accountants at least once a year as we do our taxes, and we communicate with investment advisers more often. In comparison, we often leave estate planning lawyers out of the loop. A 10-minute phone call to your lawyer can identify events that may be significant. Let your lawyer know if you:

❧ Have lost your spouse

❧ Have a new child or grandchild

❧ Have substantially more or less money than when you last did your estate plan

❧ Have been diagnosed with a serious illness

❧ Are approaching age 70½

❧ Recently received a large inheritance or learned about one you may receive in the future

❧ Are thinking of selling your company

❧ Have started a promising business or made an investment that may pay off handsomely

❧ Want to make a significant gift to charity

❧ Have bought real estate or other costly assets

❧ Want to sell your home

❧ Plan on moving to a different state

Glossary

After born child – offspring not included in a parent's estate plan, because the will or living trust was signed before the child was born and not updated. In most states the law protects them from disinheritance, but other complications can arise.

Alternate beneficiary – see *contingent beneficiary*.

Alternate valuation date – a date six months after someone dies that may be used instead of the date of death to measure the fair market value of his assets to see if the estate will be subject to tax. The alternate valuation date is used when it would reduce the tax owed, but whatever date the heirs choose must apply to everything in the estate (for example, they can't use one date for the house and another for the stock portfolio). For property sold or distributed within six months of the death, the alternate valuation date is the date of that transaction.

Annual exclusion – the amount (currently $14,000 for individuals, $28,000 for married couples) that can be given annually to each of as many recipients as the donors choose without incurring gift tax. (The amount is periodically adjusted for inflation, in $1,000 increments.)

Applicable exclusion – the sum of the basic exclusion amount and the deceased spousal unused exclusion amount.

Applicable federal rate (AFR) – the interest rate, announced each month by the Treasury, that is used for loans and installment sales between family members. The rate depends on whether the loan is short term (three years or less), midterm (more than three years but no more than nine) or long term (more than nine).

Ascertainable standards – specific guidelines that a trustee must follow when making payouts to the beneficiaries of a trust (for example, "health care, education, maintenance and support"), in contrast to a trust that leaves distributions solely to the trustee's judgment.

Asset protection – the process of trying to make it impossible, or at least more difficult, for potential future creditors to require the liquidation of certain property or accounts to settle their claims.

Attorney in fact – one or more people appointed to act as agent under a durable power of attorney. The term is confusing because the agent need not be a lawyer. In fact, most lawyers do not want to take on this time-consuming role, which also carries the responsibility of acting as fiduciary.

Bargain sale – selling an asset, such as tangible personal property or real estate, for less than its fair market value. When the sale is to a charity, the donor can take a charitable income tax deduction for the difference. When the sale is between family members, it is considered part sale and part gift, for tax purposes.

Basic exclusion amount – the amount that we can each transfer tax-free during life or at death. That amount is $5.43 million, adjusted for inflation.

Basis adjustment – an increase or decrease in the cost basis of inherited assets to reflect their fair market value either on the date of death or on a date six months later. An increase in the cost basis could reduce or eliminate the capital gains tax that heirs have to pay if the property is sold.

Beneficiary – a person or charity entitled to money or other assets under an estate planning document, such as a will or trust.

Beneficiary designation – a clause in a document that indicates who should inherit certain assets that do not pass under a will or trust. Examples: retirement accounts and the proceeds of a life insurance policy. See *designated beneficiary*.

Bequest – what a person or organization receives according to the terms of a will or trust.

Bomb clause – a provision in a will or living trust indicating how assets would be distributed if the individual creating the document and her closest heirs are wiped out simultaneously, as in an accident. The purpose is to provide for the distribution of assets among people or charities who might not otherwise receive anything.

Buy-sell agreement – an agreement among business owners covering what would happen to their interest in the company if events like disability, death, divorce or personal bankruptcy occur. By requiring a sale under certain circumstances (known as trigger events) and by specifying the terms beforehand, a buy-sell can prevent one owner from becoming an unwilling partner with another owner's heirs or leaving a surviving spouse illiquid because the remaining owners refuse to buy the survivor's inherited shares.

Bypass trust (or *credit-shelter trust* or *family trust*) – a planning tool that serves a variety of purposes. When the first spouse dies, the trust is funded with assets up to the basic exclusion amount. It distributes income and principal to the survivor or other family members while the surviving spouse is alive, then passes on whatever is left to family. Funds in the bypass trust are covered by the basic exclusion and are not taxed when the first spouse dies. Nor are they considered part of the survivor's estate, so they are not subject to tax when she dies. There are two other ways for couples to each use their full federal estate tax exclusion amount. One is to leave assets outright to people other than a spouse – for example, to children. Another is to rely on portability. Some couples might want to use these trusts for other purposes, including: sheltering assets from state estate taxes; avoiding estate tax on any increase in value of the assets; applying the generation-skipping transfer exemption; and protecting inherited assets from creditors.

Carryover basis – the original price paid for an inherited asset. Typically, this information is not relevant to heirs. See *basis adjustment*.

Charging order – a term connected with the use of a family limited partnership or a limited liability company, to achieve asset protection. It refers to the fact that creditors generally cannot take all the assets in the entity or force a liquidation, no matter how much they are owed. The most they can get is a court order giving them the right to the debtor's distributions up to the amount of the debt.

Charitable gift annuity – a contract in which the donor contributes assets, typically cash or marketable securities, and the charity agrees to pay a fixed amount of money annually to that person and perhaps to the surviving spouse. The annuity can be paid immediately or deferred until the donor reaches a specific age (which might be some time during retirement).

Charitable lead trust – see *charitable remainder trust.*

Charitable remainder trust – one of two split-interest arrangements in which charitable and non-charitable beneficiaries each get a share of the trust assets but at different times. In a charitable remainder trust, individual beneficiaries (or a trust for their benefit) receive income for whatever period of time is specified – their lifetimes or a term of up to 20 years. When this interest ends, the charity receives what is left, known as the remainder interest. The charitable lead trust reverses the priorities: The charity receives its payout up front for the period selected by the person creating the trust. When this payout ends, the non-charitable beneficiaries, usually family members, get what is left. Each of these vehicles is irrevocable and carries significant tax advantages.

Codicil – an amendment to a will, which must be signed with the same formalities as a will.

Conservator (or guardian) – someone appointed by a court to oversee the finances of an individual who can no longer handle her or his own affairs and has not made prior arrangements about who should play this role.

Contingent beneficiary – the alternate, or secondary, beneficiary (a person, charity or trust) named on a beneficiary designation form to receive assets if the primary beneficiary has died or chosen to turn them down. See *disclaim.*

Credit-shelter trust – see *bypass trust.*

Cross-purchase agreement – a form of a buy-sell agreement used by business owners in which the surviving owner has the obligation or right to buy the share held by the other's estate.

Crummey power – the right for a limited time, usually 30 or 60 days, to withdraw from the trust the yearly gift intended for each beneficiary. Each year, the trustees must send a letter, called a Crummey notice, to the beneficiaries (or the parents, guardian or representative, if the beneficiaries are minors) advising them of this right. Any trust that includes this power is a Crummey trust, although the trust may be named for other distinguishing features.

Custodial account – an account at a bank, mutual fund company or brokerage house that designates an adult to oversee the assets of a child until the child is able to withdraw them under state law (usually at age 18, 19 or 21). See *Uniform Transfers to Minors Act.*

Custodian – the bank or financial institution that holds a retirement account, or the individual or institution that holds a custodial account.

Decant – to pay out funds from one trust to another. State laws that allow decanting essentially permit amendment of irrevocable trusts.

Deceased spousal unused exclusion, or ***DSUE, amount*** – an awkward phrase introduced by the 2010 tax law. It refers to any part of the basic exclusion amount (currently $5.43 million and adjusted for inflation) that was not used by the spouse who died most recently. See *portability.*

Decoupled – when a state has an estate tax and the state exemption amount is less than the federal one.

Designated beneficiary – a term defined in the Internal Revenue Code, with further elaboration in IRS regulations, that refers to people named to receive IRA assets when the account owner dies and to certain trusts that also qualify for a stretch-out (defined on page 340).

Devise – an arcane and rarely used word that in the past referred to a transfer of real property at death, in contrast to a bequest, which referred to a gift of personal property, and a legacy, which covered money. A document written in plain English today might simply describe a gift or distribution instead.

Digital assets – a new category of assets that emerged with the Internet age. From an estate planning perspective, the question is whether what we leave behind is purely a digital footprint or something that we can transfer through a will or trust. Often the primary issue involves giving other people access to online accounts, even if they have little or no monetary value, as is generally the case with e-mails, family photos stored online and social media accounts. Other digital assets, such as domain names, Bitcoin or Web pages and blogs, may be more valuable and may be transferred.

Direct skip – a term that involves the application of generation-skipping transfer, or GST, tax. Refers to an outright gift to an individual or money put into a trust that exclusively benefits skip persons. In this case, the person making the transfer or her estate (rather than the recipient) generally pays any GST tax.

Disclaim – to decline an inheritance (typically, with the intent of benefiting another person or a specific charity) – usually for tax reasons. People who disclaim, known as disclaimants, are generally treated as if they had died before the person from whom they are inheriting. The assets go to the person next in line as designated in the estate plan or under state law if the plan makes no such provision, or to a specific charity if that is what the estate plan specifies.

Distribution – payout from a trust, partnership or a retirement account, or according to the terms of a will.

Domestic asset protection trust (or ***self-settled spendthrift trust***) – a trust designed to give the grantor access to the income and principal of the trust while protecting the assets from the claims of future creditors. These trusts are allowed in 14 states: Alaska, Delaware, Hawaii, Mississippi, Missouri, Nevada, New Hampshire, Ohio, Rhode Island, South Dakota, Tennessee, Utah, Virginia and Wyoming.

Domicile – the state someone calls home. While residency determines liability for income taxes, domicile determines whether a person's estate is subject to state estate tax. It is generally based not just on time spent in a place (the test for residency), but also on additional evidence that it's the place a person is most closely connected to, as demonstrated by voting records, a safe deposit box rental and memberships in local clubs, for example.

Donor-advised fund – a popular alternative to a private foundation that can be funded during life, through an estate plan or a combination of the two. Contributors make irrevocable gifts to a non-profit that administers the fund in conjunction with funds set up by other donors. The donor or the designated successor advisers can recommend which non-profit organizations should receive grants from the account.

Drop-down trust – a trust that receives a personal residence or vacation home at the end of the term of a qualified personal-residence trust. See *QPRT*.

Durable power of attorney – appoints a family member, friend or adviser as an agent to act on a person's behalf in a variety of financial and legal matters and authorizes actions even after the person's disability.

Dynasty trust – a trust designed to continue in perpetuity (or for a very long time) and pass wealth through multiple generations without incurring estate, gift or generation-skipping transfer taxes. Perpetual trusts are allowed only in states that have abolished the rule against perpetuities. These include Alaska, Delaware, South Dakota and Wisconsin. Residents of other states can choose one of these states as the situs, or location, of a trust; in most cases, some connection to the state is needed and certain conditions apply.

Elective share – a minimum portion of a spouse's estate that the surviving spouse is entitled to under state law. A spouse can waive her right to the elective share in a prenuptial agreement that specifies how assets will be distributed if the couple is married when one of them dies.

Engagement letter – a contract between a lawyer and client that describes the terms under which they will work together. It should cover the scope of the work, the fee and how disputes will be resolved.

Escheat – the process by which the state acquires property that has no owner. This can happen if someone dies without a will or living trust. See *intestacy*.

Estate – everything a person owns when she or he dies, including house and personal property; all investments, whether in the form of bank or brokerage accounts, retirement plans, real estate or alternative investments; and any interests in a family business or partnership.

Estate tax exemption – the amount that can be passed on to heirs tax-free before the 40 percent federal estate tax kicks in. That amount is $5.43 million, adjusted for inflation, plus any unused amount that a widow or widower carries over from the spouse who died most recently. The 2010 tax act uses the term "applicable exclusion" rather than "exemption," but this word is not likely to disappear from common parlance.

Executor (personal representative) – the person or institution that administers an estate and remains in charge until it is legally closed.

Exhaustion rule – an IRS rule that requires the party paying a private annuity to have assets sufficient to continue the payments not just for the seller's actual life expectancy but until he reaches age 110.

Family limited partnership (FLP) – along with a limited liability company (some lawyers are more familiar with that structure), this family-controlled entity is used to minimize the tax cost of transferring assets. A senior family member puts assets such as marketable securities, real estate or shares of an operating business into the entity, then sells or gives away shares in the entity – rather than the assets themselves. Since the interests can't readily be sold outside the family, their value is discounted for *both* lack of marketability and lack of control (often a total discount of 20 to 30 percent).

Family trust – see *bypass trust*.

Fiduciary – a person or institution (such as a trust company) that is legally obliged to act in the best interest of those whose assets it manages. Examples include a trustee, an agent designated under a durable power of attorney or the custodian of a custodial account.

Forced heirship – laws in some countries designed to avoid disinheritance of a spouse or child. These laws, which may apply to property U.S. persons own in that country, entitle certain family members to a preset share of assets left by a relative who has died. Forced heirship rules can frustrate estate planning strategies that are popular in the U.S. (Louisiana, which has some laws based on the Napoleonic Code, still requires forced heirship in certain cases.)

Foreign Bank Account Report (FBAR) – a form that must be filed with the Treasury Department by June 30 each year, reporting foreign investment accounts, such as bank accounts or brokerage accounts, held during the previous year.

Formula clauses – provisions in a will or trust that include phrases like "that portion," "that fraction" or "that amount" (without saying what it is) instead of naming a specific sum to be distributed – to a person, a trust or a charity. For example, these clauses might refer to an amount up to the estate tax exemption that is to go into a bypass trust or express the sum as a percentage of whatever the limit happens to be when the person dies.

Fraudulent conveyance – a term used in the context of asset protection that refers to a transfer with the intent to hinder, delay or defraud creditors, typically in anticipation of a lawsuit. State and federal laws prohibit such transfers. Unfortunately, no hard-and-fast rules spell out what these terms mean, and they are applied on a case-by-case basis. If a court finds there has been a fraudulent conveyance, it can declare the transfer void and order the assets be made available to creditors.

Future interest – something beneficiaries can't use right away, as opposed to a present interest, which they can. The distinction is important in estate planning because a future interest will not qualify for the annual exclusion. Including Crummey powers in a trust is one way to address this issue.

Generation-skipping transfer, or *GST, tax* – the tax that may apply when assets are given directly to grandchildren, or trusts are set up, or added to, that benefit this generation or future ones. The GST exemption is $5.43 million, adjusted for inflation; a 40 percent tax applies once you have exceeded this limit. See *skip persons.*

Gift-tax exemption – the amount a person can give away during life without triggering gift tax. Once a person has passed the limit, which is currently $5.43 million per person, adjusted for inflation ($10.86 million for married couples), a gift tax of 40 percent applies. On the estate tax return, the tax-free amount available when someone dies is reduced by the sum he or she has used for lifetime gifts. If a person exceeded the limit, heirs can take a credit for the gift tax that was paid for making lifetime gifts. The 2010 tax act uses the term "applicable exclusion" rather than "exemption," but this word is not likely to disappear from common parlance.

Gift-splitting – when married couples combine their annual exclusions to give away up to $28,000 to each of as many people as they choose each year. A gift-splitting couple can give $14,000 each, $28,000 from a joint account or $28,000 from one of their individual accounts. Couples can also gift-split with their applicable exclusion amount and together transfer up to $10.86 million through lifetime gifts.

Grantor – the person who sets up and funds a trust. See *settlor*.

Grantor retained annuity trust (GRAT) – a short-term irrevocable trust that makes an annual payment to the grantor for the entire trust term based on a rate set each month by the Treasury. Any appreciation in the trust when the annual payments end above the rate set by the Treasury passes tax-free to remainder beneficiaries.

Grantor retained income trust (GRIT) – an irrevocable trust set up by someone who retains the right to get income from the trust for a specific number of years. When that term expires, all the trust assets, including any appreciation, go tax-free to the named remainder beneficiaries.

Grantor trust – a trust in which the person who creates the trust, known as the grantor, retains certain rights or powers. The term refers not to a single variety of trust but to a set of characteristics that can be incorporated into various types of trusts. A grantor trust is not treated as a separate entity for income tax purposes and the grantor, rather than the trust or its beneficiaries, must pay tax on trust earnings. This amounts to a tax-free gift from the grantor to the beneficiaries.

Guardian – someone appointed to care for a person, her money or both. The guardian, who in many states is subject to court oversight, may be appointed by a court, as in the case of someone who is no longer able to handle her finances and has not signed a durable power of attorney (in this context the guardian is sometimes called a conservator). Parents should appoint a guardian, through their wills, to care for a child who is a minor or who has special needs. To handle the child's money, the parent would need to designate a financial guardian or, better yet, set up a trust that puts these matters in the hands of a trustee and provides more direction about how the funds should be spent.

Health and Education Exclusion Trust (HEET) – a complex estate planning technique used to fund health care or education for multiple generations while avoiding generation-skipping transfer tax. A HEET must incorporate two features: The trust must make payments directly to the schools or care providers and the trust must have a charity as a co-beneficiary.

Health care agent – see *health care proxy*.

Health care power of attorney – see *health care proxy*.

Health care proxy (also known as health care power of attorney) – authorizes someone, known as a health care agent, to make medical decisions on behalf of the person signing the proxy.

Health Insurance Portability and Accountability Act – see *HIPAA*.

HIPAA (Health Insurance Portability and Accountability Act) – the federal law designed to protect medical privacy; it prohibits doctors and hospitals from sharing medical information without a patient's permission.

HIPAA release – gives doctors and hospitals permission to share medical records with specific people in addition to a person's designated health care agent.

Homestead law – a law in certain states that makes all or part of the equity in a personal residence exempt from the claims of creditors.

"I love you" will – the practice, common among spouses, of leaving everything to each other. All the assets then qualify for the unlimited marital deduction and are not taxed when the first spouse dies. But those assets become part of the survivor's estate and could be subject to tax when the surviving spouse passes away.

In terrorem clause – see *no-contest clause*.

Incapacity – a mental state in which people do not know who their family members are, what assets they have or what they want to do with them. Once someone becomes incapacitated, it is generally legally too late to make changes in estate planning documents.

Inclusion ratio – reflects what portion of assets are exempt from the generation-skipping transfer tax when exempt and non-exempt assets have been mixed in the same trust. Estate planners try to design trusts covered by the GST-exemption that have what's called a zero inclusion ratio, meaning that the trust is completely GST-exempt. That way, there isn't any tax on either a taxable distribution or a taxable termination.

Income in respect of a decedent – income that wasn't taxed before a person's death and would have been taxed if the individual had lived long enough to receive it. The most important example involves a traditional IRA that is inherited. Because the IRA owner did not pay income tax on the funds in the retirement account, the person or entity (such as a trust) that is a beneficiary of the IRA must pay tax as the money is withdrawn.

Installment sale to an irrevocable grantor trust – an estate planning technique in which senior family members sell assets to a trust that will benefit younger relatives and, in exchange, receive an interest-bearing promissory note. Assuming a sale at fair market value and interest at the applicable federal rate, there is no gift and, therefore, no gift tax.

Instrument – an estate planning document that looks like a contract and is used to create an entity such as a trust.

Inter vivos – an estate planning vehicle that takes effect during life, as opposed to one that is testamentary and takes effect when someone dies (for example, an "inter vivos trust" or an "inter vivos transfer").

Intestacy – a ranking of inheritors in order of priority for people who die without a will or living trust. Typically, the spouse comes first, then children, parents and siblings. See *escheat.*

Irrevocable – an estate planning document that cannot be changed. Examples include an irrevocable life insurance trust (ILIT), a grantor retained annuity trust (GRAT) and a qualified personal-residence trust (QPRT).

Irrevocable life insurance trust (ILIT) – a trust created to purchase and own a life insurance policy. Its main purpose is to avoid a situation in which the person insured owns a policy on his own life, because that could result in estate taxes. An ILIT can also benefit minors, who are not allowed to own the policy directly but only through a custodianship or a trust. Another trust can be the beneficiary of an ILIT (for example, a special needs trust or a generation-skipping transfer trust), and an ILIT can be the remainder beneficiary of a trust (such as a grantor retained annuity trust).

Issue – an arcane word for descendants. Still used in some wills, and occasionally by estate planners in conversation.

Joint tenancy with rights of survivorship – a popular form of ownership in which both owners have access to the assets during life, and when one of them dies, the survivor immediately becomes the sole owner of the whole property, regardless of what the will says or whether there is a will. See *tenancy in common* and *tenancy by the entirety.*

Legacy – traditionally, a gift at death of money but now used to refer to a gift of real property or personal property as well. Increasingly, the word also refers to passing along family values and traditions.

Leveraging – applying various strategies to pack as much value as possible into both the lifetime exemption and the annual exclusion. Examples include using annual exclusion gifts to fund the premium of a life insurance policy and using a grantor retained annuity trust (GRAT) or a qualified personal-residence trust (QPRT) to discount the value of the interest being transferred.

Life estate – the right to own or use an asset (typically real estate) that ends when someone dies.

Lifetime exemption – see *gift-tax exemption* and *applicable exclusion*.

Limited liability company – see *family limited partnership*.

Living trust (revocable trust) – safeguards assets and provides for the care of someone who can no longer handle his or her affairs, then determines who will receive the property when that person dies.

Living will – expresses preferences about certain aspects of end-of-life care rather than leaving them up to the person named in a health care proxy.

Marital deduction – an unlimited deduction from estate and gift tax that postpones the tax on assets inherited from each other until the second spouse dies. It applies only if the inheriting spouse is a U.S. citizen. See *QDOT*.

Marital share – assets left to a spouse. They are covered by the unlimited marital deduction as long as they go to the spouse either outright, through a qualified terminable interest property trust or through a trust with a power of appointment.

Minimum required distribution – the amount that owners of traditional retirement accounts and inheritors of traditional accounts or Roth IRAs must withdraw in a given year unless they inherited the account from a spouse. The required payout is based on the account balance on Dec. 31 of the previous year divided by the individual's remaining life expectancy, as listed in IRS tables. See *stretch-out*.

No-contest clause – a provision in a will or living trust designed to avoid legal disputes by indicating that anyone who formally challenges the document gets nothing. Some states prohibit these clauses. Also called an in terrorem clause.

Non-exempt trust – a trust that would ordinarily be subject to generation-skipping transfer tax. This tax can be avoided by allocating an individual's exemption to assets as they are put into the trust. If the exemption has already been used up, the tax would have to be paid.

Non-probate assets – money or other assets that pass by contract or by operation of law rather than under a will or living trust. These include retirement assets, life insurance and savings bonds, as well as jointly titled bank accounts, brokerage accounts and real estate. For many people, these non-probate assets represent a large part of what they leave behind. Who gets these assets is determined by the paperwork you fill out and what type of account they are in; it's important to coordinate them with the rest of your estate plan.

Non-resident aliens – citizens of another country who do not live in the U.S.

Offshore trusts – trusts in certain foreign jurisdictions, generally set up for asset protection purposes.

One-lung trust – a single trust left to a spouse, instead of setting up both a marital trust to provide for the spouse and a separate bypass trust to provide for the spouse and other relatives. This strategy involves giving the executor the option of making the QTIP election over some of the trust funds when the first spouse dies. To make this possible, the bypass trust must be "QTIP-able," meaning that it provides (or could provide, as the result of the election) that the spouse will get all the income and that nobody else is entitled to any distributions from the QTIP portion of the trust.

Outright bequest – gives recipients immediate ownership of their inheritance. In contrast, the assets can go into a trust, which puts a person or company in charge of managing the assets and distributing them according to the wishes of the grantor, as expressed in the trust instrument.

Payable on death – see *transferable (or payable) on death*.

Pecuniary bequest – a transfer at death of a fixed dollar amount, which can be expressed as a specific number or as a formula.

Per stirpes – when a beneficiary dies, inheritances that get passed down to a beneficiary's descendants rather than going to other members of her own generation.

Perpetual trust – see *dynasty trust*.

Personal property – see *tangible personal property*.

Personal property memorandum – provides guidance or direction (depending on state law) to an executor about whom should receive jewelry, art and other personal property not described in the will.

Personal representative – a word used in two contexts, as a synonym for executor and as a reference to someone who has the right to a person's medical information under the Health Insurance Portability and Accountability Act, HIPAA.

Portability – the ability of widows and widowers to add the unused estate tax exclusion of the spouse who died most recently to their own. A concept introduced by the 2010 tax law (although the term was invented by tax geeks and does not appear in the legislation), portability was made permanent by the 2012 tax law. To take advantage of portability, the executor handling the estate of the spouse who died will need to transfer the unused exclusion to the survivor, who can then use it to make lifetime gifts or pass assets through his or her estate. The prerequisite is filing an estate tax return when the first spouse dies, even if no tax is owed. This return is due nine months after death with a six-month extension allowed. If the executor doesn't file the return or misses the deadline, the spouse loses the right to portability.

Pot trust – a trust with multiple beneficiaries at the same time, as opposed to just one.

Pour over – a provision in a will directing that, after certain distributions have been made, all remaining assets be paid to a trust, referred to as a pour over trust.

Power of appointment – the right of a trust beneficiary to name the next person to receive the trust property. This power may be special, meaning that she must designate someone from a certain group, or general, meaning that she can appoint anyone she chooses (or her own estate).

Power of attorney – see *durable power of attorney.*

Pre-arranged-sale rule – a rule that applies when a donor has a binding obligation to sell any non-cash asset, including real estate, before giving it to charity. This rule forces the donor to pay tax on the gain.

Precatory – wording in an estate plan that expresses a preference, but not a requirement, about something you want done after you die. For example, "If I die with an unused estate tax exclusion, the executor must file an estate tax return electing portability," makes it a requirement, while precatory language might ask the executor to file the return, "if my surviving spouse requests it."

Present interest – see *future interest.*

Principal – the assets used to fund a trust plus any appreciation or capital gains associated with those assets. Distinguished from trust earnings, which are considered income.

Private annuity – a sale of assets in exchange for an unsecured promise to pay an annuity for the rest of the seller's life. The payout is based on the seller's life expectancy under government actuarial tables.

Private foundation – a tax-exempt legal entity set up by an individual or a family to make grants to charities or individuals. Unlike a donor-advised fund, donors may have total control over both investment management and grant-making.

Probate – the process through which a court determines that a will is legally valid.

Protector – a neutral party, such as an attorney, accountant or family friend, who provides checks and balances by supervising agents under a power of attorney or trustees of a trust.

QDOT, or ***qualified domestic trust*** – a trust used to leave assets worth more than the basic exclusion amount when they are going to a spouse who is not a U.S. citizen. Without this trust, anything above the exclusion amount would be taxed immediately. Any time the QDOT distributes principal, it must withhold estate tax – at the rate that was in effect when the spouse died.

QPRT, or ***qualified personal-residence trust*** – an irrevocable trust that removes part of the value of a costly home from the estate and shelters future appreciation. The grantor puts her primary residence or vacation home into an irrevocable trust, retaining the right to live there rent-free for a specified number of years. During that time the trust, of which she could be trustee, owns the property. When the period ends, ownership can pass to the beneficiaries, usually children, or go into another trust, often called a drop-down trust, for the rest of her life. Meanwhile, the QPRT has removed both the property and any future appreciation from the estate. Because the trust freezes the house at its fair market value when it's transferred to the QPRT, no additional tax is due after that.

QTIP, or ***qualified terminable interest property trust*** – a trust designed to hold the marital share and qualify for the unlimited marital deduction. The trustee is required to pay all income to the surviving spouse for life and can also make distributions of principal. Distributions to anyone other than the spouse are not permitted while the spouse is alive; after that, the assets can go to whomever the trust documents specify.

QTIP election – a formality that must be observed in order to apply the marital deduction to the QTIP. The executor, who signs the federal estate tax return, Form 706, must elect to treat the trust property as if it has passed to the surviving spouse. In the process of making this election, the executor can decide how much should go to the marital share and how much to a bypass trust.

Qualified domestic trust – see *QDOT.*

Qualified personal-residence trust – see *QPRT.*

Qualified state tuition programs – see *Section 529 plans.*

Qualified terminable interest property trust – see *QTIP.*

Real property – real estate, as distinguished from tangible personal property, such as art, and intangible personal property, such as stocks.

Redemption agreement – a form of buy-sell agreement used by business owners in which the shares of the owner who died will or may be sold back to the business.

Related use rule – a rule that limits the deduction for tangible personal property donated to charity. In order for a donation to qualify for a full fair market value deduction, the charity must use the asset in a manner related to its exempt purpose. A donor who gives violins to an orchestra can deduct the fair market value if the orchestra uses them rather than sells them.

Remainder – a future interest in assets, as opposed to a current one, which typically takes effect when a predetermined event occurs. For example, remainder beneficiaries of a trust might not receive distributions until the current beneficiary dies or the trust term ends.

Required minimum distribution – see *minimum required distribution.*

Residuary estate – what is left after estate expenses, creditors and taxes have been paid and gifts of specific items or specific sums of money have been satisfied.

Revocable – a document, such as a trust, that can be amended (for example, by adding beneficiaries). The most common example is a living trust. Trusts set up to save estate taxes usually have to be irrevocable.

Revocable trust – see *living trust.*

Roth retirement account, such as a Roth IRA or a Roth 401(k) – a retirement account consisting of after-tax dollars, so no tax is assessed when the money is withdrawn.

Rule against perpetuities – a law in many states that prevents a trust from lasting indefinitely and sets a maximum term. Traditionally, it was measured by "lives in being plus 21 years." In that case, the best choice for the "measuring life" is typically someone who is young at the time the trust is created. A simpler approach, now used in many states, is to limit the term to 90 years from the time the trust is created. In states that have abolished the rule against perpetuities, it is possible to have a dynasty trust, which can last forever (assuming its assets are not depleted).

Section 529 plans – qualified state programs that can be used for higher education costs and are available in all states and the District of Columbia. These plans allow an individual to set up a separate account for each family member. A private money manager chosen by each state typically manages the funds. Withdrawals are federal-tax-exempt, provided the money is used for college or graduate school.

Section 2503(c) trust – one of a handful of trusts that meet the present interest requirement. (Another is a Crummey trust.) This irrevocable trust must have only one beneficiary, give the beneficiary the right to withdraw the assets at age 21, and must not restrict the trustee from making distributions of principal and interest before that. The trust must be includable in the beneficiary's estate if the beneficiary dies.

Section 2642(c) trust – an irrevocable trust that generally does not give rise to generation-skipping transfer tax. It can benefit only one grandchild, and the trust document must specify that if the grandchild dies before the funds have been fully distributed, the remaining funds become part of the grandchild's estate, making them potentially subject to estate tax.

Section 7520 rate – an assumed interest rate, set each month by the U.S. Treasury. The Section 7520 rate is 120 percent of the current midterm applicable rate, rounded to the nearest 0.2 percent. It is used to calculate the value of any annuity (for example, in a grantor retained annuity trust), any interest for life or a term of years (such as in a charitable remainder trust) or any remainder interest (for example, in the personal residence donated to charity).

Self-canceling installment note (SCIN) – a financing technique used in connection with the sale of assets to family members or to a trust for their benefit. With an ordinary installment note, if the seller dies while the note is outstanding, the balance is payable to the estate. With a SCIN, the debt is forgiven if the seller dies during the note term.

Self-settled spendthrift trust – see *domestic asset protection trust*.

Self-settled trust – a trust in which the person who sets it up and funds it is also a beneficiary.

Settlor – see *grantor*.

Situs – the place where an entity, such as a trust, is legally situated. This determines which state's laws apply to the trust.

Skip persons – in a family, anyone other than a spouse who is two or more generations younger than an individual; outside of the family, anyone more than 37.5 years younger than an individual. The term is used in the context of applying the generation-skipping transfer, or GST, tax.

Special needs trust – a trust to benefit an individual (whether a minor or adult) with physical, emotional or cognitive needs who may some day qualify for state or federal assistance. Having more than a certain sum of money in his or her own name disqualifies the recipient from assistance. Keeping assets in a specially designed trust avoids this restriction.

Special trustee – see *protector*.

Spendthrift clause – a provision in a trust preventing the beneficiaries from assigning their interests.

Split-dollar arrangement – a financing tool in which two parties, such as a trust and a family member, share the premiums and the proceeds of a life insurance policy. Typically used to fund permanent life insurance (as opposed to a term policy).

Step-up in basis – see *basis adjustment*.

Stretch-out – the strategy, available to an IRA owner or beneficiary, of extending minimum required distributions from a traditional account or any inherited account over her life expectancy. The longer the withdrawals can be extended, the smaller each payout will be. This allows the money to compound tax-deferred in the case of a traditional IRA and tax-free in the case of a Roth IRA.

Supplemental needs trust – see *special needs trust.*

Tangible personal property – personal possessions, such as cars, boats, clothing, jewelry and artwork, in contrast to real estate and intangible assets, such as stocks, bonds and bank accounts.

Tax-deferred retirement accounts – traditional accounts, including IRAs and employer-sponsored plans such as 401(k)s and 403(b)s, with which the owner can take a tax deduction when making contributions and there is no need to pay tax as investments in the account grow. Income tax is due on funds as they are withdrawn by the account owner or beneficiaries. See *Roth retirement account, such as a Roth IRA or a Roth 401(k).*

Tax exclusive – refers to a system of tax in which there is tax only on the sum given away, not on the money used to pay the tax. Gift tax, for example, is applied on a tax exclusive basis. In contrast, estate tax is said to be tax inclusive, meaning that the amount of tax owed is based on the entire estate, and the tax due is paid with after-tax dollars.

Taxable distribution – a payout to a skip person from a trust that benefits both skip persons and older family members.

Taxable termination – when the interests of all non-skip persons in a trust have ended and skip persons are the remaining beneficiaries. This event could generate GST tax; if so, the tax is paid by the trustee using funds in the trust.

Tenancy by the entirety – a form of joint ownership, available only to spouses, in which each spouse automatically inherits the other's share. In most states, only the couple's joint creditors have access to the asset. See *joint tenancy with rights of survivorship* and *tenancy in common.*

Tenancy in common – a form of joint ownership in which each co-owner owns part of the property, known as an undivided interest. When one co-owner dies, only that person's share gets included in his or her estate. See *joint tenancy with rights of survivorship* and *tenancy by the entirety*.

Testamentary – an estate planning vehicle that takes effect at death, as opposed to one that is inter vivos, which takes effect during life (for example, a "testamentary trust" or a "testamentary transfer").

Testator – the person whose property is covered in a will. Arcane term used in old wills instead of referring to the individual by name.

Transferable (or payable) on death – terms used interchangeably, but the exact wording may depend on state law and the type of asset. For example, you can make savings bonds "payable on death" to the person you name, while brokerage accounts are labeled "transfer on death." The net effect is the same. These assets do not pass under a will or living trust. When the owner dies, the person named can promptly collect the money by presenting the death certificate and filling out any paperwork the institution requires. In contrast with joint ownership, the named people have no access to the money while the account owner is alive.

Transfer tax – gift tax that applies to certain lifetime gifts, estate tax that may be an issue for assets that pass at death and generation-skipping transfer, or GST, tax that applies to some transfers made at either juncture that benefit grandchildren.

Trust – a legal wrapper for holding assets, such as cash, real estate, an insurance policy, shares in a closely held company or publicly traded securities, created by a document that looks like a contract and is called the trust instrument, declaration or agreement.

Trust adviser – see *protector*.

Trust protector – see *protector*.

Trustee – in a trust, the person or company that manages the assets and distributes them according to the terms of the trust document. A trust can have one trustee or several.

Unified credit – see *applicable exclusion*.

Uniform Transfers to Minors Act (UTMA) – the law most states have adopted to regulate custodial accounts. Under this law, children are legally entitled to the money when they reach the age specified under state law (usually at age 18, 19 or 21).

Unitrust – one that bases payouts to beneficiaries on the value of the trust assets, recalculated each year, rather than requiring the trustee to pay income, which can reflect only the annual earnings on stocks and bonds (not capital gains). This can be done by defining income as a unitrust amount, a fixed percentage of the trust value each year (typically 3 to 5 percent or a specific figure within that range) that is sometimes averaged over a three-year period. A more flexible approach is to give trustees broad discretion to invade principal along with distributing income but, again, limited by the formula; this is called a "power to adjust."

Unrelated business taxable income (UBTI) – income to a charity financed by debt or generated by business activities unrelated to its tax-exempt purpose. This income falls outside the tax-exempt status that charities usually enjoy. It, therefore, defeats one purpose of donating the asset to charity, which is to avoid the tax a donor would have to pay himself.

U.S. persons – U.S. citizens and resident aliens who hold a green card.

Will – the cornerstone of many estate plans, it should transfer assets, appoint a guardian for minor children and name an executor.

Resources and Further Reading

Listed below are sources you may find helpful to tie up loose ends or cope with other difficult issues that directly or indirectly affect your estate plan.

Finding a Lawyer

American Bar Association
A national lawyers' trade association, divided into sections. The one on Real Property, Trust and Estate Law has its own area on the ABA's Web site, providing basic information to the public.
http://bit.ly/1Bveagl

The American College of Trust and Estate Counsel
A group of trust and estate lawyers elected to membership based on their experience and scholarship. The public area of the ACTEC Web site includes "Find an ACTEC Lawyer," which allows you to search by location, and "Resources," with an abundance of useful links.
www.actec.org

Martindale-Hubbell Law Directory
The most complete nationwide listing of attorneys by location and area of practice.
www.martindale.com

National Academy of Elder Law Attorneys
Many estate planners work with elderly clients. Members of this group focus on some of the elderly's particular concerns, including Medicaid

planning, maintaining independence and geriatric care. Provides a tool for finding an elder law attorney nearby.
www.naela.com

Special Needs Alliance
A national network of attorneys dedicated to assisting families with special needs planning. Many became involved in the field because members of their own families were affected.
www.specialneedsalliance.org

Books

The following books cover in greater detail some of the special concerns addressed in this book.

Advice for the newly widowed. On top of everything else, losing a spouse leaves you saddled with financial paperwork. *On Your Own: A Widow's Passage to Emotional and Financial Well-Being* (2011, On Your Own Publishing Company), by Alexandra Armstrong, a financial planner, and Mary R. Donahue, a psychologist, is the classic guide for women who were accustomed to having their husbands manage the money. Financially savvy women (and men) will likely find much of the advice too basic but still appreciate the hand-holding, divide-and-conquer approach.

Those still coping with grief can relate to *A Widow's Story: A Memoir* (2011, Ecco), in which the author Joyce Carol Oates describes in excruciating detail the pain of suddenly losing a spouse after 48 years of happy marriage. In eloquent prose, she covers all aspects of early widowhood, from insomnia to probate court.

Confronting mortality. Life is finite. Estate planning reminds us of that. So does old age and terminal illness. Roz Chast, a cartoonist for *The New Yorker* magazine, covers the former with words and drawings in *Can't We Talk about Something More Pleasant?* (2014, Bloomsbury USA), a brutally honest memoir about her parents' end-of-life care. We empathize with her nightmare, welcome the occasional comic relief and realize that we are not alone.

Atul Gawande takes a more philosophical approach in *Being Mortal: Medicine and What Matters in the End* (2014, Metropolitan Books). With graphic examples drawn from his personal life and work as a surgeon, the author shows how modern medicine delays the inevitable and forces us to think about what it means, in Ronald Dworkin's terms, to "be the author of your own life." Gawande concludes that if we are given the chance by compassionate caregivers and the health care system, we can continue to find purpose and meaning, right up until the end.

Living well is the flip side of planning for our mortality. Two books, about men who gracefully faced death, inspire us to make the most of every day. *Tuesdays with Morrie* (2002, Broadway Books) is the sportswriter Mitch Albom's memoir about his Brandeis University professor and mentor Morrie Schwartz. While Schwartz is dying of Lou Gehrig's disease, Albom visits him weekly to chronicle his declining health and enduring wisdom.

Inspired by his diagnosis with terminal cancer, former Carnegie Mellon professor Randy Pausch speaks for himself in *The Last Lecture* (2010, Hyperion Books). He dispenses good life advice for his kids, who were young when he died, at age 47, about everything from pursuing your dreams to the lost art of thank-you notes. All the rest of us can benefit from it, too. In a reminder of how fragile life really is, Pausch's co-author, the former *Wall Street Journal* columnist Jeffrey Zaslow, died in a car accident, at age 53, two years after their best-selling book was published.

For sensible advice when bad health strikes, there's Jane Brody's *Guide to the Great Beyond: A Practical Primer to Help You and Your Loved Ones Prepare Medically, Legally, and Emotionally for the End of Life* (2009, Random House). Brody, a *New York Times* columnist and noted authority on health, deploys her eminently readable writing style to tackle this weighty topic. Martin M. Shenkman writes about what he knows in *Estate Planning for People With a Chronic Condition or Disability* (2009, DemosHealth). He is a CPA and estate planning lawyer whose wife has multiple sclerosis.

Dysfunctional families. This subject may be so familiar that you don't feel the need to read about it. Or you might conclude your family is normal compared with the one described in *Mrs. Astor Regrets: The Hidden Betrayals of a Family Beyond Reproach* (2008, Houghton Mifflin Harcourt), by Meryl Gordon. It's a saucy tale of events leading up to the criminal trial of the New York philanthropist's son and lawyer, who were convicted in October 2009 of conspiring to take advantage of Brooke Astor's diminished capacity. Though the author doesn't say so, there are lessons here for us all: Anticipate your possible mental decline, and go outside the family for help if you can't trust your kin.

Hendrik Hartog gives a view of the other side – disappointed heirs – in his book *Someday All This Will Be Yours* (2012, Harvard University Press). It's a comprehensive, scholarly window on misunderstandings and broken promises. If you think anything that has happened in your own family is aberrant or unique, Hartog offers two centuries' worth of court cases to prove you have plenty of company.

How not to spoil your kids. Family wealth can be a blessing or curse. Thayer Willis writes from experience in two books, *Navigating the Dark Side of Wealth: A Life Guide for Inheritors* (2003, New Concord Press) and *Beyond Gold: True Wealth for Inheritors* (2012, New Concord Press). For another take on the subject, refer to *Silver Spoon Kids: How Successful Parents Raise Responsible Children* (2002, Contemporary Books). The authors Eileen Gallo, a psychotherapist, and her husband, Jon, a trust and estate lawyer, team up to offer a highly creative approach to teaching children about money.

(Even) more about IRAs. For many Americans, retirement accounts are their largest and least understood asset. Without dispute, the bible on the subject for lawyers and financial advisers is *Life and Death Planning for Retirement Benefits* (2011, Ataxplan Publications), by Natalie Choate, now in the seventh edition. Consumers with an appetite for detail may also find it a valuable resource; among other things, it includes sample letters to use when communicating with financial institutions.

Another resource, geared specifically to consumers, is Ed Slott's *The Retirement Savings Time Bomb...and How to Defuse It* (2012, Penguin Books). It's written by a CPA who uses plain English and comical metaphors without compromising substance. Another CPA, Michael J. Jones, dishes up advice from the trenches for inheritors (and their financial advisers). His book *Inheriting an IRA: How to Create a Lifetime of Paychecks* (2014, Paddleboard Press) covers everything from how to avoid some common mistakes to navigating your way out of the oddball situations.

The intricacies of insurance. Much of the literature (if you can call it that) about insurance is written by those who have ties to the industry. A notable exception is *Smarter Insurance Solutions* (1996, Bloomberg Press), by Janet Bamford. Though out of print, it is available on the used-book market.

You can find another independent perspective in *Making the Most of Your Money* (2010, Simon & Schuster), by Jane Bryant Quinn. In this comprehensive desk reference, the eminent columnist, who once took on the insurance industry, offers a guide to all aspects of personal finance.

Estate planning for pets. Whether your pet is a rescue you adopted or a purebred worth many thousands, you can't put a price tag on what it's worth to you. So you ought to take steps to provide for this family member after you are gone – just as you would for any other. The go-to book on the subject is *Fat Cats & Lucky Dogs: How to Leave (Some of) Your Estate to Your Pet* (2010, Prism Publishing). The authors, Gerry W. Beyer, a professor at Texas Tech University School of Law, and Barry Seltzer, a Toronto lawyer, have joined forces to produce a historical, whimsical and highly practical guide for people who are serious about estate planning for their pets.

Building a charitable legacy. Among other things, estate planning involves dividing the pie among family, charity and the tax man. *Wealth in Families* (2008, Harvard University), by Charles W. Collier, now in the second edition, is a classic for advisers and families who want to foster a spirit of giving. Written by Harvard's former senior philanthropic adviser and intended for the university's fundraising, the book looks at motivations and methods for being philanthropic.

Newsletters and Magazines

Chronicle of Philanthropy
With its non-profit news and grant announcements, this bi-weekly newspaper is required reading for fundraisers, and the heartwarming success stories will inspire donors.
www.philanthropy.com

Ed Slott's IRA Advisor
Addresses both consumers and advisers with monthly updates and rec-

ommended strategies from Slott and other leaders in the field.
www.irahelp.com

Steve Leimberg's Estate Planning E-mail Newsletter
In the rapidly changing world of estate planning, staying current is essential. With frequent updates on breaking news and analysis by leading experts (I admit I have been an enthusiastic contributor), this newsletter, delivered electronically, fills a pressing need.
www.leimbergservices.com

Taxwise Giving
Conrad Teitell, a writer, speaker and authority on the law of charitable giving, leavens his advice with plenty of puns and homespun humor. His artful turns of phrase make this monthly newsletter interesting to both fundraisers and donors.
www.taxwisegiving.com

Software

Brentmark Software Inc. (www.brentmark.com)
A go-to source of software for professionals. Products include tools to analyze estate planning decisions, such as whether it makes sense to use a bypass trust or convert a traditional IRA to a Roth. I'm proud that *Estate Planning Smarts* is featured in Brentmark's booth at professional conferences.

Tiger Tables Actuarial Software (www.tigertables.com)
Created by Lawrence P. Katzenstein, a trust and estate lawyer, this software computes the value of the interests transferred and those retained through a variety of tools for estate planning or charitable giving, including: grantor retained annuity trusts, charitable remainder trusts and qualified personal-residence trusts. The program incorporates the mortality tables used by the Internal Revenue Service for various purposes and automatically updates the Section 7520 rate – an assumed interest rate, set each month by the IRS, that is used in the calculation. A free demo is available on the site.

Web Sites

www.estateplanningsmarts.com
The home of this book, where material will be updated to reflect legal developments that might affect your estate plan. You can register at the site to receive e-mail notifications about these changes and follow me on Twitter: @djworking

www.fairmark.com
Hosted by Kaye A. Thomas, a tax lawyer and author, this site provides consumers with a wealth of information about personal finance.

www.savingforcollege.com
State-by-state information on Section 529 accounts.

Blogs

Many estate planning blogs sell products or services. The following ones offer an independent perspective.

TaxProf Blog
http://taxprof.typepad.com/taxprof_blog
Paul L. Caron, a professor at the University of Cincinnati College of Law, curates coverage from academic journals and the media.

Wills, Trusts & Estates Prof Blog
http://lawprofessors.typepad.com/trusts_estates_prof
Daily posts by Gerry W. Beyer, a professor at the Texas Tech University School of Law, are a tasty smorgasbord, summarizing articles that have appeared in newspapers, magazines, professional journals and other blogs.

IRS Publications

Helpful Internal Revenue Service publications can be downloaded from www.irs.gov. They are a lot simpler to read than the tax code, though they are not binding, as only the law can be. Here are some that may be useful.

519   *U.S. Tax Guide for Aliens*

555   *Community Property*

559   *Survivors, Executors, and Administrators*

590   *Individual Retirement Arrangements (IRAs)*
Includes all three Life Expectancy Tables used to calculate the minimum required distribution from an IRA. The two that most people will need are the Uniform Lifetime table, which applies to IRA owners, and the Single Life Expectancy table, which applies to inheritors. Both of these are in the Appendix of this book. The third table is the Joint Life and Last Survivor Expectancy table, which applies only when the spouse is the sole beneficiary and is more than 10 years younger than the IRA owner.

970   *Tax Benefits for Education*

Single Life Expectancy

For use by beneficiaries*

Age	Life Expectancy	Age	Life Expectancy
0	82.4	28	55.3
1	81.6	29	54.3
2	80.6	30	53.3
3	79.7	31	52.4
4	78.7	32	51.4
5	77.7	33	50.4
6	76.7	34	49.4
7	75.8	35	48.5
8	74.8	36	47.5
9	73.8	37	46.5
10	72.8	38	45.6
11	71.8	39	44.6
12	70.8	40	43.6
13	69.9	41	42.7
14	68.9	42	41.7
15	67.9	43	40.7
16	66.9	44	39.8
17	66.0	45	38.8
18	65.0	46	37.9
19	64.0	47	37.0
20	63.0	48	36.0
21	62.1	49	35.1
22	61.1	50	34.2
23	60.1	51	33.3
24	59.1	52	32.3
25	58.2	53	31.4
26	57.2	54	30.5
27	56.2	55	29.6

*Spouses who are the only beneficiary and more than 10 years younger than the IRA owner need to consult the Joint Life and Last Survivor Expectancy table, included in IRS Publication 590, available at www.irs.gov.

Source: Internal Revenue Service

Single Life Expectancy

For use by beneficiaries*

Age	Life Expectancy	Age	Life Expectancy
56	28.7	84	8.1
57	27.9	85	7.6
58	27.0	86	7.1
59	26.1	87	6.7
60	25.2	88	6.3
61	24.4	89	5.9
62	23.5	90	5.5
63	22.7	91	5.2
64	21.8	92	4.9
65	21.0	93	4.6
66	20.2	94	4.3
67	19.4	95	4.1
68	18.6	96	3.8
69	17.8	97	3.6
70	17.0	98	3.4
71	16.3	99	3.1
72	15.5	100	2.9
73	14.8	101	2.7
74	14.1	102	2.5
75	13.4	103	2.3
76	12.7	104	2.1
77	12.1	105	1.9
78	11.4	106	1.7
79	10.8	107	1.5
80	10.2	108	1.4
81	9.7	109	1.2
82	9.1	110	1.1
83	8.6	111 and over	1.0

*Spouses who are the only beneficiary and more than 10 years younger than the IRA owner need to consult the Joint Life and Last Survivor Expectancy table, included in IRS Publication 590, available at www.irs.gov.

Source: Internal Revenue Service

Uniform Lifetime

For use by:

- *Unmarried owners*
- *Married owners whose spouses are not more than 10 years younger*
- *Married owners whose spouses are not the sole beneficiaries of their IRAs*

Age	Distribution Period	Age	Distribution Period
70	27.4	93	9.6
71	26.5	94	9.1
72	25.6	95	8.6
73	24.7	96	8.1
74	23.8	97	7.6
75	22.9	98	7.1
76	22.0	99	6.7
77	21.2	100	6.3
78	20.3	101	5.9
79	19.5	102	5.5
80	18.7	103	5.2
81	17.9	104	4.9
82	17.1	105	4.5
83	16.3	106	4.2
84	15.5	107	3.9
85	14.8	108	3.7
86	14.1	109	3.4
87	13.4	110	3.1
88	12.7	111	2.9
89	12.0	112	2.6
90	11.4	113	2.4
91	10.8	114	2.1
92	10.2	115 and over	1.9

Source: Internal Revenue Service

Index

A B Bernstein, 46, 91
ABLE (Achieving a Better Life
    Experience)
        accounts, 95, 172-174
adjusted gross income (AGI)
    charitable deductions and, 136, 193,
        274, 276-277
    Coverdell Education Savings
        accounts and, 160
    deducting unreimbursed medical
        expenses of a dependent, 172
adoption
    married couple and non-biological
        children, 88, 90
    partner in unmarried couple adopts
        biological child of partner, 86-87
    previous marriages, children from,
        90, 305
    single person, 88
    unmarried couple and non-
        biological children, 86-87
advance directive. *See* living will
advisers. *See* lawyers and advisers
after born child, 91, 319
AFR. *See* applicable federal rate
agency account, 175
Alaska
    community property, opt in, 78
    domestic asset protection
        trusts in, 293
    dynasty trusts in, 237
aliens. *See* domiciliaries; non-citizen
    spouse; non-citizens; non-resident
    aliens; resident aliens
alternate beneficiary. *See* contingent
    beneficiary
alternate valuation date, 50, 319

Alzheimer's, 2
Amazon, 15
American College of Trust and Estate
    Counsel, The, 312, 343
American Council on Gift Annuities, 268
American Jobs Creation Act (2004), 210
American Taxpayer Relief Act of 2012,
    129, 299
annual exclusion. *See also* gifts
    amount 57-58, 177, 185, 205, 206,
        210, 246, 307
    appreciating assets and, 247-248
    cash gifts using, 170, 171, 234,
        247, 248
    Crummey notices, use of, 103,
        149, 177
    deadline for making gifts with, 249
    death (imminent) and use of, 308
    defined, 57, 319
    determining what gifts qualify for,
        238-239
    expatriate rules, 225-226
    foreigners and, 219
    funding ABLE accounts with, 173
    funding Section 529 plans with, 159,
        179, 234-235
    funding life insurance premiums
        with, 143, 146-147, 149, 237
    funding trusts with, 103, 109, 163-
        164, 206, 210, 238-239, 251-252
    generation-skipping transfer tax and
        cash gifts, 234
    grantor trusts and, 252
    leveraging gifts with life insurance,
        143-144, 237
    partial interests, giving away,
        185-186

About the Author

Deborah L. Jacobs is a lawyer and award-winning journalist specializing in legal topics. In her best-selling book, *Estate Planning Smarts,* she draws on 17 years of writing about the stressful issues that surround estate planning. Her articles for *The New York Times, Bloomberg Wealth Manager, Forbes, Business-Week* and many other publications have been widely cited and circulated by both advisers and consumers. Readers appreciate her clear, concise explanations of complex subjects and her ability to combine real-life stories with reassuring, practical advice. A former senior editor at Forbes and now columnist for Morningstar, she has also been interviewed as an expert by reporters from many different media outlets, including *The New York Times, Bloomberg News, Reuters, U.S. News & World Report, MarketWatch* and CBS TV.

A dynamic speaker, Jacobs has addressed audiences of professionals and consumers. Listeners say they feel like they're sitting at the kitchen table with a knowledgeable, trusted friend.

Jacobs has been a syndicated newspaper columnist, newsletter editor and entrepreneur – she has had her own company, producing a variety of written products on legal and financial matters, for most of her career. She is the author of *Small Business Legal Smarts* (Bloomberg Press).

A graduate of Barnard and Columbia's Law School and Graduate School of Journalism, Jacobs lives in New York City with her husband and son.

Keeping Current

To keep readers current between editions, Jacobs tweets (@djworking) and posts material on the book's Web site, www.estateplanningsmarts.com. You can register at the site to receive e-mail notifications of updates as they become available.

At Least 10 Ways
To Use This Book

So much has happened since the first edition of *Estate Planning Smarts* was published. The book has been widely and favorably reviewed, become a best-seller and been embraced by a wide audience of consumers, lawyers, accountants, fundraisers and financial advisers.

Individuals of all ages have used the book as a source of information. Some have ordered multiple copies and given them to family members as they prepare to discuss this complicated topic.

Professionals have relied on *Estate Planning Smarts* as a business development tool, giving it to clients and prospects. For this purpose, it can be personalized by adding a company logo to the cover and up to 16 pages of customized text.

Advisers have also used *Estate Planning Smarts* to:

1 Provide clients background before a meeting

2 Reinforce their own recommendations afterwards

3 Reduce the time they must spend with clients who are sensitive about fees

4 Present an independent perspective about controversial subjects, such as the drawbacks of do-it-yourself documents

5 Facilitate family meetings

6 Suggest next steps, referring to the action-oriented To-Do lists at the end of each chapter

7 Serve as continuing education course materials

8 Educate colleagues who are less familiar with the subject

9 Prepare for the Certified Financial Planner exam

10 Enrich law school courses they teach. Both full-time and adjunct faculty have adopted *Estate Planning Smarts* as an "uncasebook," leaving more class time for experiential learning

Photo Credits